INTRODUCTION

by

the Rt. Hon. Gerald Kaufman MP

Is diplomatic immunity necessary?

Here in Britain, apart from being able to speak their minds in the House of Commons itself without risk of slander or libel actions, Members of Parliament are as much subject to both the civil and criminal law as anyone else. MPs continue to carry out effectively the job they are elected to do, and democracy continues to flourish. If domestic legislators do not need to be above the law, why should overseas diplomats be different?

Well, there is, of course, a very major difference. Countries have a propensity to fall out with each other, and it is necessary in such circumstances to ensure the physical safety of ambassadors and their staffs. The transfer of confidential documents can be vulnerable to interference, and it is only proper that a host government should be prevented from yielding to the temptation to take a look at its rivals' – or even its friends' – secrets.

Such standards of civilized behaviour are accepted (in principle, at any rate) by all governments in the world. Many would also agree that the almost sacrosanct nature of the premises of a foreign mission must be available as asylum for political fugitives. Even though it did not like it, the Hungarian Government thirty years ago resigned itself to Cardinal Mindszenty's being sheltered in the United States Embassy in Budapest; in 1986 the South African Government did not tamper with nationals of their country who sought refuge in a British diplomatic mission.

When the obverse of such niceties of behaviour takes place, and the inviolability of diplomatic premises is invaded, the reaction is horror. The holding of many of the American Embassy staff as hostages by the Iranian régime was, perhaps, the ugliest example of such violation.

Accordingly, and rightly, most countries pride themselves on maintaining proper standards of behaviour towards guest missions, even from nations with whom their relations are far from cordial. At the same time, there is an uneasy feeling that this propriety is too often being unpardonably exploited. That feeling is documented by this disturbing book.

Of course, we all know of the grossest and most horrific examples of the abuse of diplomatic immunity. For us in this country the worst by far was the murder by a member or members of the Libyan mission in London of a young woman police constable, Yvonne Fletcher. That the premises of the so-called People's Bureau were used as a base for her shooting was repugnant enough. If anything, even harder to stomach was what came next. The guilty person or persons together with accomplices and accessories, having themselves abused their diplomatic status to commit a vile crime, then insisted on that same status being respected by requiring the bereaved British police to escort them to safety aboard their departing aircraft.

Ashman and Trescott dramatically start their story with the Fletcher murder. From there they go on meticulously to document dozens – hundreds – of less well-publicized violations of immunity, some of which are almost as disgraceful and all of which are unacceptable within the civilized commerce of nations. The majority of cases cited took place either in Britain or the United States.

There is among most of us anger that diplomats flout the traffic laws – and get away with it. This book provides the statistics: the extraordinary number of 104,690 parking tickets cancelled in London in 1984 because the cars were registered to diplomats; one vehicle in New York whose driver was unpunished after collecting 671 parking tickets during a ten-month period. Such infractions, though unpardonable, may be little more than annoying. Other violations of traffic law, involving speeding, dangerous driving and drunken driving, can have far worse consequences. The case is cited here,

OUTRAGE

By the same authors

KISSINGER – THE ADVENTURES OF SUPER-KRAUT
MARTHA MITCHELL – THE MOUTH THAT ROARED
THE ADVENTURES OF BIG BAD JOHN CONNALLY
THE CIA–MAFIA LINK
THE STRANGE DISAPPEARANCE OF JIMMY HOFFA
THE FINEST JUDGES MONEY CAN BUY
THE GOSPEL ACCORDING TO BILLY GRAHAM

OUTRAGE

The Abuse of Diplomatic Immunity

Chuck Ashman
and Pamela Trescott

With an Introduction
by Gerald Kaufman

W.H. ALLEN · LONDON
1986

Set in Palatino by
Input Typesetting Ltd, London
Printed and bound in Great Britain by
Mackays of Chatham Ltd, Kent
for the Publishers W. H. Allen & Co. Plc
44 Hill Street, London W1X 8LB

British Library Cataloguing in Publication Data

Ashman, Chuck
Outrage: the abuse of diplomatic immunity.
1. Diplomatic privileges and immunities
I. Title II. Trescott, Pamela
341.3'3 JX1672

ISBN 0–491–03713–9

almost physically painful to read, of the excruciating physical sufferings and crippling financial consequences of one breach of the law by a diplomat which immunity made unpunishable.

Even more alarming are the accounts of the use of diplomatic premises or pouches for major crimes, especially drug-smuggling, and the exploitation of personal diplomatic immunity to escape the legal pursuit of other crimes, particularly rape and sexual assault.

These ugly excesses stem partly from the growth in size of diplomatic missions. In 1985, 4,524 diplomats in London enjoyed full immunity, along with over 10,000 members of diplomats' families. These totals compare with a maximum of 1,084 less than half a century ago. Partly they derive from a hazy zone of international agreements – is the person immune or is he or she not? – in which governments and police forces give infringers of the law the benefit of the doubt. Partly they result from governments and police turning a blind eye to breaches of the criminal law by persons who by no reasonable criteria possess immunity but whose countries, for reasons of policy good or less than good, Foreign Offices or State Departments do not wish to offend.

As described and documented in this book, the present situation is clearly unacceptable to most sensible people, and especially to those with profound respect for the principle stated by Sir Anthony Kershaw: 'Immunity is immunity, and it depends on people being civilised and claiming only the immunity that is necessary to them, and not behaving in the barbaric way that has become fashionable in certain parts of the world recently.'

Plainly changes need to be made. It is odious that an embassy can be used as a murder base, that a diplomatic pouch can be misused to transport lethal weapons or even the live body of a kidnapped prisoner (which latter circumstance, as Ashman and Trescott point out, has happened more than once). It is infuriating that diplomats, their wives, sons and servants should be able to escape the consequences of crimes which, in their own countries possibly more than in those where they committed them, are subject to severe penalties.

There is no unilateral remedy. One country's concept of diplomatic immunity may not be another's. To cut the Gordian knot by expulsion (frustrating in itself when involving the escape scot-free of a violent criminal) may invite reprisals on innocent persons in the home country of the expelled diplomat. Re-negotiation of the Vienna Convention governing diplomatic immunity seems the most logical step. This book will have made an important contribution if it plays its part in creating a climate that leads to such a re-negotiation. If that can be achieved, perhaps Yvonne Fletcher will not have died in vain.

Gerald Kaufman

House of Commons
April 1986

FOREWORD

THIS BOOK REALLY began four years ago when we interviewed a rape victim in New York City. She had been beaten, robbed and sexually assaulted by the son of an Arab delegate to the United Nations. The police caught him and he admitted his crimes while boldly claiming immunity from American law.

While the victim was in a hospital recovery room after five hours of surgery, the rapist was released from police custody. He had been held less than one hour before diplomats arranged his release. He insisted on stopping at his favourite bar to toast his good fortune. Eight hours later, he boarded a plane to the Middle East. His final gesture was an obscene one made to the arresting officer who had come to the airport to see him off. The officer became a member of a growing fraternity of frustrated policemen whose arrests are nullified by political dealings.

The victim has never fully recovered physically or emotionally.

While that was the beginning of this book, our mandate came outside the Libyan Embassy in London. The day photographers from throughout the world focused on policewoman Yvonne Fletcher's cap lying on the bloody ground, the writing of this book became an urgent necessity.

That killing, more than any other single event, seemed to highlight the arrogance that has become a routine part of diplomatic relations. But it is not an isolated case. There are in fact too many similar incidents of diplomatic outrages for the authors to discuss them all in one volume. We have assembled several of the most offensive, most bizarre and most outrageous crimes. We have talked with the victims and their families, prosecutors, police, judges, journalists, social workers and members of the diplomatic corps. Many believe the time is right for change.

The basic concept of affording special consideration to visiting dignitaries is not in question. But changes in the law to prohibit or punish the constant abuse of diplomatic immunity are long overdue.

It is bad enough to know there will be rapes and robberies every day and that many of the guilty will never be caught. But no civilized nation can accept that the guilty may be apprehended and then set free because of a stamp on their passport which reads, 'DIPLOMAT'.

OUTRAGE

CHAPTER ONE

'Keep Calm'

On April 17, 1984, Yvonne Fletcher was fatally shot in the back by a Libyan assassin. Eleven others, Libyan exiles peacefully protesting against the dictatorship of Muammar el-Qaddafi, were wounded. Yvonne's fiancé, Constable Michael Liddle, who was also assigned to the demonstration detail, watched helplessly as she fell to the ground just a hundred yards away. For days after she lost her life in front of London's Libyan embassy, her black and white uniform hat lay abandoned in St James's Square, a grim reminder of the heinous act.

Memories of the petite policewoman they nicknamed 'Super Fletch' still haunt her fellow officers. At Salisbury for her funeral, Tim and Queenie Fletcher listened with 1,500 assembled mourners as Yvonne's commander, Chief Superintendent Bryan West, eulogized their daughter: 'She was one of my best officers.'

Eighty-three miles away, thirty Libyans waited at Heathrow Airport to board a plane for home. One of them had got away with murder, the others had been accessories, all were free. Their sealed diplomatic baggage could not be opened. It almost certainly contained the murder weapon. In the history of diplomatic immunity, few incidents have so dramatically demonstrated the kind of abuse that so outrages ordinary citizens.

Yvonne Fletcher was remembered fondly by many. She was liked and respected by her police colleagues, adored by her family, and popular with everyone in the small town of Semley where she grew up.

A tomboy who only wore a dress when her mother

insisted, Yvonne excelled in sports. She represented her school in hockey and swimming. She played football on equal terms with boys. At the age of eleven she began judo lessons.

Not only was Yvonne physically confident as a girl, she also developed into a natural leader with a strong sense of duty. When she eventually found a career that suited her, it was sure to be demanding and responsible.

When Yvonne learned in school how Sir Robert Peel had founded the London police force in 1829, she was fired with enthusiasm and the history of the force increased the young girl's commitment to her new ambition. She was determined to become a WPC.

At about seventeen, Yvonne stopped growing at only five feet two and a half inches, an inch and a half short of the minimum required for most British police work. Though disappointed, she was never daunted. She had unshakeable faith that somehow she could demonstrate her commitment, her ability, her talent. She knew that she would be good at it. She had no self-doubts, no false hopes, she simply *knew*.

Once she had her heart set on something, Yvonne was the sort of person to go all out to achieve it. While still at school, she applied to about a dozen police forces. At eighteen and a half, the eligibility age for the Metropolitan Police, she applied, wording every answer just right. She posted her application and waited optimistically.

She had waited before, and disappointment had been her thanks. Rejections by several police forces were based on her height, or rather her lack of it. But she was so determined to pursue her dream that she considered moving to Hong Kong. The Hong Kong police had no such height requirement.

The wait seemed like years, but word came in about six weeks. Yvonne was invited to Hendon in north-west London for an interview. She was ecstatic. Hendon, she knew, was where all Metropolitan Police applicants go for a two-day interview and later, if accepted, for their training. This was definitely a step in the right direction.

When the time came for her eighty-mile trip to Hendon, the young applicant was nervous as a bride. She'd spend her first night away from home in a hotel with other hopefuls. Like herself, at least half of them would be from outside London.

The first day at Hendon includes a medical exam and a written exam on general information. The second day is a gruelling fitness test – hour after hour of exercises and running.

Yvonne returned home exhausted, but exhilarated. She thought she had done well, but was too hopeful to be cocky. Several weeks passed slowly. Finally, in March, 1977, the envelope marked 'The Metropolitan Police' came. She wasn't sure if she should open it. As long as it remained sealed, hope remained intact.

Finally, she ripped it open. Her smile lit up the room and her eyes danced down the page. Accepted for training! They considered her an outstanding candidate for the force. Her parents joyfully joined in her celebrations. Her younger sisters congratulated her. For her family, it was the end of a happy era and they would miss her. Yvonne looked forward to her starting date at Hendon.

The twenty-week training course was rigorous, both physically and mentally. Acceptance in the force is provisional, and depends on performance over a two-year probationary period. Yvonne knew she could fail at any time while she was a probationer. After all, many did.

The days at Hendon passed quickly with frequent tests on laws, protecting evidence, crowd psychology, report procedure and court testimony. There were practical simulations in which she and the other trainees took turns assuming the role of constable. So much was covered: how to investigate a crime, how to question a suspect, community relations. There was even a language lab to hear the many foreign dialects she would encounter in London.

Physically, training at Hendon was like being in an Army training camp. Yvonne and her fellow classmates were required to have strength, endurance and as much control over their bodies as they had over their emotions.

Men outnumbered the women by ten to one at Hendon, a ratio that applied to the force as well. Twenty-four thousand men and 2,400 women comprise the London Metropolitan Police. But whether man or woman, passing training is only the first hurdle.

'This is no average police station,' the officers at the famous Bow Street Station proudly proclaim. 'This is one of the top police stations in the country.' Following her twenty weeks of training, Yvonne was posted to Bow Street. Whether or not it was the luck of the draw, she considered it a feather in her cap.

Yvonne took a flat in London and frequently visited her family in the Wiltshire valley that was home.

Bow Street is one of the busiest police stations in London; perhaps in Western Europe. Its jurisdiction covers a bustling business centre by day and the entertainment centre of Soho and Leicester Square by night. From businessman to prostitute, from tourist to tramp, constables are likely to encounter every type of person in their work here.

Besides the 250 constables posted there, Bow Street has three chief inspectors, thirteen inspectors, thirty-seven sergeants, and a large civilian staff under the Chief Superintendent. Though there are only 3,000 permanent residents, over a quarter of a million people pass through the area every day. The station hums with activity twenty-four hours a day.

Built in 1917, the Bow Street Station and Magistrates' Court hasn't changed much over the years. A three-storey red brick building with large windows, it houses a communications centre, mess hall, locker rooms, booking area, a lockup, criminal investigation division, and offices. The high-ceilinged corridors and rooms are painted a cheerful yellow or white.

West End Central Police Station, Vine Street Station, and Bow Street comprise 'C' or the St James's District, one of twenty-three Metropolitan Police Districts, each one distinguished by a letter of the alphabet.

Over the remainder of her two-year probationary period, Yvonne continued to be tested. As a probationer, she was rotated through the various duties of constable: communications, desk duty, traffic control and street duty.

Periodic assessments recorded that Yvonne was progressing well. Other probationers were weeded out gradually, largely for temperament – finding out or being told that they didn't have the most important single quality necessary for police work, control of your emotions. Yvonne had it in large measure, as well as other requisites like understanding people and common sense. Besides that, 'Fletch' (as she was known) was well liked by her fellow officers. She got on well with everybody, a decided asset in a job with more than a little human interaction.

After two years of application, determination and hard work, Yvonne's dream was realized; she was confirmed as a regular constable. Now she officially wore the hat she had tried on in her imagination. She wore it proudly. As she always knew it would, it fitted her exceptionally well.

The years passed and Yvonne came of age in the police force. Now a seasoned professional, she had developed into a confident, self-possessed young woman. She kept fit with regular squash and swimming. Her brown belt in judo was a tribute to her strength and agility.

One evening, a fight broke out among about a dozen football supporters in a Covent Garden pub. A call to the station sent nearby officers to the scene. Yvonne, having been the closest, arrived there first. Immediately, she chose the largest of the trouble-makers and good-naturedly confronted him. 'All right,' she said, 'you've had a good evening here. Don't let's spoil it by forcing me to make arrests.'

Other officers burst into the pub only to find the brawl ended, and the last two fighters apologizing for their behaviour.

On another occasion, a highly disturbed young man had been arrested for creating a fracas. He was to appear in Bow Street Magistrates' Court, but escaped from his probation officer. Yvonne came across him on her patrol. Standing in the rain, the cheerful young policewoman calmly talked with him on the street, and eventually led him back to the court. She stayed with him until it was his turn to sit in the dock.

Then, she accompanied him and sat there holding his hand while the magistrate discharged him for hospital treatment.

Yvonne met Michael Liddle, another constable stationed at Bow Street. They got to know each other through their work and fell in love. They had become engaged and planned to be married in 1984.

The solid green flag of Libya hung over the door to its embassy in St James's Square. Like the other 145 accredited missions to the Court of St James, the elegant grey stone Georgian embassy appeared the height of respectability. Inside, the seventy rooms were decorated with gold leaf and graceful chandeliers. A richly panelled front hall led to a stately stairwell on the right. Upstairs, luxuriously appointed reception rooms and offices flowed from one to another.

The old-world ambiance of this London embassy, though, was an inappropriate setting for its present occupants. With the military take-over of Libya by rebel leader Colonel Muammar el-Qaddafi in 1969, life changed radically for its three million citizens. Dress regulations are strictly enforced. Police have been known to splash paint on the legs of women whose skirts are considered too short. Men with long hair have been given haircuts, courtesy of the government. The use of jewellery and make-up is restricted and Arab women must wear veils.

The country's conduct of international diplomacy changed, too. No ambassador from Libya had been formally accredited to the Foreign Office since 1979, when, on September 2, a 'Revolutionary Committee' took over Number Five, St James's Square. People's Bureaux were also established that month in Paris, Bonn, Rome, Madrid, Athens and Brussels. Twenty-three more People's Bureaux were declared in world capitals in 1980, ten in 1981, one in 1982 and six in 1983. In Arab countries, 'Brotherhood Bureaux' were established. Worldwide, Libya has over 80 missions.

Libya's attitude to the rest of the world was no longer one of statesmanship and peaceful coexistence. When the new breed of diplomats weren't peddling the country's main export, oil, they were investigating Libyan emigrants living abroad. All exiles, including the 6,500 living in England, were considered by the fanatical regime to be traitors. Colonel Qaddafi openly threatened to 'liquidate' them. New appointments to the embassy helped him make good on his word.

Since Qaddafi came to power in 1969, political parties are no longer allowed in Libya. The national parliament remains dissolved. All officials are appointed by Qaddafi and free elections are deemed 'unnecessary'. The north African country now purports to be ruled by a twelve-man military junta called the Revolutionary Command Council, but in reality, the Council is controlled by its Chairman and President, Muammar el-Qaddafi. A 22,000–man army enforces Qaddafi's iron rule.

Qaddafi's terrorist activities are not hidden like shameful secrets; he brags openly about them. He backed an attempt on the life of King Hassan of Morocco. Palestinian guerrillas receive generous subsidies from Libya as do other terrorist groups around the world. Following the massacre of Israeli athletes at the 1972 Olympics, a special five million dollar bonus was proudly presented by Qaddafi to the terrorist group Black September. When Qaddafi offered cash to African nations who broke ties with Israel, all but four agreed to do so. He has been described by one British diplomat as a cross between Adolf Hitler and Idi Amin.

Within a few weeks of his 'liquidation' threat, ten Libyan exiles were murdered in London, Rome, Athens, Bonn and Beirut. Italian police apprehended the murderer of one who was shot in the head in a Rome cafe. He simply said his victim was an 'enemy of the Libyan people and of Qaddafi, which are one and the same'.

Henchmen are posted in world capitals under the dignified and well-protected guise of diplomat. The week of the Iranian Embassy siege in London, in May, 1980, the US government drew the line, closed its embassy in Tripoli, and ordered its diplomats home. At the same time the State Department declared 'unacceptable' four of the so-called diplomats at the Libyan People's Bureau in Washington and they were ordered to immediately leave the country. They had been harassing other Libyans within the US, promising physical harm and even death if they did not return to Libya to face 'charges'. The 'crime' was opposing Colonel Qaddafi.

When the State Department ordered the four Libyans out, the People's Bureau suddenly changed their tune. They now insisted the four were not diplomats, they were students. As students, Libya contended, the State Department had no authority to expel them. The four diplomats/students/gunmen holed up inside the five-storey red brick embassy in Washington. Because embassies are immune from entry, eight carloads of police and FBI agents waited outside to deport them when they emerged. It became a stalemate.

Article 22 of the Vienna Convention prevented officials from entering the People's Bureau. 'The premises of the mission are inviolable,' states the Convention, which has been ratified by 141 countries. 'The agents of the receiving states may not enter them except with the consent of the head of mission. The premises of the mission . . . shall be immune from search.'

Finally, in May, 1981, President Reagan went a step further. Although he had closed the US Embassy in Tripoli, he had not formally severed relations with Libya. Now he did so, ordering them to close their 'People's Bureau' in Washington because of 'a general pattern of unacceptable conduct' and 'support for international terrorism'.

Rather abruptly, the Libyan government decided to recall the diplomats in question. At an airport press conference staged before their departure, the quartet denied the terrorist charges and said, 'We wanted to finish our studies.'

Britain, too, has had a history of problems with Libya's so-called diplomats; problems that foreshadowed the events that would lead to the taking of Yvonne Fletcher's life. Several murders in London, the result of feuds among Arabs or between Arabs and Israelis, were suspected to have been carried out by Libyans. Scotland Yard believed that the weapons used in the Iranian Embassy siege were smuggled into the country in Libyan diplomatic pouches and supplied to the terrorists who held twenty-one hostages in the Iranian

Embassy until the shoot-out that freed the hostages and killed the terrorists.

London's Iranian Embassy siege in 1980 set a construction boom in motion at the People's Bureau. The Libyans spent one million of their petrol pounds fortifying the People's Bureau against such an attack. A steel lining able to withstand a rocket blast was installed inside the wood-panelled front doors. Roof-mounted motion detectors could alert inhabitants to the slightest movement. Wall and ceiling sensors could detect intruders. The fortress housed a basement shelter stocked with weapons, flak jackets and gas masks. There was a firing range for submachine gun practice in the basement.

The Secretary of the People's Committee and the man Her Majesty's Government recognized as the head of the Libyan People's Bureau, Musa Kusa, was expelled from Britain shortly after his appointment. Two Libyans living in Britain who opposed the Qaddafi regime were murdered. Kusa, in a statement to *The Times*, approved the decision of the 'Revolutionary Committee' to kill them. After he was told to leave the country by Deputy Foreign Secretary Sir Ian Gilmour, Kusa promised more would be murdered on London streets and his country would continue to fund Irish terrorists.

Kusa used the publicity as an opportunity to proclaim that Libyans living in Britain 'are criminals'. He denied charges that diplomatic bags were used to smuggle guns into Britain, offering a rather unique defence. 'A gun costs forty pounds on the British black market,' Kusa explained. 'That's cheaper than in Libya.'

Following the expulsion of Kusa, Members of Parliament called on Mrs Thatcher's government to re-examine diplomatic immunity for those who use their embassies as headquarters for criminal activities. The British government warned Libya that 'criminal actions in the United Kingdom must cease' and promised to screen persons at the Libyan mission. That did not solve the problem.

The prohibition, under British law, of the acquisition and possession of fire-arms by a foreign mission was the subject of stern circular letters sent by the Foreign Office to all embassies in January and April of 1980, and again in 1982. Evidence presented at the trial of Barry Howson, a British arms dealer subsequently convicted of trying to export guns illegally, showed that the Libyans were ignoring the Foreign Office's warnings.

Howson, it was shown, bought ten hand guns from a dealer in St Martin's Lane. He took them to St James's Square where he met a Libyan agent and loaded them into the boot of the agent's car. One of the guns sold to Howson and passed to the Libyan was used to murder a Libyan journalist near Regent's Park mosque.

Several Members of Parliament again called on the Thatcher government to close down the Libyan Embassy for harbouring what one MP called a 'gang of thugs'. But the People's Bureau remained open.

On February 18, 1984, the leadership of the People's Bureau in London was seized by a student revolutionary group. The British embassy in Tripoli was notified that Mr Adam Kuwiri, who had acted as Secretary-General of the People's Committee of the Libyan Mission and was recognized by the Foreign Office as the chargé-d'affaires, ceased to be the head of mission. No replacement was named. The four-man student committee took up the running of the People's Bureau. The 'diplomats' now reported to them.

The student committee wasted no time introducing themselves to the constituency of Libyans they were ostensibly in England to protect. On March 11, five bombs injured twenty-six people in London. The next day, two more bombs went off in Manchester where there is a large concentration of Libyan students. One of those bombs exploded under a car belonging to a Libyan opposition leader and the other injured a Syrian family of four.

In April, 1984, thirty-five persons were recognized to have diplomatic status at the People's Bureau of the Socialist People's Libyan Arab Jamahiriya. Many of their family members also enjoyed immunity from the law. Under the terms of the Vienna Convention, ratified in 1961 and passed into British Law in the Diplomatic Privileges Act of 1964, diplomats enjoy immunity from prosecution. In addition, they are exempt from certain taxes and utility charges. Their missions are inviolable, and Britain is obliged to protect them and 'the dignity of the mission', an obligation met by the Diplomatic Protection Group. Events were soon to prove how little the Libyans were concerned with dignity and diplomacy.

On Tuesday, April 17, PC Michael Liddle and WPC Yvonne Fletcher were both on the 6.30 a.m. shift at Bow Street. Accustomed as they were to the early shift hours, they arrived at the station in their usual good humour.

Dashing down the station's red linoleum-covered stairway to the basement, Yvonne headed for the women's locker room. Since there were so few women constables, it made sense for them to share toilet and shower facilities with the women traffic wardens. The door marked 'Women Police Only' opened to the exclusive province of the WPCs. Here, in the fourteen by eighteen foot room furnished with about thirty grey steel lockers and a bench, Yvonne changed into her uniform: the starched white shirt, neat tie, dark blue wool tunic and skirt topped with black and white hat. Uniform meticulously in place, she crossed the rear courtyard and descended the stairs to the parade room. Making it with her usual five minutes to spare, she exchanged greetings with the other constables on the 6.30 shift.

When the inspector entered the parade room, everyone sprung to attention. Ritually, each presented a constable's accoutrements: the key to traffic lights and emergency boxes, the handcuff key and the silver whistle of the Metropolitan Police.

Inspection passed, they stood at ease to receive their duty assignments for the day. Half a dozen of them were assigned to public order duty in St James's Square. A demonstration was scheduled from 10.00 to 10.30 a.m. in front of the Libyan People's Bureau. They were expecting some skirmishes today, as there had been a similar demonstration on September 30. Several members of the armed Diplomatic Protection Group were also to be on hand at the Square.

*

April marks a special tradition in Libya – it is the month for public hangings. Today's demonstration in St James's Square was prompted by a public hanging in Libya two weeks before when two students from Tripoli University, denounced as traitors, were executed by the Qaddafi regime. Demonstrators had notified the police of this planned gathering well in advance, not for approval but in the interest of public safety. Experience of the Iranian demonstrations proved that a crowd's anger could easily turn into violence. Police have the power to stop parades and marches, but not to ban a demonstration of like-minded people, no matter what their cause. Every year, about 400 such demonstrations take place in London.

About midnight the night before, two members of the People's Bureau presented themselves to the duty officer at the Foreign Office to protest against the demonstration. About the same time, a message was delivered to Her Majesty's Embassy in Tripoli. Both conveyed the same threat. The Libyans said they 'would not be responsible for the consequences' if the demonstration proceeded as scheduled. The Foreign Office relayed a message to the Home Office: 'The Libyans seem very agitated and are unpredictable.'

Inside the People's Bureau, terrorist diplomats and their henchmen met under the framed colour photograph of Colonel Qaddafi to plan the day's events. Portraits of Qaddafi were featured prominently in every room, every corridor, every stairwell. Like Big Brother, his countenance seemed to watch you every minute, a reminder that 'treason' is punishable by death.

The once elegant rooms were in crowded disarray. Banks of filing cabinets cluttered each room. Desks were littered with paperwork spilling out of file folders. On every desktop was an Islamic desk diary, published and distributed by Qaddafi's regime.

As is common in countries who use a different calendar than the West, each page had two dates, one counting from the death of the Prophet and the other its corresponding Gregorian calendar date. The pages also contain two quotes for the day: one from the Koran and one labelled 'Sayings by the Moslem revolutionary Muammar Qaddafi.' Every thirty or so pages was a full colour photo insert immortalizing the leader, Qaddafi. He prays at a mosque; he speaks to the people; he attends conferences. Like a propaganda scrapbook, there were magazine covers, news headlines and booklets bearing his name. In a chilling centre spread, captioned 'Christian terrorism in Lebanon', photographs depicted a husband being dragged off as his wife screams, a soldier executing civilians in the street with an automatic pistol and the faces of children burned to near skeletons.

The People's Bureau received instructions that morning from Tripoli that they were not to react 'passively' to the day's demonstration. They were under instructions to 'meet the demonstration with violence'. They solidified their plan and began to filter out into St James's Square in discreet groups of two or three so they wouldn't be noticed. Each headed in a different direction.

A desk diary is turned to the day's date. On the page marked April 17, 1984, the quote from the Koran reads: 'May justice prevail among our people. You are the Supreme Judge.'

After parade, Yvonne and the rest of the shift walked across the courtyard to the station itself to check out radios. Yvonne took a fresh battery out of its charger and was officially on duty.

The first bit of business for the public order detail at St James's Square was to set up the steel barriers in front of the embassy and in front of the demonstration area across the street. The police plan was to separate the two factions with barriers which would slow down any confrontation and cool heated emotions. From the People's Bureau there was a line of steel barriers, the roadway, more barriers and then the demonstrators. Wherever the trouble originated, the plan would provide maximum containment of the expected disorder.

Inspector Alex Fish of the Vine Street Station was one of those in charge of the public order detail at St James's Square. The experienced fifteen-year veteran explained the logic of the plan: 'The numerous similar demonstrations in the past had all followed a similar pattern. Members of the staff came out of the embassy and tried to attack the anti-Qaddafi supporters, or the anti-Qaddafi demonstrators tried to provoke something of an attack on the embassy. We spoke to the embassy staff that morning and made it abundantly clear that if there was any trouble that morning, it was a police matter. It wasn't for them to come out and deal with it.'

Constables began setting up the steel barriers on the pavement in front of the embassy. Several members of the People's Bureau rushed out into the early morning and demanded that the police should not set the barriers there. The barricades would interfere with their plan to drag whatever demonstrators they could into the embassy where they intended to punish them.

Two of the People's Bureau members were especially agitated. The abusive and vociferous pair were taken away to the Vine Street Station. Dr Omar Sadani was not arrested because he had diplomatic immunity. He and his companion were calmed down.

All barriers had been in place for about an hour when about 70 demonstrators arrived by coach at Charles II Street. Police inspectors boarded the buses and reviewed the ground rules. Demonstrators would be ushered around the corner into the barricaded area. They would carry their banners and shout their slogans for thirty to forty-five minutes and then would be escorted back to their coaches which would be waiting in Pall Mall. There was to be no loitering about the Square after the allotted time.

'We didn't like the idea of them parading through the streets with masks over their faces,' Inspector Fish recalls, 'but they explained their position quite categorically. Most weren't prepared to show their faces because they would be photographed. They felt, therefore, their lives were at risk if they were identified, which, in hindsight, I see was probably very accurate.'

There were two policewomen on the schedule for policing

the event that morning which was comprised of C District constables from Bow Street, Vine Street and West End Central Police Stations.

Inspector Fish took the two women aside. 'There is sure to be trouble today,' he said, 'perhaps a struggle with us in the middle. I need the strongest force possible to be in the Square. One of you will have to stand guard with the coaches in Pall Mall to make certain the demonstrators are ready to go when their time is up.'

Neither of the two WPCs wanted that duty, Fish recalls. Both expressed a preference for duty in the Square. He would have to choose who stood duty in Pall Mall and who was in the Square. 'Yvonne,' he said, 'you'll be on the cordon in the Square.'

The officers took their positions around 9.40 a.m. The protesters were accompanied to the site across the street from the Libyan People's Bureau.

The demonstrators began chanting: 'Qaddafi hangs students. Qaddafi is a murderer.'

Before too long, a pro-Qaddafi faction numbering about two dozen arrived on the Duke of York Street side. A second pro-Qaddafi group of similar size approached the demonstrators from the Charles II Street side. These two groups walked towards the masked picketers shouting their slogans. Police, expecting confrontation, moved in, positioning themselves between the two groups on either side. Another line of police stayed in position between the embassy and the demonstrators. Instead of engaging in contact, though, the opposition groups stopped unexpectedly on the fringe. Three television cameras and a student cameraman recorded the scene.

Crouching down below the sill, the gunman slid the window open. Carefully positioning the rifle out the window, he took aim. A second gunman at the adjoining window likewise adjusted his sights.

At 10.18, the shots rang out. The demonstrators screamed.

At first, police thought it was merely a recording of machine-gun fire being broadcast over loudspeakers from the embassy. On previous occasions, the Libyans had broadcast loud music to drown out the anti-Qaddafi slogans. Sometimes they played the sounds of automatic weapons fire.

But this time it was no idle threat reeling through a cassette to frighten dissenters into compliance. This time a young woman, shot in the back, would lose her life.

Inspector Fish remembers the police reaction: 'Initially, we couldn't possibly believe that a machine gun would be fired out of a diplomatic premises into what was, in fact, a peaceful demonstration on the street. I don't think *anybody* could believe that it really happened. When we saw Yvonne, we thought, "She's fainted." But then you stop and see the blood everywhere. It's all a reaction that seemed a fraction of a second. It seemed like it was happening in slow motion. Then everyone realized it was real.'

Two officers rushed to Yvonne's side – PC John Murray and Sergeant Howard Turner. The two officers, acting without the slightest regard for their own safety, surrounded Yvonne Fletcher as she lay mortally wounded. The gunshot had ripped through her so severely they felt that moving her would aggravate the injury. Conscious and aware of what had happened, she lay on the pavement in a pool of her own blood. As the very life flowed out of her, she thought not of herself but of those around her. She looked up at them. In the true spirit of the seasoned professional she was, she said her last words: 'Keep calm.'

The machine-gun fire mowed down the demonstrators just after Yvonne was hit. Eleven of them fell wounded. Chaos ruled in St James's Square. The police went into action, commanded not by orders but by years of training and experience. Michael Liddle and other constables hurried the group of demonstrators and counter-demonstrators out of the line of fire and into Charles II Street. The eleven wounded demonstrators had been hit in the arms and legs. They bled profusely. An office worker across the square was injured. Police barricades had kept the demonstrators at a sufficient distance so that the bullets had lost much of their power and none of the demonstrators was fatally wounded. Officers transported them out of the line of fire. Assistance was called in.

Once he reached the action, Michael saw Yvonne. Fellow officers wrestled to restrain him from running to her in the Square. The two fellow constables hovering over Yvonne were still in the line of fire, like sitting ducks. Reluctant to move her because movement would aggravate her wound, they didn't think of their own peril. The danger was too great, though, and Yvonne had to be moved. They carried Yvonne over to the Charles II Street side to wait for the ambulances.

Within a few short minutes, this well-planned, routine demonstration became the scene of a vicious crime, and the assassins who called themselves diplomats had created an international crisis. In the street lay Yvonne's black and white hat. It would never be worn again.

Confusion surrounded the Square. Workers poured out of the nearby buildings to see what the commotion was. Police vehicles sped to the scene from all directions. Ambulance sirens wailed. The wounded screamed in pain. Yvonne was unconscious and had stopped breathing. Sergeant Lewis gave her resuscitation. She revived momentarily, then lapsed into unconsciousness again. He breathed life into her twice more, not wanting to believe his efforts were futile, not wanting to watch life leave her. Michael Liddle ran the perimeter of the sealed off area to be by her side.

Police tried to contain the disaster. The five streets leading to the Square were sealed off. Traffic in the West End became a tangled mess. The ambulances fought for twenty minutes to get through. At 10.40, the ambulance arrived in Charles II Street. Yvonne was rushed to Westminster Hospital. Michael had got there too late to go with her, so he sped to the hospital after her.

At the Bow Street Station, Chief Inspector Bryan West sat at his large wooden desk in his third-floor office, engaged in the routine of running the busy station under his command. Communications officers, alerted by radio from the Square, relayed the horrible news: one of his constables had been shot. A moment later he learned it was Yvonne.

Bryan West had a special friendship for Yvonne and Michael and knew them well. He knew their records as outstanding police officers and had been happy to learn of their engagement. West and his wife had met and fallen in love twenty-five years before when they were both young police officers stationed at Hammerford, so he felt a special bond with the young couple.

Mr West's thoughts moved to action instantly. He ordered police to rush Yvonne's parents and youngest sister from Wiltshire to the hospital. He hoped they would make it in time. Then he rushed to hospital himself.

In the hospital corridor, Michael waited in vain outside the operating theatre for some good news. His Chief Inspector knew it would be some time before doctors could determine the outcome, so he took Michael back to his office. The phone call came. The news was tragic. Bryan West sadly told Michael that Yvonne never revived from her final coma at the Square. The cause of death was a bullet wound from the Sterling submachine gun fired from the Libyan Embassy.

The drivers who were rushing her parents and her youngest sister, Debbie, to London phoned the station half way, hoping for an improvement to report. They learned that Yvonne had died, but couldn't bring themselves to tell the distraught parents. Twelve-year-old Debbie, Tim and Queenie were brought to Inspector West's office at Bow Street. There, he broke the terrible news.

Later on, Yvonne's two sisters, Sarah and Heather, who had followed in their sister's footsteps to live and work in London, came to the Chief Inspector's office where they too heard that Yvonne was dead. Michael and the family whom Yvonne had loved so much, consoled each other at the station. Through their tears, they tried to find comfort in one another. The coroner's report would read: shot by person or persons unknown.

In St James's Square, the police had a massive job to do. The rear garage entrance to the People's Bureau was not sealed off for at least ten minutes after the shooting. During that time some of the occupants are known to have fled the building.

Every building in the Square had to be evacuated. A communications centre, code-named Zulu Control, was established in the offices of the D'Arcy, MacManus & Masius advertising agency. It became the heart of the operation. Senior officers, support services, technical services, communications personnel and special armed officers from D–11 rallied there for logistics, planning and negotiations with the Libyans. Representatives of the Home Office, the Foreign Office and the Metropolitan Police planned their strategy.

With Mrs Thatcher that morning en route to Lisbon for a three-day state visit and Sir Geoffrey Howe, the Foreign Secretary, in Peking, Leon Brittan, the Home Secretary, headed the government during the crisis. Sir Kenneth Newman, Metropolitan Police Commissioner, worked closely with him on all strategic matters.

The Libyan authorities in Tripoli were requested to instruct those inside the People's Bureau to leave the building so it could be searched for weapons and explosives. The request was denied.

The entire Square was sealed from view with enormous blue plastic tarpaulins. Traffic in central London was completely halted. It was 8.00 p.m. before C District constables were allowed to return to their stations to be debriefed. The morning's 'routine duty' seemed so long ago.

Word of the London shooting no doubt reached Colonel Qaddafi via telephone or radio very shortly after it took place. Before long, the British Embassy in Tripoli was surrounded by about 60 revolutionary guards. The twenty-five Britons inside, including eleven women and two children, were under an undeclared house arrest.

The inviolability of a diplomatic mission as outlined in the Vienna Convention meant that the British police were unable to storm the embassy in St James's Square and that the revolutionary guard were unable to enter the British Embassy in Tripoli.

Sir Francis Vallet was on the drafting committee of the Vienna Convention and was a member of the International Law Commission from 1973 to 1981. He recalls, 'The prospect of an embassy being used for that kind of purpose (terrorist activities) was not in contemplation in 1961. If you look at the kind of amendments which were submitted on Article 22, you see the kind of risk foreseen was the risk of something happening in the embassy which would threaten the lives and property in the vicinity, a fire or an epidemic, and not deliberate acts being taken from the embassy outward.'

Ironically, the original draft of Article 22 of the Convention gave the agents of the host country power of entry 'in an extreme emergency, in order to eliminate a grave and imminent danger to human life, public health or to safeguard the security of the state'. The shooting in St James's Square certainly would have fitted this description, but Sir Gerald Fitzmaurice, a British representative, was one of the chief movers in having it rejected. He persuaded the International Law Commission, which was drafting the Convention, that if an exception were there, it would be used all too often.

Colonel Qaddafi, as always, was willing to ignore the rules. Mr Douglas Ledingham, the 35-year-old manager of British Caledonian Airways stationed in Tripoli, was arrested by the Libyan authorities. He and two other British citizens remained under detention for several hours. Since they were not diplomats, they were not immune from detention. Several attempts on the part of British Caledonia to get an explanation from the Libyan government or a release proved fruitless. Had it been stated, the threat could not have been plainer.

On the advice of the Foreign Office, Tuesday's British Caledonia flight to Tripoli, already over Italy, headed back to Heathrow Airport.

Tension among Britain's 8,000 citizens in Libya grew. British residents of Tripoli were advised via the BBC World Service to keep a low profile. Virginia Ledingham and her four children waited anxiously by the telephone for news.

The *Daily Express* contacted the British Embassy in Tripoli on the night of the 17th. When asked for a comment, a spokesman replied laconically: 'Situation? What situation?' The sixty revolutionary guards still surrounded them.

The urgent priority emergency committee of ministers, who meet in the Cabinet Office Briefing Room (Cobra), were in session almost continuously overnight on the 17th. Strategists thought through every scenario. What would be the consequences of a Special Air Service strike? With 8,000 British citizens in Libya, the consequences would be hard to predict.

History records one incident in 1973 when Pakistan demanded access to the Iraqi Embassy to search for smuggled arms. The Iraqi Ambassador refused admission but armed police raided the embassy anyway. They found huge consignments of arms as they suspected they would. The invasion was in violation of the Vienna Convention, but no action was taken by the International Law Commission.

The Home Secretary told the British people that the government had protested to Libya in the strongest possible terms how 'Without warning, provocation or excuse, gunfire commenced from the window of the Bureau and there was the most disgraceful and barbaric outrage that London has seen for a very long time.' He described the incident as 'the outrageous abuse of the premises occupied by the Libyan People's Bureau.'

On the morning of the 18th, Mr Oliver Miles, the British Ambassador to Libya, was allowed to drive out of the embassy to go to the Foreign Liaison Bureau. The Ambassador's wife, Mrs Julia Miles, told reporters she had spoken with the families of all British diplomats by phone. 'Morale is very high,' she said, 'despite what's going on. We have plenty of food, everything is perfectly normal. We are happy, the dog is happy, the sun is shining, we have water and electricity . . . We are carrying on as normal.' Mr Miles made a formal protest about the Libyan containment and asked that the inhabitants of the People's Bureau in London leave the building. Observing the dignified protocol of diplomatic convention provided a stark contrast to Qaddafi's diplomatic assassins.

Cobra hoped to pressure the Libyans into waiving immunity, as in the case of the London Iranian Embassy siege of 1980, when the head of mission had agreed to do so. There were several snags, however. Unlike the Iranian Embassy siege, during which the embassy was held by outside terrorists whose hostages included several members of the Iranian mission, the Libyans cornered in the Bureau *were* the members of the mission. Also, since February 20, there was no head of mission. Terrorists had not just staged the show; these terrorists were running the show.

Ironically, Libya was the birthplace of the British army's elite Special Air Service, founded in 1942. These commandos, whose rigorous training includes field exercises with live ammunition, are skilled in demolition, lock picking, sabotage, hand to hand combat, skiing, diving and parachute jumping. SAS members always work masked, to protect their identities. Frequent simulated field exercises to liberate hostages from planes, trains and buildings keep them in top form. Their split-second timing and fearless determination to get the job done make them one of Britain's most valuable assets.

Shortly after the shooting on the 17th, SAS commanders selected a twenty-five man squad to fly to a jump-off point near London should they be needed. They were armed with Browning pistols, submachine guns and stun grenades, the same weapons they had used in the Iranian Embassy siege.

Their breathtaking attack in that siege, an attack that was rehearsed on a full scale model of the Iranian Embassy, was on everyone's mind. From the time of their arrival on the 17th throughout the eleven days of tension, the squad meticulously prepared for action. The SAS motto, 'Who Dares Wins', encapsulated what many British people were thinking.

Media reports of the SAS arrival near London sparked fear in Qaddafi's gunmen. The Libyan News Agency Jana reported the British police were preparing to storm the People's Bureau. To the report was added this threat: 'The committee warns against the consequences of such an action and places full responsibility for it on the British government . . . An act of this magnitude will not go unanswered by the Libyan people, who know how to avenge themselves.'

On the 18th, Libyan representatives to the United Nations filed a complaint citing British 'provocation' and 'inhumane' behaviour in its handling of the crisis. A letter sent to UN Secretary General Javier Perez de Cuellar accused British police of taking Libyan students hostage and mistreating them.

Lower Regent Street was crowded with onlookers gathered behind police barriers waiting in anticipation of decisive action. A 39-year-old woman told a telephone operator that a bomb inside the People's Bureau would go off if Mrs Thatcher did not act. Though the threat was idle, the woman was arrested. She was given a three-month suspended sentence.

The British police maintained the position that they wanted 'the Libyans out and the police in, to search the embassy'. Two Libyan diplomats who were not in the embassy at the time of the shooting acted as intermediaries during the crisis. One of them, Muftah Fitouri, was formally recognized as the Bureau's charge d'affaires. The two Libyan intermediaries made several trips into the People's Bureau carrying messages from the police.

Negotiations became futile and the Libyans were notified that diplomatic relations would terminate at 6.00 p.m., April 22. They were told that all persons were to have left the Bureau by midnight, April 29. The Libyan government said they would send a representative to witness the evacuation.

Heathrow Airport, where 270 Libyans were enrolled in a British Airways engineering course, was the centre for several incidents. A bomb exploded in a luggage hall on the 20th, injuring twenty-five people. A car going through the Heathrow tunnel was stopped and armed officers took two Libyans away for questioning. Four more Libyans were arrested at Terminal 2 while waiting for a Libyan Airways flight.

The tension-filled days passed slowly for Cobra members, negotiators and the Metropolitan Police, who worked in twelve-hour duty shifts in and around the People's Bureau. On Friday, one of Yvonne's fellow constables retrieved her hat from the place where it had fallen on Tuesday. Though he acted against orders, he wanted the hat for her coffin.

While the eyes of the world focused on St James's Square,

the government, mindful of the 8,000 British citizens it had to protect, tried to resolve the situation by patient diplomacy. The Libyans responded with threats and violence.

The semi-official weekly newspaper *Green March* hinted that Libya might retaliate against Britain again by donating generously to the IRA.

In a staged television interview broadcast in Libya, Qaddafi said the British police had launched an armoured attack on the People's Bureau and accused Britain of causing the death of Yvonne Fletcher. At a press conference, Qaddafi warned a group of British and American reporters: 'The Libyan people are very angry and I cannot anticipate what will take place.' When a reporter asked if he intended to continue to eliminate his enemies abroad, the Colonel replied, 'I have no enemies because I am not in power here; it is the people who are in power.'

Home Secretary Leon Brittan, in a television broadcast he was sure was being watched in the People's Bureau, denounced Yvonne Fletcher's murder: 'Diplomatic status does not convey the right to shoot people with machine guns . . . Our aim is to ensure that everyone comes out and then the police can make their enquiries and search the building for weapons and explosives . . . But it is not a question of getting permission to go in – the police will not be deterred from doing what is necessary.'

We may never know what threats the Libyans made behind closed doors. Over the course of days, hopes for arresting a murderer became futile; negotiations were in progress to provide safe passage for the besieged Libyans.

Once funeral plans for Yvonne Fletcher were announced, Chief Inspector Byran West recalls, the police knew the Libyans would pick that day for the evacuation of the Libyan People's Bureau. 'Call it police sense,' he says, 'we just knew they would want the most publicity possible in the world press.'

Helicopters flew overhead and the air was filled with tension, as the cream of the police's sharp-shooters trained their sights at the portal of the People's Bureau. On April 27, at 8.47 a.m., the evacuation began. Security precautions were thoroughly planned and executed. The manner and means of the evacuation and the transportation of the Libyans had been negotiated to the finest detail. Neutral intermediaries from Turkey, Syria and Saudi Arabia would be present every step of the way.

Four large canvas bags, each closed with a diplomatic seal, were carried out of the People's Bureau. The bags were handed over the police barricade to intermediaries and the weight nearly caused one to be dropped. The bags were loaded into the back of a white van. Their contents were no secret; one of them contained the rifle used to kill Yvonne Fletcher.

The murder weapon and ammunition were returned to Libya the same way they arrived – under the protection of the diplomatic bag, accorded safety by Article 27 of the Vienna Convention which states: 'The diplomatic bag shall not be opened or detained.' The Convention stipulates no restrictions on the size as long as the 'packages' bear 'visible external marks of their character and may contain only diplomatic documents or articles intended for official use.' Lethal weapons were now apparently official instruments of Muammar el-Qaddafi's government.

By 11.00 a.m., all thirty 'diplomats' and 'student revolutionaries' had evacuated the Bureau and were under safe conduct to Heathrow. One hundred and thirty-seven of their dependents were also given free and protected passage out of the country.

In Tripoli, thirty British Embassy employees and their dependents waited at the airport for permission to leave for home. Julia Miles, the Ambassador's wife, led the British nationals in a chorus of 'Rule, Brittania', as they marched to their jet.

At Salisbury Cathedral, mourners gathered to pay tribute to a very brave young woman. As the Libyans boarded the plane for a hero's return to Tripoli, the sun shone brightly on the honour guard of fellow police officers who stood at attention outside the cathedral.

Chords of organ music wafted out of the 750-year-old

Gothic cathedral as an overflow crowd of 1,500 filed in. Nearly everyone from Yvonne's native village of Semley attended. About 800 police officers, including the entire staff of the Bow Street Station, mourned there that day. The Chief of Scotland Yard and Home Secretary Leon Brittan paid their respects.

Escorted down the aisle by six uniformed Metropolitan Police pallbearers, Yvonne's coffin was draped with the blue flag of Scotland Yard. Placed on top of the flag were a bouquet and Yvonne's hat. Dozens of wreaths filled the sacristy; one from the family of WPC Jane Arbuthnot, who was killed by an IRA car bomb outside Harrods in December, 1983.

The Bishop of Salisbury, the Right Reverend John Austin Baker, conducted the forty-five minute service. 'As each new act of corruption is reported,' he told the assembled crowd, 'we slip too easily into saying of the perpetrators, "They must be mad.". . . The problem is not madness but wickedness. Yvonne was the victim of an evil act.'

Bow Street Chief Superintendent Bryan West eulogized Yvonne touchingly: 'Here was a girl, loving and in love. She was warm-hearted in the best sense of the phrase. She tackled every task – no matter how irksome or inconvenient – with happy willingness and an infectious chuckle that was her particular mark. There was never any complaint from her, only good humour and generosity, applied to standards far above the norm. She was affable and courageous, she had tenacity and determination.'

That day the free world mourned the tragedy of a young life lost while her murderer went safely home. The abuse of diplomatic immunity has never been so apparent. While the hue and cry was widespread and vociferous, nothing has changed. The day before Yvonne Fletcher's death no one would have believed such a thing was possible. Now we can only wait and see what further outrages tomorrow may bring.

The file on the murder of Yvonne Fletcher was never closed, nor has she been forgotten. Forensic experts continue to investigate her murder, preparing their ballistic evidence, much of it gathered from the People's Bureau after the Libyans' departure, so that should the day ever come when her murderer can be tried, the evidence will be conclusive.

At 4.10 p.m., April 30, police cautiously entered the Bureau accompanied by a representative of the Saudi Arabian Embassy. Though fearful the Libyans had left booby-traps, the search went smoothly. The building was then sealed.

Following the inspection of the premises, police announced the discovery of a spent cartridge case near the upstairs window from which witnesses saw a gun emerge. Thirty Beretta pistols, some Browning pistols, two ammunition clips, two pistol grips for submachine guns and an enormous cache of ammunition were recovered from inside the People's Bureau. The diplomatic bags must have been too full to carry it all back to Tripoli.

Qaddafi, who never publicly varied his indignant insistence that the shots were fired from outside the embassy, accused the police of falsifying the evidence, even though investigators were accompanied by Saudi witnesses. In a hollow effort at justification, Libya announced the discovery of arms inside the British embassy. Qaddafi repeated his threat to resume aid to the IRA as a means of punishment for the expulsion of his murderous diplomats.

The Metropolitan Police cherished Yvonne and they cherish her memory. A watercolour portrait of her, smiling brightly in her uniform, hangs in a place of honour at the Bow Street Station. Those who worked with her, from Chief Superintendent West to the probationers, will never forget her. 'She was always smiling,' a fellow officer remembers. 'It was almost as if her personality was two sizes too big for her.'

The British people have not forgotten her either. Donations to police charities in memory of her death topped £28,000. A cherry tree planted in her memory in St James's Square will bloom every April. Nearby, a marble and stone memorial stands as permanent reminder of the young woman who died at the hands of a terrorist protected by diplomatic immunity.

Queenie and Tim Fletcher struggle to reconcile themselves

to their tragic loss. 'I suppose we do feel bitter,' says Queenie. 'Her life was short, but it was happy. She did a lot in her life – probably more than some people will however long they live. Joining the police was what Yvonne wanted to do – and she loved it.'

Reflecting on what Yvonne herself might have thought about murderers who are not held accountable for their actions, Queenie says, 'She had such a strong sense of fair play, I'm sure it must bother the police force as a whole – it must always be in the back of their minds that it could happen again.'

CHAPTER TWO

Diplomatic Immunity And Its Abuse

'BEFORE OUR COMMITTEE starting looking at the situation, I really had no idea of the size of the problem. Occasionally I would notice a newspaper story or someone would mention an incident. But now I am well aware of the dimensions of our problem. Do you know we have 15,000 diplomats here in London and that they commit at least one serious crime a week – that is, a crime that could be punished by at least six months' imprisonment. If we don't begin eliminating this situation, it could well overwhelm us.'

The speaker is Sir Anthony Kershaw, the distinguished chairman of the Foreign Affairs Committee. For almost a year following Yvonne Fletcher's tragic death, Sir Anthony's committee was charged with investigating the entire problem of the abuse of diplomatic immunity in Britain and to report back to the House as a whole with its recommendations for changes both in the law of diplomatic immunity and the way it is applied by the Foreign Office.

Sir Anthony was not entirely accurate when he said that there were 15,000 diplomats stationed in London. In fact, according to the Foreign Office, as of February 1985 there were eighty-eight embassies and forty-one high commissions in London, staffed by 4,524 diplomats who enjoyed full diplomatic immunity: they cannot be charged with any crime nor can they be brought into a civil court to answer any action there. While they enjoy full immunity, so do 'members of the family forming part of the household', in the words of Article 37 of the Vienna Convention. When these 'family members' are added to the diplomats, the number of persons enjoying total immunity amounts to the 15,000 Sir Anthony talks about.

Then, in addition to this number who enjoy full immunity, there are another 2,654 who enjoy limited immunity: complete immunity from criminal prosecution and limited immunity from civil suits in respect to acts carried out as part of their official duties.

In recent years there has been a tremendous leap in the number of protected diplomats. In 1913, the number of diplomatic personnel in England with immunity was 543. Even by 1938, that number had only doubled to 1,084.

But in the years following World War II, the number of diplomats, consuls and attachés stationed in world capitals grew inexorably. Before World War II, missions were smaller and had more limited interests. Since the end of the war, there has been a proliferation of attachés assigned to every mission. Every embassy now incorporates in its official delegation military attachés, political, agricultural and cultural attachés, trade, labour, science and legal attachés, economic attachés and many others besides. All of them and their dependents are entitled to immunity. As well as the increase in the staffing of already established missions, between 1945 and 1970 more than sixty new nations came into existence and they, too, have sent their diplomats out into the world.

By 1955, the proliferation of legation members was causing concern. Alfred Robens, a Labour MP from Blyth spoke before the House of Commons that year about the expansion of diplomatic operations following World War II. He cited the 'general anxiety in many people's minds about the growing army of civilians receiving diplomatic immunity'.

If anything, the problem of diplomatic proliferation is even greater in the United States because not only does the US grant immunity to those diplomats representing foreign governments but also extends diplomatic immunity to the personnel of institutions like the World Bank, the International Monetary Fund, and the OAS who work in Washington, DC.

To this already sizeable total must be added the employees

and officials of the United Nations Secretariat, observer nations, employees of foreign government missions, and members of the mission of the Organization of African Unity and their families. Immune residents of the New York area alone total over 15,000. In the United States as a whole there are some 36,000 people with full immunity and another 13,000 with partial immunity.

The idea that diplomats should be free from hindrance in the performance of their duties is by no means a new concept. It was codified into English law by the Diplomatic Privileges Act of 1708 which granted virtually complete immunity from both criminal prosecution and civil suit to diplomatic 'agents', their families, their staffs and their personal servants. 'Agents' in turn had the broadest definition and covered just about everyone in an embassy or mission. Under the statute, anyone with diplomatic immunity could simply ignore any kind of summons or court document because it was without force; and in fact a person or government official could actually be prosecuted for initiating a suit or arrest against a person he knew to have diplomatic immunity.

By the late 1950s, there was general agreement that this blanket granting of immunity to the ever-increasing diplomatic community was a situation that was getting out of hand. So in 1961, eighty-one nations, including Britain, met in Vienna at a UN sponsored Vienna Convention on Diplomatic Relations, their purpose to draft a new international treaty on diplomatic relations. Of the fifty-three articles agreed to at the conference, twelve dealt directly with the subject of personal diplomatic immunity.

Two major changes were adopted at Vienna. The first distinguished between the public and private acts of those enjoying immunity and in Article 37 divided the personnel in a diplomatic mission into different classes giving each a varying degree of immunity. The four different divisions are: diplomatic agents; administrative and technical staffs; service staffs; and personal servants.

Article 31 granted the broadest immunity to diplomatic agents and their direct families (courts have held 'direct family' to be spouses and children although some countries including Britain also occasionally extend immunity to a diplomat's parents if they are living with the diplomat and even to a diplomat's brothers and sisters under some circumstances). This group were given complete immunity from criminal prosecution and from civil suits except when a diplomat acts in a purely private way.

A major difference of interpretation is given to exactly who is a diplomatic 'agent'. Some nations, especially those in the Eastern Bloc, define it very narrowly: the top two or three members of the delegation. Other nations, including Britain and the United States, tend to interpret it more broadly, granting full immunity to a much larger number of individuals and their families on an embassy's staff.

Members of the administrative and technical staff and their direct families were given full immunity from criminal prosecution but are immune from civil suit only regarding official acts. By definition, family members cannot undertake 'official acts'.

Members of the service staffs, which would include cooks, drivers, etc., have both criminal and civil immunity only as regarding official acts, and their families receive no immunity whatsoever.

Personal servants received no immunity.

If a family member is a citizen of the host state there is no immunity.

Another slight change is that if a diplomat initiates a suit, he automatically waives immunity from any counterclaim that results. (Although the courts have held he does not waive immunity for the execution of any judgment that might result from the counterclaim.)

Both Britain and the United States signed the Vienna Convention, as it has become known, in 1961. Its provisions were enacted intact into British law in the Diplomatic Privileges Act of 1964. But for varying reasons, the US Senate did not ratify the convention until 1965 and even then delayed its effective date until 1972. But when it did ratify the Vienna Convention it did not repeal the existing broader diplomatic immunity act which dated back to 1790 and which was modelled after the British law of the time. Thus in 1972, when the Convention became effective, the US in effect had two contradictory laws on its books. The State Department continued to adhere to the broader law until 1978 when Congress got around to passing what is known as the 'Diplomatic Relations Act of 1978' (DRA).

Under both the UK's Diplomatic Privileges Act and the US's Diplomatic Relations Act, no diplomatic agent or member of his family can be arrested or even detained on criminal charges once his identity has been established and it is confirmed that immunity exists. There is an exception to this. If the holder of immunity is deemed a threat to public order, or to himself, he may be held for a reasonable amount of time until that threat has passed.

In the case of immunity from civil proceedings, the granting of immunity is not automatic and cannot be given directly to either the Foreign Office or the State Department. It can only be granted by the courts, and usually only after the individual has put in a court appearance and the Foreign Office or State Department has certified that the individual is entitled to immunity. But in practice, since lawyers know that bringing a suit against immune diplomats is an exercise in futility, few suits are ever brought where it is clear that this defence will be invoked.

Traditionally, the Foreign Office has seen as its main mission the preservation of good relations with foreign states. This entails the suppression whenever possible of any details of abuses by diplomatic lawbreakers or, if details do leak, the minimizing of their impact.

In a case we will view in detail in a later chapter, Mrs Lynn Reynolds, a young mother, was sexually molested in Kensington Gardens by a Jordanian diplomat in front of her two small children.

When the details of the incident slipped out, the press was livid and stories of the incident began appearing with calls to do something about perverted diplomats. So the Foreign Office decided to do something – something to protect the reputation of the Jordanian who had been granted immunity from charges of indecent sexual assault and who had left the country.

The Foreign Office issued a formal statement saying that Scotland Yard had determined that even if the man in question had not had immunity, and had not fled the country, he would not have been formally charged. Lack of evidence, said the Foreign Office. It was only Lynn Reynolds' word against his; there were no other witnesses save her two children and they were too young to testify. The story the Foreign Office was trying to sell was that in the end the man had not escaped because he had immunity, he had got off because of lack of evidence.

But in the same announcement, the Foreign Office also said that it had sent a strongly worded letter to the Jordanian mission reminding its members of their obligation to obey the laws of their host country. A very strange letter indeed, considering Foreign Office insistence that there was not enough evidence to bring the man to trial had he not had immunity.

But the St James's Square murder and the attempt to kidnap former Nigerian government official Umaru Dikko from the streets of London and ship him back to Nigeria in a crate under diplomatic protection have finally forced the government to remove some of the secrecy that surrounds cases of diplomatic abuse, and to admit for the first time the extent of the problem.

The facts, as presented by the Foreign Office to Sir Anthony Kershaw's committee, are appalling. Over the last ten years, foreign diplomats assigned to the eighty-eight embassies and forty-one high commissions in London committed 546 serious crimes. Of these crimes, about forty percent were for theft and another forty percent were road traffic offences, mainly driving while under the influence of either alcohol or drugs.

The statistics show the problem is worsening. In the period between January, 1982, and May, 1984, there were 123 incidents of diplomats avoiding prosecution for serious offences. Of this number, sixty-two were road offences and forty-one were incidents of theft, mainly shoplifting.

By way of comparison, the 6,800 diplomats of the British Foreign Service and their families stationed abroad in the service of the Queen committed a total of nine such offences in the same period. And of these nine offences five were in Eastern Bloc or Third World countries not considered friendly to Britain, and could therefore possibly be regarded as 'political' in nature. In other words, in the last ten years, 546 crimes were committed by diplomats stationed in Britain while as little as four like crimes were committed by British diplomats and their dependents stationed abroad.

Listening to facts like this quickly turned Sir Anthony from a casual observer to a leading expert on the subject of diplomatic abuses.

'I was very surprised, I must admit, at the size of the problem. I was also surprised at the laxness of the Foreign Office in many of these matters. Take the Libyan affair. They knew for more than eighteen months that things were out of hand at that mission. Yet they let the matter go until we had a tragedy.'

After the murder of WPC Fletcher, everyone in the Foreign Office expressed shock that such a thing could happen. 'How is it possible that diplomats could use their own embassy to committ an act of terrorism?' was the question most often heard. Yet, as Sir Anthony points out, they did have many different warnings.

Demonstrations outside the Iraqi Embassy on Queen's Gate resulted in violence by diplomatic personnel on at least two occasions. In 1982, a mission employee came out of the embassy during a demonstration and, in an ensuing scuffle, assaulted a policeman. Since he had diplomatic immunity, the clerk was released. Then, only days before the demonstration in St James's Square, demonstrators entered the Consular Section of the embassy where they were held captive for several hours. The Iraqi Embassy refused to allow police to enter, invoking the inviolability of the mission.

If Sir Anthony Kershaw, who as chairman of the Foreign Affairs Committee has available to him resources that are matched by few in Britain, was surprised at the scope of the diplomatic abuse problem, what then of the shock of the average citizen at learning that diplomats can kill, rape, maim, steal and generally flaunt the laws of our country with virtual impunity? Not only can they do this, but as Sir Anthony so directly points out, they *do* so each and every week. Moreover, they are often protected and shielded by the Foreign Office which sees its primary function not as the protection of British citizens but as the maintenance of good diplomatic relations – no matter the price that must occasionally be paid by some unsuspecting citizen.

The Thatcher government formally responded to the events of St James's Square and the investigation of the Foreign Affairs Committee with a White Paper on diplomatic abuses issued in April, 1985. In it, the government noted: 'The main abuse lies not so much in the comparative number of alleged offences or in their relative gravity, but in the reliance on immunity to protect individuals for offences without any obvious connection to the efficient performance of the functions of a diplomatic mission.'

No case better illustrates this fact than the antics of a Syrian diplomat named Ahmed Walid Rajab, who became embroiled in a dispute that was to eventually outrage all of Britain.

In early 1982, businessman John Chaffey, his wife Suzanne and their two children, Samantha, then aged ten, and Daniel, eight, had the opportunity to move to the United States for six months on a temporary business assignment.

Not wanting to see their handsome £85,000 three-bedroom flat in Stonor Road, West Kensington, stand empty, the Chaffeys decided to rent it out for six months, more to have it occupied than to earn income. They advertised it for lease and had several calls. One came from a woman who said she was Lebanese and that she and her husband and two daughters had just arrived in Britain on a six-month assignment and were looking for accommodation.

The two women met and the match seemed perfect. A six-month lease calling for rent of £125 per week was entered into and the Chaffeys left for America. The new tenant, Ahmed Walid Rajab, his wife and two daughters, Rawan and Roula, moved into the flat. Later, Chaffey would learn that

Rajab was the Counsellor Advisor on Arab League Affairs at the Syrian Embassy and was not on a six-month assignment.

The Chaffeys' stay in America turned out to be longer than anticipated and so, in a phone conversation, it was agreed that the Rajabs would continue living in the flat for an additional three months at the same rent. In October, the Chaffeys returned to Britain and called the Rajabs to tell them it was time to leave the flat. They then received a shock. The Rajabs really liked the place and they had no intention of moving.

Based on the fact that the Chaffeys had continued to accept rent payments after the expiry of the six-month lease, Rajab was able to petition a local Rent Officer to be declared the statutory tenant of the flat. Moreover, the Rent Officer reduced the rent from 125 to 100 pounds a week.

Chaffey immediately contacted his solicitors and received a rude shock. He was told that he was completely in the right but that the only way he could regain his home was to bring suit against Rajab for possession and that Rajab could and would fight any such suit or any writ arising from a court judgment on the basis of diplomatic immunity; moreover, Rajab would win. Diplomatic immunity blocked anything he could do, he was told.

Chaffey could not afford to buy another home so the only answer was for the family to split up. Mrs Chaffey went to live with her mother, Mr Chaffey moved in with friends and the two children went to live with another friend.

An entire year passed with the situation at a stalemate. Then one day, Mr Chaffey noticed that the Rajabs had gone on holiday. So, using his front door key – the locks had not been changed – the Chaffeys moved back in, reunited for the first time in over twelve months. They had a moving company come and put the Rajabs' furniture in storage.

The Rajabs were soon back from their trip and they were not pleased that the Chaffeys were living in 'their flat'. They immediately went to the West London County Court and got an order evicting the Chaffeys. Back went the family to their nomadic existence, back into the flat came the Rajabs.

Then in March of 1984, the Chaffeys received from Rajab's

solicitors what they call the 'blackmail letter'. After setting forth their position that no judgment against Rajab could be enforced because of his diplomatic immunity, the letter went on to say that Rajab might be willing to move 'if he receives a sum of money to compensate any damages he may be claiming'. Mr Chaffey indignantly rejected the offer.

Another six months passed and then Rajab made what was to prove a tactical error. Amazingly, he brought suit against the Chaffeys for £10,000, claiming damages for the three weeks the Chaffeys had reoccupied the flat and for loss of goods that had been placed in storage.

Because of the suit Rajab had effectively waived his right to claim immunity. So the matter finally moved into the courts.

By this time, John Chaffey wanted simply to be done with the matter, so on the advice of his counsel, an agreement was worked out which the court approved and which was made the subject of a binding court order. Chaffey would pay Rajab £8,500 in settlement of the suit with the money to be placed into a trust account to be paid over on the day Rajab vacated the flat. But as part of the agreement, Rajab was to be allowed to occupy the flat, rent free, for an additional three months. It was agreed the Rajabs would vacate the flat on February 28, 1985.

That day came and went and still the Rajabs would not move out. Once again the defence of diplomatic immunity was being raised. But now Chaffey was armed with a court order. His wife then came up with an idea. The law was now clearly on their side, so she sat down and wrote long letters to the Queen and the Prime Minister outlining the family's plight and begging for help.

She also sent copies of the letters to major newspapers and soon the dispute was front page news. Rajab was called 'The Squatter Envoy' in newspaper headlines to which he indignantly replied, 'I am not a squatter. I am not against the law. I respect the law. It is they who do not respect my immunity.'

One major daily's front page questioned: 'Why does the Foreign Office continue to sit on its hands while the Chaffey family, virtually broke and demoralized, lives through this nightmare?'

Suddenly the Foreign Office was galvanized into action. Reportedly, the sudden interest in the case was the result of a direct order from Mrs Thatcher. In early April a letter was written to the Syrian Ambassador asking that he take action to see to it that Rajab obeyed the court order. Nothing was received in reply and Rajab continued to occupy the flat. Finally, Foreign Secretary Sir Geoffrey Howe is said to have become personally involved and the Syrian Ambassador, Dr Loutof Allah Hadar, was called in on June 10, and told, in no uncertain terms, that the matter could go no further.

Suddenly the next day, Rajab announced that he had found a new flat and would be moving the next Friday. The move was then put off until the following day, but finally on June 12, after fighting for more than two years, the Chaffeys got their flat back.

The Chaffeys were delighted to be home although the experience had left them all but broke. It had cost them £9,000 in legal fees plus the £8,500 settlement to the law suit. Upon moving back into the flat, John Chaffey said, 'This has been the most terrible experience of my life, to see how the law is powerless against diplomats. But the children have been marvellous and this has taught me that one's family is what matters most. All I want now is for Mr Rajab to get out of the country.'

But even as they were leaving the Chaffeys' flat, the Rajabs were still indignant. Daughter Roula told a reporter how angry her father was over all the attention he was getting in the newspapers, how the family had found a new 'and nicer' flat weeks before and had planned on moving all along. 'We are very angry about all this and how we have been made to be the villains.' As she passed Samantha Chaffey, Roula was heard to growl, 'Don't think this is the end of it all. It is only the beginning.'

Asked by a reporter if he would leave Britain, Ahmed Rajab shot back: 'Of course not. This has been simply a civil matter.'

But apparently Rajab's public display of displeasure at

being forced to obey a court order was the last straw. Richard Luce, Minister of State, notified Ambassador Hadar that Rajab's conduct was found to be unacceptable and that he had fourteen days to leave. John Chaffey had got his fondest wish, Ahmed Rajab was on his way out of Britain.

Another bizarre example of diplomatic immunity being used to avoid a minor problem unrelated to an official function occurred in September, 1984, on a quiet residential street in the suburb of Roehampton in south-west London.

George Line, a company director, was looking out of his window and saw the whole scene unfurl.

'I heard a commotion and looked out the window and saw a sheep being dragged out of the house bleating something awful. There were about four men, two women and a couple of children.

'While the group looked on, two men held the struggling animal over a street drain. Another man came out with a watering can and sprinkled the animal's head. Then another man with a long white apron slit its throat with a long knife. The sheep struggled and died almost at once. I have seen this kind of thing in the Middle East but never on a London street.'

After the sheep stopped struggling, the men held it for a while over the drain and allowed it to bleed some more. Then it was taken into the house. A man then came out and washed the blood down the drain with a garden hose.

At least three other neighbours saw the slaughter of the sheep and the police were called. By the time they arrived, all the people were back inside the house. The constables went to the door and knocked and the man who answered identified himself as Seyed Abolghassem Mokhtari, First Secretary of the Iranian Embassy. He refused to allow the police to enter his house nor would he discuss the incident. He claimed diplomatic immunity. Later he would deny to a newspaper reporter that any sheep had been slaughtered. 'It is a total lie made up by some anti-Khomeini people,' Mokhtari said.

Later in the day, another neighbour, Mrs Rosolinde Fitzgibbons, reported, 'We noted the smell of burning flesh and wool wafting from the garden. It was very unpleasant.'

Had Mokhtari not invoked diplomatic immunity, he could have been charged with a violation of the 1911 Cruelty to Animals Act. The incident also brought an outcry from the Royal Society for the Prevention of Cruelty to Animals.

Calling the act 'absolutely horrifying', an RSPCA spokesman said, 'It is bad enough any animal being killed without pre-stunning but to do it in a street without even the limited safeguards of the slaughterhouse is absolutely appalling.' The RSPCA called for the Foreign Secretary to declare the Iranians involved as *persona non grata*, and to expel them from the country.

But the Foreign Office's response, after receiving a full report of the incident from Scotland Yard, was to send a mildly worded letter to the Iranian mission reminding them of their responsibility to respect the laws and customs of their British hosts.

Immunity also means that diplomats do not have to go to court to answer embarrassing questions. In 1980, police had what they thought was a perfect arrest. They caught four burglars loading their night's loot into the boot of their car. The stolen goods was valued at over £2,000 and included 10,000 cigarettes as well as many cases of brandy, wine and spirits.

The problem was that the four had just robbed the Chinese Embassy in Portland Place, Marylebone. The Chinese, citing diplomatic immunity, refused to come to court to give testimony or even to identify the loot as their property. The police had no choice: without the testimony of the property owner they could not prove the goods were stolen and the four men were released.

On October 4, 1984, a man died in a blazing car crash in Hendon, north London. As in all fatal crashes, police convened an official inquiry, scheduled for October 10, to try to determine the cause of the crash. This inquiry had to be adjourned because the dead man had been identified as thirty-year-old Hartmut Linser, a third secretary at the East German mission in London.

The East Germans, citing immunity, refused to supply anyone to give testimony about what Linser was doing in Hendon. Further, they refused to allow the authorities to examine Linser's body to determine if he had been drinking or if there was a medical reason for the accident. The crash raised many questions, but because of the East Germans' claim of immunity, these questions went unanswered.

When the framers of the Vienna Convention met in 1961, they tried to insert some measure of protection for receiving states in the new compact. But one complaint heard by the Foreign Affairs Committee in its investigation of diplomatic abuses is that quite often the Foreign Office sides with diplomats against the interests of British citizens even when it does not have to. In many cases, loop-holes placed in the Convention to favour the host country are all but ignored by the Foreign Office in its willingness to bend over backwards to protect diplomats by using the broadest possible interpretation of the law.

Take for example a case we will examine in more detail in a later chapter, an attempt by a Saudi diplomat to use diplomatic immunity to avoid paying a firm of decorators for remodelling his lavish London flat.

One of the provisions of the Vienna Convention, which in turn was adopted into British law in the 1964 Act, is that a diplomat forfeits much of his immunity if he is considered to have become a resident alien. This proviso was put into the Convention to counter the practice of many Third World and Middle Eastern countries of conferring diplomatic status on their nationals who have taken up residence in Western countries.

In the case of the Saudi diplomat, he was carried on the rolls of the Saudi Embassy with full diplomatic status. But he was actually a long-time resident of Britain and reportedly had developed extensive private business interests in London. It could have been very reasonably argued that he had become a resident alien and therefore subject to suit. But to do so might have angered the Saudis, a nation that the Foreign Office treats with extreme deference.

Then there is the case of the Mercedes that ran over a little boy. In September, 1983, seven-year-old John Costello was on his way to school, crossing the road, as he had been taught by his parents, on a zebra crossing.

Around the corner came the Mercedes, and hit the boy, knocking him off his feet and stunning him but, miraculously, not injuring him seriously. Police were there within minutes and arrested the driver who entered a surprise plea before a magistrate. He claimed diplomatic immunity based on the fact that his wife was a third secretary in the Syrian mission in London. The Foreign Office was consulted and they agreed that the man, a doctor, was entitled to immunity. Not only were all charges dropped, but the immunity protected him from a suit by the boy and his parents for damages.

In point of fact, the doctor had lived and practised medicine in London for a number of years, having secured the necessary work permits. By almost any definition, he came under the resident alien exemption built into the Vienna Convention. In most Western countries which follow exactly the same set of rules as Britain, he would have been denied the protection of diplomatic immunity.

Then there was the 1980 case of the eighteen-year-old son of an Egyptian military attaché at his country's embassy in Washington.

The young boy was on his way from Cairo to Washington when he changed planes at Heathrow airport. Going through a security check before boarding the Washington-bound flight, he was found to be carrying some ten thousand pounds' worth of marijuana. He was detained and charged with drug possession. But he claimed diplomatic immunity and was released into the custody of Egyptian officials who put him on a plane back to Cairo.

The Foreign Office said it granted the boy immunity based on Article 40 of the Convention which states that if a diplomatic agent passes through a third country on his way to a diplomatic posting, 'that country shall accord him inviolability'. But many countries, including the United States, have interpreted that Article to mean that immunity shall be granted if, and only if, the diplomat has been granted a visa to enter the country and has actually done so. There have been at least three cases in the last five years in the US where, in exactly the same circumstances – a diplomat in transit, changing planes, found with drugs – immunity has been denied and the diplomat made to answer for his crime.

A similar situation which resulted in a questionable granting of immunity occurred early in 1984, when a young man stepped off a plane from Uganda at Gatwick airport. Because of his diplomatic passport, the young man would normally have passed through customs without much formality, but he had the bad luck to arrive on a day when there was a drug-sniffing dog on duty at the airport. The dog became quite excited over the young man's luggage.

Feeling they had proper cause, customs agents opened the bag and found forty-four pounds of marijuana. The young man then identified himself as the son of an African President, and claimed diplomatic immunity.

Although he was travelling on an official passport, he was clearly not a diplomat. He was arriving in England to attend school. Nevertheless, he was granted immunity and was turned over to officials of his country on the condition that he immediately leave Britain.

The Foreign Office now says that it recognizes that it may have been too lax in the past in too broadly granting immunity and now says that it will mend its ways. This 'new' policy may actually have started after a young man was stopped by police on Percy Street at 4.00 a.m. on September 1, 1984, for speeding and drunken driving. His Mercedes had diplomatic plates but a check showed that they had been issued for a motorcycle. The added charge of driving with false plates was also entered against the young man.

He identified himself as a Saudi prince and demanded that he be released on the basis of diplomatic immunity. But because he was not listed on the diplomatic rolls, he was bound over for a court appearance.

It turned out that in fact the young man was one of the many sons of the late King Saud, the half-brother of the current King of Saudi Arabia, King Fahd. He was living in London while attending the Royal Military Academy at Sandhurst.

When he appeared before a Clerkenwell magistrate, he again raised the defence of immunity. The Foreign Office said it was not ready to take a position on whether the young man deserved immunity, apparently fearing that if it did not grant the immunity it would anger the Saudis, but also fearful that if it did grant immunity, it would be setting a precedent for the dozens of members of the extended Saudi royal family that are in London on any given day.

Finally, after months of agonizing over the problem, they decided to oppose granting immunity. But when police went out to re-arrest the young man, he was nowhere to be found. Sandhurst officials said he had left the Academy and that they understood he had returned to Saudi Arabia.

Another problem heard by the Foreign Affairs Committee was that, in a great many cases, once a diplomat is granted immunity – even for a serious crime – he is still allowed to stay in Britain. Here again the facts are rather appalling.

During the period between January, 1982 and May, 1984, diplomats committed 123 serious offences. Yet in only twenty-four of these cases did the Foreign Office ask that the offender leave Britain. In another nine cases, the head of mission voluntarily sent the offender home.

Or take 1979 as another example. In that year a total of 284 diplomats in Britain claimed immunity to avoid being charged with crimes ranging from assaulting a police officer to shoplifting and including one charge of gross indecency, one of indecent assault, one of incest, two of drug possession and 215 for non-parking traffic offences. Of this number, 120 were considered potentially serious criminal offences. Yet of these 120 diplomatic criminals, only seventeen were either forced to leave the country or left voluntarily.

Even repeat offenders were allowed to stay in Britain. One study done in 1980 showed that of fifty-one diplomats or dependents who had claimed diplomatic immunity on more than one occasion, twenty-four were still in Britain.

One Valeriy Egochine's escapades are typical. A second secretary in the political section of the Soviet Embassy, he was fondly known to his neighbours in Earls Terrace, Kensington, as the 'Red Menace'. If the implications were not so serious, this would be a funny story.

Egochine apparently had a slight problem: when he got behind the wheel after having a few too many vodkas, he tended to run into things. In 1981, he was detained twice after running into lampposts. In each case, the only damage done was to his own car and the lampposts. Then, in April 1983, he hit a moving target, colliding with another car at an intersection. The officers who arrived at the scene said Egochine had clearly been drinking.

But Egochine's finest moment came during Christmas 1983. Teresa Greenless remembers the night well. She was hosting a small party in her Kensington flat when she heard a loud crash, or more exactly, a series of loud crashes. Rushing out into the street, she saw Egochine struggling to get out of an almost demolished black Triumph Acclaim. The street looked as if a battle had just been fought.

'I don't know how he managed to do it,' Ms Greenless says, 'but he had managed to destroy a whole row of perfectly parked cars.'

What had happened was that Egochine had turned into the quiet residential street, most probably at high speed, and had failed to negotiate the curve. As a result, he had mowed down a whole row of six parked cars before his own car finally stopped.

Police arrived almost at once and Egochine came out of what was left of his car waving his diplomatic card. But police still administered a breath test which they told onlookers he had failed badly. By this time the Soviet mission had been notified and several Soviet diplomats arrived in a black limousine into which they bundled Egochine and then disappeared into the night.

The next morning, a Soviet official appeared on the scene with a representative of the Black Sea and General Insurance Company offering apologies and handsome settlements to the shocked residents who emerged from their homes to find what was left of their cars. Meanwhile, a Soviet spokesman said, 'I don't know why they are making such a big deal out of this – accidents happen all the time.'

Sir Anthony Kershaw, for one, was not amused by this incident. Saying 'This Russian is clearly a drunk,' he demanded that Egochine be expelled. The Foreign Office talked with the Soviets who announced they were voluntarily sending Egochine home.

This is only one of many instances where persons freed on claims of diplomatic immunity have committed multiple offences. There was the case of the son of a technical employee of the Ghana High Commission, who, in 1981, became something of a one-man mini crime wave. First he was arrested for purse snatching. Upon identifying himself as a diplomatic dependant he was released into the custody of his father.

Then some weeks later, on successive nights, he was arrested again. In the first incident, he snatched the till from a flower seller in Sloane Square tube station. The next night he was arrested with a number of other youths after an altercation in the King's Road, Chelsea. In each case he was quickly released after he identified himself as a diplomatic dependant and claimed immunity. After this third arrest the Foreign Office strongly suggested to the high commission that the young man be 'voluntarily repatriated'. Officials thought the matter closed until a few weeks later when a youth was arrested outside Sloane Square tube station for purse snatching. It was the young boy once again.

This time the Foreign Office finally demanded that he be sent home and within twenty-four hours the high commission announced he had been returned to Ghana for his compulsory military service.

In another case, police stopped a man driving through Piccadilly at 1.45 in the morning for not wearing a seat belt. The man had clearly been drinking heavily and so police took him to the Vine Street Station where a breath test was administered. The test showed he had fifty-four micrograms of alcohol per 100 millilitres of breath, well above the legal limit of thirty-five.

As they were about to charge him for drunken driving, the man identified himself as an assistant attaché at the Iraqi mission, and demanded to be released. A check with the Foreign Office showed that he had Grade 1 immunity so he was immediately released.

A check through the records later showed that this was the second time he had been arrested for drunk driving and that he had been stopped but not arrested on several other occasions. Each and every time he had been let off because of his diplomatic immunity. The Foreign Office then announced that it would consider expelling him. But while the matter was being discussed in Whitehall, the Iraqi mission announced he had voluntarily left the country.

A legendary case of a person remaining in Britain after being freed on a grant of immunity from a serious offence took place in the mid–1970s. An Indian diplomat tried to extort £20,000 from Selfridges. When caught red-handed, the Indian High Commission employee claimed diplomatic immunity and within hours was a free man.

On the day of his arrest, Sri Natwar-Singh, then the Indian Deputy High Commissioner in London, said that 'if we find that these charges are proved, and I have no reason to doubt the police, this man will most certainly be sent back to India.' Case closed, everyone thought.

Not quite. Six months later, a London newspaper found that the man was still in England, still living in the same, nice, three-bedroom flat in Temple Road, Cricklewood, that he was living in the day he was arrested for his extortion attempt. When asked for an explanation, Assistant High Commissioner Natwar-Singh said that because of the charges brought against him, the man had promptly been fired by the high commission. But since he was now a private citizen, he was not subject to their authority and thus could not be sent, by them, back to India. 'As far as we are concerned he no longer has immunity and can be tried here in Britain under British law.'

Did this mean that India had waived the man's immunity? 'Oh no,' Natwar-Singh replied, 'he just no longer has immunity since we fired him.'

So could he now be tried? No, said the Foreign Office. He had immunity at the time of his crime, claimed that immunity, was granted that immunity, so all charges had been dropped. 'No action can be taken retrospectively,' said Whitehall.

Then, after studying the matter for awhile, it was even further decided that the man could not even be deported, because he had never been convicted, only accused, of a crime. The ex-diplomat may still be in Britain to this day.

A person may not waive his own diplomatic immunity. It is up to his country to do so, and in serious cases, almost routinely, the Foreign Office makes the request of the sending state, and almost as routinely, it is denied. But in one major case something extraordinary happened.

On February 24, 1985, acting on a tip, Scotland Yard Drug Squad officers followed a minicab to a house in a London suburb. There they arrested the driver who had in his possession a little over two kilos of pure heroin with a street value estimated at about half a million pounds. This was a major drug seizure, and the police took it very, very seriously.

Under intense questioning the arrested man indicated that he had obtained the drugs at a house at 25 Arran Court, Colindale, north-west London. Police and customs officers rushed to the house, entered it, and began a search of the premises over the shouted objections of the occupant.

About fifteen minutes into the search, the occupant of the house identified himself as a third secretary of the Zambian mission to the UK, claimed diplomatic immunity and ordered the police out of his house. A call to the Foreign Office confirmed that he was entitled to immunity so the search was stopped and the police and customs officers withdrew.

The next day, Zambian officials at the mission denounced the search as a violation of the man's diplomatic status. Police officials defended their actions, saying that they broke off the search and left the premises as soon as the man had identified himself as a diplomat. But, nonetheless, the

Foreign Office promptly issued an apology for the police action.

Police investigators, after further questioning the man caught with the drugs, had reason to believe that the diplomat was bringing the drugs into Britain under diplomatic seal and they passed this information on to the Foreign Office. They called in Zambian High Commissioner (Ambassador) Lieutenant General Peter Zuzu and demanded that the man's immunity be waived. According to one observer at the meeting, Zuzu again stated his displeasure at the search of the man's house. But he said that he would pass the request back to his government.

The result was both swift, and to diplomatic professionals, shocking. Zambian President Kenneth Kaunda promptly waived the immunity and did so in a letter which was publicly released in London. President Kaunda wrote:

> Diplomatic immunity was never intended to prevent the investigation of serious crimes. I myself have a horror of all addictive drugs. It destroys human beings. How can such activities be protected by diplomatic conventions?
>
> In Zambia we have virtually no addiction problems. But I am told by Interpol that our country is being used as an important link for the storage and smuggling of heroin. So I feel that I am acting to protect my people and also the people of Britain and indeed of the whole world.
>
> When the request for the waiver of immunity reached me I did not hesitate for a second. It was, I am told, an almost unprecedented action. But in this fight we all must wage against this terrifying menace I am convinced that I am right.

The Secretary was arrested immediately. As President Kaunda noted, his action in waiving immunity is almost unprecedented. More typical is the situation faced by a woman architect who walked into a London hospital one night early in 1985, battered and bleeding.

She told hospital authorities that she had been beaten by

her husband. She said she feared that she would be beaten again and asked hospital officials to call the police.

The police came, questioned her, and set off to find the husband. When they did he gave them short shrift. He identified himself as a financial counsellor to the Indian High Commission and claimed diplomatic immunity.

As with the Zambian case, a request was made for a waiver of immunity. The Indian response was just as quick: no.

A spokesman for the high commission said of the request, 'It is not a matter for the British courts. If she wants to seek justice she should do so in an Indian court and not here where her husband might be embarrassed or his career put in jeopardy over what might be a false accusation. We don't want to see one of our diplomats dragged through the courts unnecessarily.'

But the lady still feared for her safety. So she went into a British court in an attempt to at least get an order forbidding her husband from beating her again. In doing so she said, 'I want to show that my husband cannot behave as he wants just because he is a diplomat.' But through solicitors engaged by the high commission, the husband opposed the granting of a writ, based on his immunity. The court had to agree and dismissed the action.

CHAPTER THREE

Rape

A WOMAN FACES a unique fear: the terror of rape. For those to whom it has not happened, it is a dread based on the many stories they've heard. Those unfortunate enough to have experienced the horror, carry it with them for the rest of their lives. Fear, outrage, a terrible sense of violation and invasion, and a real inability to understand '*Why*' it happened, colour the rest of their lives. What she would have thought were irrational actions and fears before the rape become a part of the rest of her life. It is an experience that deadens the soul.

Carol Holmes understands this well. So do 'Jane Doe' and 'Kelly'. But even worse they carry a special burden because the men who have raped them have gone free and unpunished due to the magic of diplomatic immunity. While their lives have been changed forever, their attackers are able to continue living the good life back in their own countries, or even in the same neighbourhood where their victim still lives.

1. JANE

'You remember a case like this forever. It sticks with you,' said New York Police Detective Sergeant Pete Christiansen. 'The law says you cannot arrest them so you just let them go. It's tough, a case like this, very tough. You just don't forget that they're back on the streets!'

The case Pete Christiansen cannot forget began in November, 1980, in the Yorkville area of Manhattan. 36-year-old Christiansen had been a member of a special Sex Crimes

Unit for about eighteen months. Established by the Police Commissioner in 1960, the unit contained some of New York's best and brightest investigators – all of whom had been specially trained to deal with victims subjected to these terrorizing ordeals. Working from the Twelfth Precinct house on West Eighty-Second Street, the unit covered the entire island of Manhattan. When you've worked in the Sex Crimes Unit for a while, you believe you've seen it all. Usually you're right. But in the case of Manuel Ayree, Pete Christiansen found out he was wrong.

'At the time,' Christiansen told me, 'this was a very hot case. We knew this guy was working the neighbourhood. He had committed a lot of rapes, at least ten of which had been reported. Since so many women don't report rapes, this probably meant he had committed many more. The first one took place in early November 1980. They were happening frequently. He was still on the street so we thought we had a good shot at grabbing him.'

Christiansen pays attention to every detail. He's a trained professional; frustrated but still determined to be fair. About five foot seven inches tall, he sports a reddish-blond moustache and wears a three-piece suit, starched shirt and windsor-knotted tie. An investigator since he graduated from the Police Academy, he is outgoing, conservative and above all methodical. He looks like a businessman or a stockbroker but he's not. He is a hunter, and one of the best.

In Christiansen's work you have to be systematic. Without detailed, often boring, detective work, you won't make an arrest. But after weeks spent investigating one savage attack after another, the pressure and frustration build up. You work hard and though you try not to, you take the case home with you. When you look at your wife and your two young daughters it makes you think, and so you go back to the hunt even more determined.

Rush hour that Thursday in January, 1981, was no more rushed than most other winter days when the temperature in Manhattan is around twenty degrees. When it's this cold, you move, and you don't mind crowded buses or standing so close to strangers. By four o'clock it gets gloomy, and by five it's as dark as midnight. It's depressing when it's dark before you leave work, but by January you're used to it. It was January 8.

Her bus headed up Third Avenue loaded with its cargo of yuppies going from their Midtown offices to the fashionable residential areas of the Upper East Side. The 26-year-old media buyer for an advertising agency we can know only as 'Jane Doe' boarded the crowded bus, shifted her purse and her briefcase to her left hand and she pulled seventy-five cents from her trouser pocket. Finding no seat, she stood.

The bus lurched and swayed, manoeuvring in the traffic past Bloomingdale's and PJ Clarke's, a popular night spot. She looked out of the window. Maybe her boyfriend would call tonight. She wished he could have been in town for Saturday night, but he wasn't due back until midday Sunday. Her stop was coming up. She rebuttoned her coat, adjusted her purse on her shoulder and squeezed her way to the back door.

Briskly, she headed for the small grocery on the corner. She liked to stop there on her way home from work. To her it signalled the end of the work day. Anyway, it was easier to buy a little every day rather than struggle up five flights of stairs with a week's worth of groceries.

With the brown bag tucked safely under her arm, she crossed the street. This was a pretty neighbourhood; it was convenient for restaurants and cinemas where you could meet your friends. Rents were reasonable by the standards of a city as expensive as New York. Lots of young people lived in the area on their way up to high-status addresses like Central Park South or Sutton Place.

The neighbourhood bustled with life all hours of the day and night. German in the days of the big European immigrations, its beer halls and brathauses had made way for bars with tiffany lamps. Block after block of multi-family tenements were converted to smaller apartments – studios and one-bedrooms. To some it had become 'Mr Goodbar' country – home of the swinging singles. At 5.45 p.m., Jane Doe mounted the steps to her building's small entrance.

Inside, she stopped as she always did to check her mailbox, before unlocking the inside door and heading upstairs. Before the door locked itself shut, she saw a young black man catch it and come in. His keys were in his hand and he smiled at her, the kind of half smile a neighbour might give. Under his raincoat, she noticed his neat shirt and tie, his trim, well-pressed slacks. He looked like he belonged. He took off his hat and fell in behind her. Leisurely, he climbed the stairs, stopping to light a cigarette. He arrived at the fifth floor landing shortly after she did and went to the door across the hallway from hers. Once her key opened the lock, her personal nightmare began.

Suddenly he pressed against her back. 'Do everything I say or I'll kill you. I have a gun,' he said in a thick, staccato accent.

'I'll do anything you want. Please don't kill me.' Surprised at how calm she sounded, her heart pounded inside her. She was terrified, on the verge of panic. Her eyes focused on the partially opened door. Her mind raced.

He gave her a little push. She knew it meant for her to go inside. She thought quickly of how much money she had, of what she could give him to go away. Right through the door was the tiny kitchen. From the draining board, he grabbed a serrated steak knife, threw his burning cigarette on the floor and stamped it out.

'Do everything I say, or I'll kill you,' the man later positively identified as Manual Ayree threatened.

Jane felt the knife at her stomach. Her mind searched for a way out. There seemed none.

'I'll give you all my money, everything I have, as long as you leave me alone,' she offered, trying to take control of the situation, trying to get him to go away.

She put her purse down next to the sink and reached in for her wallet.

'Do you live alone?' he asked, looking around.

'No,' she lied.

'If you don't tell me the truth, I am going to kill you. Do you live alone?' Ayree demanded.

Should she bluff him out? Could she pretend her boyfriend would be here any second? 'Yes, I do,' she admitted.

'Are you sure?' he probed.

'Yes.' She handed him the few dollars from her wallet.

'Is that everything you have?'

'Yes,' she responded emotionlessly, hoping he would leave now. But she knew he wouldn't. Not yet.

He ordered her into the studio. She could tell him she had venereal disease and he shouldn't have sex with her because he would catch it, but the words stuck in her throat.

Her convertible sofa was still left open from the previous night. He ordered her to take off her trousers and lie face down on the bed. Jane felt the knife point in her back. She knew she had no options. She took off her coat, biding her time, not believing this was really happening.

Lowering her corduroys, her stockings and her panties to her ankles, she lay on the bed. Her eyes could neither see nor close. She heard him lower his trousers. He lay on top of her and she felt him poking at her. The knife gleamed in his hand.

'You're not going to get anywhere if you don't put that knife down,' she heard herself saying. The knife rested about six inches from her head, with his hand only two inches from the handle. It was an easy wrist movement away. Suddenly, Ayree picked up the knife and got off her. He ordered her under the bed.

Thankfully, Jane pulled up her trousers and crawled underneath the pull-out bed. Exploring her studio, he opened closets, looked at her clothes, her things. From his footsteps, she knew exactly where he was.

'Do you live alone?' he asked her again.

She hoped he wouldn't talk, just take what he wanted and go. 'Yes.'

In the kitchenette, she heard him pick up her purse. He shook it. The rattle of change made her stomach sink.

'Are you sure you gave me everything?' he asked, catching her in a lie.

'No, there is more.' She tried to calm him, remembering the small change purse where she kept the two-dollar bill, the silver dollar and the half dollar her father had given her.

'Come out and give it to me.'

Obediently, she emerged and gave him the three and a half dollars.

'Are you sure that's all?' he taunted arrogantly.

She pulled another seventy-five cents bus money from her trouser pocket and opened her hand. 'Can't you let me keep it so I can get to work tomorrow?'

He ordered her back to the bed, waving the knife in the air. She knew she was going to die now. Who would find her dead in a pool of blood?

'Take off your pants. Drop it.'

He pulled his trousers down and invaded her anally.

The pain made her scream. She sobbed. He shushed her.

'Is it in your ass?'

'Yes,' she whimpered.

'I can't hear you.'

'YES.'

Humiliation and disgust rose inside her. Disbelief seized her. The knife gleamed in his hand.

He withdrew and sent her under the bed again. Grabbing at her blanket, he wiped himself. 'Where is my belt?'

'I don't know,' she said. She didn't.

'Hey, give me my belt,' he demanded.

Jane freed his belt from her ankles and threw it on the floor away from her.

Picking it up, he put it on and looked around again. 'Now you go to sleep and never wake up, right?'

'Yes,' she said, sure he meant it literally.

Turning, he walked towards the door, opened it and walked out, leaving the door open behind him.

Holding her breath, she heard his footsteps. He headed for the stairs. The quick creaking of the stairs signalled his withdrawal. Manuel Ayree left her apartment at 6:30 pm, but for Jane time had stopped. Everything had stopped. She slowly retreated to her bathroom. Finally she telephoned.

The doorbell startled her drifting mind out of its trance. Up the stairs came her boss, a woman, with her young daughter and two patrolmen. The uniformed officers questioned her, drawing out the details one by one, while the child waited in the bathroom on her mother's orders.

At Metropolitan Hospital, the patrol car pulled away leaving the two women and the child. Ten storeys high and covering the entire square block between 97th and 98th Streets, between First and Second Avenues, the huge hospital loomed in the dark. Surrounded by a chain link fence topped with barbed wire, it looked more like a prison. The bustling emergency room is housed in a smaller three-storey building on the 97th Street side.

Inside the emergency rape unit, two more policemen questioned her. She recounted her experience for an admissions clerk. Then, another two hospital workers noted her story in brief on their forms. She felt her horror fell on indifferent ears.

A male nurse came in, he too asked her questions. The doctor came in and he asked her more questions. On the table with her feet in the stirrups, the doctor examined her. A female nurse came in to take some cultures. Jane searched the nurse's eyes for compassion. There was little; she was all business and told Jane she could get dressed.

At her friend's apartment when she went to spend the night, Jane called the station. Two new officers wanted her report.

The night passed slowly, sleeplessly. She thanked God it was Friday and stayed at the apartment, hoping to sleep. She couldn't. The telephone broke the silence. It was Detective Pete Christiansen. Together, they would go to her apartment and she would tell him what happened.

In her own studio apartment, she relived her nightmare. Unable to face her memories, she couldn't sit down. She couldn't look at the bed. She didn't take off her coat. She felt like she no longer belonged there.

At the precinct house, she pored over the mug shots – hundreds of them. For three hours she felt sick, her stomach tied in knots.

Exhausted, Jane was escorted to her apartment by a friend. She didn't sleep. She felt alone, vulnerable, terrified. She didn't even want to lie down. Saturday came and went.

She went out, hoping to forget. She returned home only to remember. Sunday, she felt totally alone. Her boyfriend finally called. He was back in town. One more time, she detailed her ordeal. He came and spent the night holding her while she wept.

2. CAROL

On a freezing day during the winter of 1981, Carol, a free-lance proofreader living alone in New York, was preparing to go out. Flu or no flu, her two cats had to be fed, and she would just have to brave the late afternoon chill to run down to the store. At twenty degrees and windy, she was going to dress as warmly as she could. She pulled tweed slacks over her blue track-suit bottoms and a couple of sweaters over the matching sweatshirt. Though she was 39, with the wool beret all the way down over her ears and a muffler tied over her mouth and nose, she looked like a kid dressed for school.

Carefully, Carol locked the metal front door of her small apartment and headed down the five flights to the street. Leaving her yellow brick building and heading east on 92nd Street, the chill racked her nearly six-foot frame. She pulled her duffle coat closed at the neck and headed for the A & P supermarket on First Avenue. Even the garbage cans that lined the street seemed huddled together to keep warm. A lone Christmas tree lay discarded, its tinsel shreds fluttering in the icy wind.

Having lived in the Yorkville area of the city for over seven years, she made the two and a half block trip to the store on automatic pilot. Burdened with a sack in one arm and a shopping bag with two logs for the fire in the other, the thought of a cosy fireplace was the only thing that warmed her on the walk back. Maybe Bruce, her boyfriend of four years, would drop by after work. Carol stepped down the two stairs to the first glass door that led to the building's foyer. Once inside, she loosened the muffler and opened her mailbox.

Before the outside door closed behind her, she turned to see a young black man coming through the door, keys in hand. He looked well dressed in his turtleneck sweater, slacks, and anorak. With the turnover of tenants this building had, she felt he probably belonged. Later she realized, like Jane, it was the keys that had fooled her.

Instead of walking to his own mailbox or to the second, locked door, he came right up to her.

'That's right, that's right,' he said in his heavily accented English, 'this is not an accident.' She felt a sharp pressure at the back of her ribcage. 'I have a gun. I can kill you with it. I will kill you unless you do what I say.'

She turned to him. She saw his urgency. Slow him down, she thought, try to stop the panic, stop the violence. She sized him up. She was a bit taller, but he was powerfully muscled. With her flu, he would be the winner of any struggle, no doubt about that. Carol locked eyes with him. Trying to stare through him, she memorized his face.

'Give me your money, I want your money.'

With her customary precision, she reached into her bag. 'Here it is. I only have ten dollars. I just came back from the supermarket. I am sorry it isn't more, but you are welcome to it.'

'Put it away, put it away. I don't want it now.'

For an instant, she was confused.

'We're going upstairs. Give it to me upstairs.'

Grabbing her by the upper arm and thrusting the gun in her back, he made her open the inside door and then forced her up the stairs. The narrow stairwell was enclosed by thin plasterboard walls. But this time, no sounds filtered through from the apartments. It was totally silent.

Conscious of slowing him down, her mind raced. What can I do? She knew the people on these floors, but she couldn't think of how to attract their attention. She felt completely isolated. Turning again, she glanced back over her shoulder. She saw his hand. He had no gun!

His eyes followed hers. 'I have a knife, I have a poison knife, and I can kill you with it. I know how to use it and I will kill you.'

He's irrational, she thought. Anything can happen now.

She opened the door to her apartment. Together they entered the two foot wide hallway. They were too close. She walked straight ahead to the six foot by six foot dining area she used as her office and put her grocery bags down on the desk.

Scanning the room, his gaze stopped on the far wall at a large photograph of Bruce. 'Do you have a boyfriend? Do you live alone?'

'Yes, I have a boyfriend,' she said calmly, seeing a way out for the first time. 'No, I don't live alone.'

'When will he be back? When will he be back?' Repeating everything twice, Carol felt him grasping for control.

'He could walk in any minute.' Theoretically true, she wished he would.

Ayree shoved her towards the kitchen. In his hand was a pocket knife with a green plastic handle, the kind with several blades, a can opener, a corkscrew. 'This is my poison knife, this is my poison knife, and I know how to use it.' He pushed her backwards by the arm towards the kitchen.

'I want your money, I want your money.' He waited as she drew out the cash. 'No, I don't want it all. I want five dollars and a glass of water.'

Counting out five singles like a cashier in a bank, she handed it to him.

'No, no, put it down.'

She put it on the table. Turning away from him, she reached for a glass. On the small table there was a silver table knife crusty with the cream cheese she had had for her lunch. He seized it.

Placing the knife under her chin, close enough for her to sense it, but not touching her skin, he threatened her again. 'I can kill you with this, I will kill you.'

Could this blunt edge kill her, she wondered? Did she want to find out? She visualized it going through the soft part of her chin, spearing her tongue, sticking through the roof of her mouth.

He interrupted her thought. 'Take your clothes off, we are going to have sex.'

Slowly, Carol took off her coat. She headed for the coat hook by the front door.

'Throw it here,' Ayree demanded.

Forcefully, she turned, 'You're not going to interfere with my life.' She crossed the few feet and meticulously hung her coat on its hook. Then she walked to the sunken area of her living room and sat on the armchair at the foot of the bed. Next to her on the floor was the queen-size foam rubber mattress she had carried up the stairs herself. Carefully, she began to take her clothes off, keeping control of herself all the while. Bare and defenceless, assuming a calm and collected attitude, she sat in the chair and waited. Inside, she boiled. Sensing he wanted her to cry, but knowing her lack of emotion would keep his own volatility in check, she steeled herself to calmly await his next command.

'Lie down on the bed.'

Like an automaton, she obeyed. He took off his clothes. Eyes fully opened, she watched him impassively.

'Suck my cock.'

Sitting his muscular body on her chest, he poked her face, her mouth, with it. She stared blankly. He turned her over onto her stomach and lay on top of her, probing her.

She struggled to remain as limp as a rag doll. He entered her anus. The pain engendered a surge of anger. 'Stop that,' she roared as she turned herself over, passive no more. 'You can do what you want, but you don't have to hurt me.'

With a flick of his strong wrist, he turned her over, forced her legs open and thrust inside her.

Pulling on his trousers, he headed towards the bathroom. Though still naked, she followed him, trying to make him uncomfortable, to crowd him out of her apartment. She sat on the typing chair at the desk. He stood near her and lit a cigarette. She felt a battle of wills. He dragged deep on the cigarette. Reaching out, he twisted her bare breast until it hurt. He twirled the burning cigarette in his hand, burning her.

Suddenly, they heard a door slam loudly. Floorboards creaked, hands slapped banisters, loud footsteps could be heard. Startled, Ayree struggled to identify the sounds. Carol recognized a neighbour quickly descending the stairs on his way out. Ayree panicked and fled.

Though still completely naked, she ran out of the door after him, afraid he would escape. 'Stop him, stop him; he raped me,' she screamed. Outrage unleashed, she ran down the stairs after him. A door opened and a woman's face appeared. Carol looked at the woman. 'He raped me,' she cried. The door slammed shut.

Ayree bolted down the stairs, two at a time, pushing past a tenant who was coming up the stairs and thrusting another aside at the front door. Carol only made it as far as the third landing, where she collapsed. Her attacker had got away. In twenty short minutes, Manuel Ayree had irrevocably changed her life.

An ambulance took her to the rape unit of Lennox Hill Hospital, where she was questioned, examined and given a massive dose of antibiotics.

At the precinct house, Pete Christiansen asked her some very specific questions. He had heard the same responses at least a dozen times. He knew that for the second time in four days the Yorkville Rapist had struck again. How many more times would he strike before they caught him, if they ever did?

Although she didn't sleep that night, Carol wanted to stay in her apartment. The lights and the TV blazed all night, as they would for many, many months. Her nightmares were persistent. In some dreams, her two cats were killed. In other dreams, men came through the window and through the door, from every direction, to attack her. Her mouth opened to scream but no sound came out. Sometimes she was sure Ayree would return. She imagined him standing on the landing outside the door. She couldn't face opening that door alone. She recounted her attack to many in the building and on the block. Reports came back to her that others had seen the man in the neighbourhood.

Carol became obsessed with finding him; Bruce supported her in her quest. Knowing he was out there, she demanded justice and went out to find it. Though the thought of confronting him made her sick, she was determined to make sure he didn't get away with it.

She was equally determined that the violence that he had inflicted on her shouldn't leave permanent marks on her personality and emotions. She contacted a rape counsellor and attended group sessions with other rape victims.

Day after day, between 3.00 and 5.00 p.m., Carol and Bruce would walk through the neighbourhood, hunting her rapist. Perhaps he had followed her from the market. Maybe he worked as a delivery boy. In the cold, in the snow, unrelenting trackers seeking peace of mind, they walked. It was good for Carol. Block by block she reclaimed her neighbourhood. Though her attacker remained elusive their afternoon ritual helped heal her psychological scars.

Pete Christiansen and his fellow officers on the Sex Crimes Unit were especially frustrated by this case. They and street officers in the area were doing all they could, yet the rapes continued. The rapist's methods never varied. Posing as a resident, he followed the women into their buildings in the late afternoon. He either robbed them there or took them up to their flats. When he forced them into their flats, he would usually rape them, although sometimes he only threatened rape and robbed them. Almost all the incidents took place in a small area of the Upper East Side from about 95th Street down into the upper-seventies. The incidents were piling up and the man's increasing arrogance goaded Christiansen. Day by day, he became more determined to crack the case.

By February 6, 1981, thanks to Carol, Jane Doe and a few of the other victims, Pete at last had an accurate composite sketch of the man for whom they were looking. Most of the rapes had taken place within the city's Twenty-third Precinct so that day Pete attended the afternoon rollcall of the Precinct's anti-crime undercover unit.

Pete handed out copies of the sketch and once again described the assailant and his method of operation to the assembled undercover cops. Motivating the squad, he told them to concentrate on the Yorkville area from Eightieth to Eighty-ninth Streets. He could almost feel the circle beginning to close around his suspect.

Roving the streets in unmarked cars, in taxicabs, and on foot, the afternoon shift of undercover cops began their final operation at 4.00 p.m. that chilly winter Friday. After months at a snail's pace, it was all to be over in a matter of minutes.

Walking south on Second Avenue, Bruce and Carol paced their daily vigil arm in arm. They passed the small grocery on the corner of 89th Street and continued past the Carnegie Animal Hospital, Stuyvesant Square Thrift Shop and a take-away delicatessen, but their eyes didn't notice the shop windows. Instead, they combed the pedestrians, looking for a rapist.

Manuel Ayree left his high-rise apartment building and walked across 89th Street towards Second Avenue. As he turned south on Second Avenue past a small grocery on the corner, he may well have been searching for his next victim.

An ordinary yellow taxi, unnoticed in the Second Avenue traffic, carried two undercover policemen who had just come on duty from the Twenty-third Precinct. Besides their normal patrol today Pete Christiansen had given them another mission. On the seat next to the driver was the composite sketch of the rapist.

Just before the cab crossed 89th Street, the undercover detectives spotted a black man rounding the corner. He fitted the description of the rapist and his face was the one in the sketch on the car seat. They slowed down and began following the suspect while they radioed for assistance.

At the same moment, Detective Christiansen was also heading south on Second Avenue in his unmarked police car. The beeps from the paging device on his belt signalled him to telephone his office. Pulling his car over to the kerb at 89th Street, Pete walked towards the corner phone.

Manuel Ayree passed the Carnegie Animal Hospital and the Stuyvesant Square Thrift shop. Behind him at an unobtrusive twelve paces, the taxicab crept in pursuit.

Bruce and Carol reached 88th Street. As if by some mysterious instinct Bruce suggested, 'Let's turn around, let's not go any further south.' Bruce and Carol turned on their heels, facing north. The first face Carol saw coming towards her was *his*.

'Bruce, I think it's him.' Her eyes met her assailant's. Ayree's eyes flickered recognition. Not quite believing, Carol scrutinized him from head to toe as he walked past them. 'Bruce, it *is* him.'

That was all he needed to hear. Bruce grabbed Ayree around the neck and pulled him to the ground, the fury that had been building up in him for the last three weeks finding a sudden outlet. But Ayree fought back.

Carol kept her wits. Dashing to the pay phone on the corner of 88th, she commandeered the receiver from its user. '911, 911 [the New York City police emergency number], it's the man who raped me; he raped me.' She looked over towards the two struggling men.

Bruce was pinned in a scissor grip under Ayree's powerful thighs. The police taxi came screeching up. The two undercover officers bolted towards the fight. Two more undercover men posing as joggers were immediately on the scene.

One of the 'joggers' went up to Carol. The other ran towards the scuffle.

Up the block Pete Christiansen was dialling his office when he noticed the commotion. Not realizing that there were already policemen on the scene, he dropped the receiver and dashed down the short block. As he neared Elaine's, the fashionable restaurant, he recognized the undercover cops from the Twenty-third. He turned to cross the Second Avenue traffic.

'What's going on here?' the 'jogger' asked Carol, identifying himself as a police officer.

'He raped me, case number 444.'

Meanwhile, the three undercover cops had pulled Ayree from on top of Bruce, halting the fight. Christiansen then spotted Carol, and instantly realizing what had happened, took charge of the situation.

Ayree was shoved towards the back seat of the waiting taxicab, while he protested vociferously. He was a diplomat he claimed, and he had immunity. He couldn't be arrested. But lacking identification, he was taken in, according to procedure.

Inside the precinct house the suspect was taken upstairs to the detective area for questioning. Detective Christiansen grabbed the phone and called the Intelligence Unit to check out the suspect's ID. Bruce went to the desk to wait for news while Carol waited outside the large squad room. She was elated – her determination had paid off; she would prosecute, she would testify, she would see him convicted and put behind bars where he belonged. Her mind raced.

Bruce returned only to give her a shattering piece of news. They had to check it, he told her, but they believed that this man was the son of a United Nations diplomat from Ghana. If he had diplomatic immunity, the police were going to have to let him go.

'It can't be. It can't be. It can't be so. There's got to be a way,' Carol pleaded. Bruce felt helpless.

Pete Christiansen had work to do, and he had to move fast. He knew that in rape cases in the US only about thirty-five percent of assailants are ever arrested – mostly because their victims knew them. A meagre ten percent of rapists who are not known by their victims are ever caught. Christiansen had his man. He was sure; he had seen Carol's face.

Quickly finding numbers in his notebook, he began phoning. Some of the other victims had to identify Ayree. Together, perhaps these women could prevent him from having to release a rapist. He made several calls, each time getting no answer. At last, he reached Jane at the advertising agency.

'We've caught him. Can you come up to the precinct as soon as possible?'

She said she'd get a cab and come right up.

'There is a problem; he is claiming diplomatic immunity, he is a relative of a diplomat. If you don't get here soon, he may be gone.'

Jane was furious. She ran into her boss. 'I have to go,' she said grabbing her coat.

The Intelligence Unit had an answer within ten minutes, and it was bad news for the victims, police, prosecutors and the public. A member of the Ghana mission would come to identify Ayree. Detective Christiansen approached Carol. 'It looks like he is a diplomat's kid and has immunity. If this is true, we have to release him.' Losing control, Carol screamed that this was the man who *raped* her. How could they let him go?

Three people from the Ghana delegation to the United Nations identified the nineteen-year-old rapist as Manuel Ayree, son of the Third Attaché to the mission. His father, Seth Ayree, was there to claim him.

Carol wanted to talk to these people from Ghana. She was introduced to the boy's father and another member of the delegation. Sparing no detail, she wanted them to know exactly what had happened to her, so they could not explain it away or dismiss it.

'And then he sodomized me. Do you know what sodomy is? Do you know what that means in English?'

Jane hurried into the precinct house. She saw Carol, Detective Christiansen, the members of the mission. Pete took her right up to the diplomats. 'Here is another of his victims. Do you want her to identify him also?' They did not answer.

Standing in the viewing room, anonymous behind the double mirrored glass, Jane did not want to look at the face, but she knew she must. Looking up, she saw the man who had sodomized her.

'Would you like him to say something?' Pete asked her gently.

'Yes. Ask him to say, "Is it in your ass?" '

When she heard his voice, his thick accent, her stomach turned. It was him.

The men from the mission brought Ayree down from upstairs. Carol made eye contact with him. He was arrogant, jaunty and cocky. Though Pete and the NYPD had spent months working towards his capture Manuel Ayree walked out of the police station a free man just forty-five minutes after he had arrived. A claim of diplomatic immunity was his passport to freedom. He was laughing as he left.

Instead of spending the night as a prisoner on his way to the Rikers Island jail, Ayree spent the evening safe and comfortable inside his high-rise, luxury apartment. Occupying the block on the west side of York Avenue between 88th and 89th Streets, its balconies overlooking the river, the building is attended by round-the-clock doormen who guide residents between the circular driveway and the marble lobby. It was a convenient walk to the neighbourhood he had prowled, looking for women to rape.

Outraged that Ayree could apparently resume his normal life while hers remained irrevocably damaged, Carol called Mary Ann Grothe, a specialist in the prosecution of rape. Mary Ann found out that if Ghana waived immunity, Carol and Jane could prosecute. They had to act quickly. Working all weekend, lawyers from the firm of Beldock, Levine and Hoffman prepared a complaint.

The weekend was also a busy one at the New York District Attorney's office. Hoping the State Department would insist that Ghana waive Ayree's immunity, the attorneys worked furiously to compile the massive amount of evidence they would have to take to a grand jury for an indictment. There was no doubt in anyone's mind that Ayree was guilty.

But his father certainly wasn't going to admit his son's guilt. 'He hasn't done anything,' said Seth Ayree when he was telephoned by the *New York Times*. 'I do not want to be interrupted.' The rapist's father hung up.

US State Department officials heard much the same explanation when they called on Ghanaian officials over the weekend. 'We were told that it was all a "racial matter" and that the young man was completely innocent,' a State Department official remembers. 'We told them that crap would simply not fly and that they had better do something and do it quickly.'

Monday afternoon, February 9, at 4.18 p.m. in the United States District Court for the Southern Division of New York, the civil complaint against Manuel Ayree was filed by Beldock, Levine and Hoffman on behalf of Carol Ann Holmes and Jane Doe. A jury trial was requested. At 9:40 pm, Neal J. Sroka served Ayree's father at his apartment with notification of the suit.

At almost the same time the suit was being filed in District Court, State Department officials, officials from Ghana including its Ambassador to the United Nations and some from its embassy in Washington, along with New York police and prosecutors, were meeting in a session demanded by the State Department. The evidence against Ayree was put forward and the State Department made it clear: if Manuel Ayree did not 'voluntarily' leave the United States within twenty-four hours he and his entire family would be declared *persona non grata* and would be deported instantly.

'Freedom and Justice' reads the motto on the national crest adorning the glass door of the Ghana Mission to the United Nations. The consulate is located in a four-storey building on 47th Street, just east of Fifth Avenue. The dignified brick building houses ten consuls and about twenty members of the UN delegation, including, until late 1981, Seth Ayree, a relatively low-ranking attaché outranked by at least a dozen officials of his mission.

Inside the mission, you can pick up several publications detailing social, religious and cultural aspects of Ghana. From these publications, you would learn that Ghana is a largely Christian country where 'life is held in the greatest awe and respect' and that womanhood is regarded with 'esteem and deference'. It says it is 'a model and a showcase of pluralistic democracy.'

On Tuesday morning, Ghana called a press conference at the mission. At the session a statement was released to the press: 'In the spirit of the friendship that exists between our two countries, Manuel Ayree is voluntarily returning to Ghana and will not return to the United States.' The spokesman also said that the charges against the young man would be fully investigated and if it was judged that he could have committed the crimes he would be tried in Ghana.

That night Seth Ayree drove his son to Kennedy Airport where he put him on a flight to Frankfurt. There he connected to a flight to Accra. Officially, according to the State Department, young Ayree 'voluntarily repatriated'.

He was never brought to trial, nor to the best knowledge of the State Department, even investigated. Ghana is renowned for its coups and attempted coups and three former heads of state have been executed. In late 1981, President Hilla Limman fell to a military coup led by Lieutenant Jerry Rawlings. The Ayree case, it appears, was soon forgotten.

'A man raped me and he got away with it,' Jane said later, 'because he is not a citizen and because he is a relative of a diplomat, and he claims he has the right to rape me and I, as an American citizen, am not given the right to get justice. And it makes no sense.'

'This situation was particularly heart-breaking,' recalls Pete Christiansen, 'because the two complainants were there and I knew we had this guy dead to rights, that there was no way would he walk away. But he did and there was absolutely nothing I could do about it. We could not even hold him long enough for his victims to get up there and identify him. I'm sure if we had been able to hold him long enough to put him in a line-up for enough of the women, we could have closed a couple of dozen files, but we couldn't.'

A New York City District Attorney reports that based on their files in the case, Manuel Ayree could have been charged with rape, sodomy, assault, assault with intent to harm, aggravated assault, battery, kidnapping, robbery, use of a deadly weapon in committing a felony and carrying a concealed weapon, with penalities amounting to a total of 800 years in the New York State maximum security prison at Attica.

Patrol Guide Procedure Number 116–12 of the Police Department, City of New York, defines 'diplomats' as 'members of foreign missions, delegations, embassies and legations to the United Nations and to the United States, and their families and staff.' It states, 'Diplomats shall *not* be arrested or personally served with a summons.' The guideline continues to admonish: 'Do not detain a diplomat who is properly identified . . . Uniformed members of the service will extend every courtesy and consideration to them.'

In New York and the surrounding area, the number of people who are afforded this immunity from prosecution, detention and discourtesy is huge. Representatives of permanent missions to the United Nations, senior UN officials and their families number more than 5,000. The members of the United Nations Secretariat, observer nations, employers of foreign government missions, and members of the mission of the Organization of African Unity total another 7,800. Consular officers, who are accorded the same immunities by the police, number another 1,500. This is one of the largest diplomatic communities on earth.

The financial cost imposed by this community is huge and hard to document. The Committee for Receiving State Relations of New York City insists that these foreigners bring money to the city. After deducting the cost to the city from tax exemptions, including property tax exemptions, unpaid traffic tickets and police protection, there is little income left. In addition, taxpayers of the United States contribute twenty-five percent of the United Nations' budget, far more than any other country, and more than twice as much as the Soviet Union. Total US contributions to all UN organizations and relief funds exceeds one billion dollars a year.

The cost to citizens' safety is impossible to calculate. There are the terrorists. There are foreign protesters, frequently armed, who cause near-riots. And there are the criminals like Manuel Ayree.

Manuel Ayree's immunity came about because of the United States' very generous interpretation of a clause in the United Nations Charter and a separate US statute, The International Organizations Immunities Act, passed in 1945 to implement the immunities provisions of the UN Charter.

Article 5, Section 15 of the UN Charter and Section 287 of the International Organizations Immunities Act reads in part: 'every person designated by a Member as the principal resident representative to the United Nations of such Member or as a resident representative with the rank of ambassador or minister plenipoteniary and such resident members of their staffs as may be agreed upon between the Secretary General, the government of the United States and the government of the Member concerned . . . shall, whether residing inside or outside the headquarters district, be entitled in the territory of the United States to the same privileges and immunities, subject to corresponding conditions and obligations, as it accords to diplomatic envoys credited to it.'

What this means is that according to the UN Charter,

the United States is only bound to give immunity to full ambassadors to the UN. The grant of immunity to lower ranking members of delegations is a voluntary act on the part of the United States. But since the UN began its deliberations in 1945, in order to promote international harmony, immunity has been accorded to all members of a delegation. Thus Seth Ayree had immunity, and because he did, so did his son.

On December 15, 1980, only blocks from where Manuel Ayree committed multiple rapes and assaults, the General Assembly passed resolution 35/168. Part of the resolution suggested an intensified information programme to further acquaint the population of the City of New York with the privileges and immunities of the UN mission personnel and with the importance of the international functions performed by them. After the vote, the Netherlands expressed reservations to some of the language in the opening paragraph. The provisions of the paragraph could, they thought, give the false impression that there was a balance between the duties of diplomats and their rights to protection. A diplomat was entitled to the protection of receiving states, they wanted to make clear, whether or not he respected the laws of that State. Such are the diplomats who pledge themselves to peace, social freedom, human rights and justice.

3. KELLY

Alexandria, Virginia, is a largely middle class community in the close suburbs of Washington DC. Its 110,000 residents are primarily government workers and military personnel. There is also a noticeable contingent of diplomats, perhaps the largest in the Washington metropolitian area. Located in Fairfax County, near Washington's National Airport along the Potomac River, Alexandria's many large apartment complexes, shopping centres and schools are alive with the dress and dialects of the children of many nations.

T.C. Williams High School is the Washington DC area's largest, with 2,450 students. About twelve percent of the tenth, eleventh and twelfth grade students there are foreign, representing around fifty nationalities. Of these, many are the children of diplomats and others covered by the magical cloak of diplomatic immunity.

In January, 1983, a student we will call 'Kelly' was in her sophomore year at T.C. Williams, her first at the school. An average student with average good looks, she is softspoken and slender. Kelly is five foot five with light brown shoulder-length hair. Nothing about this fifteen-year-old would make her stand out in a group of teenage girls.

On the last weekend of the month, Kelly's parents went out of town for the weekend. Her parents felt secure leaving Kelly and her year-older brother with their neighbours across the street. Kelly didn't have much planned for the weekend. She had already seen the movie *Tootsie*, and most of the other movies that were playing nearby. Although a couple of senior boys she knew from school had asked her to a party, none of her friends were invited so she wasn't sure whether she would go.

Friday night, Kelly stayed in, listening to pop music by Duran Duran and Culture Club on the radio. By late Saturday afternoon she felt restless, the novelty of staying with the neighbours having played itself out. She was glad when the phone rang and it was for her. It was 'Boo-Boo', as the kids at school called him, inviting her to a party he was having that night while his parents were out of town. For a moment she was reluctant, but he said it was going to be a large party with many guests. Thinking her parents surely wouldn't mind, she decided to go.

The large white luxury sedan bearing the official looking diplomatic licence plates pulled up in front of Kelly's neighbour's house. Boo-Boo drove the car belonging to his father, a first secretary of the Royal Embassy of Saudi Arabia. The son of an Egyptian employee of the World Bank was with him. The two seventeen-year-olds drove Kelly a few miles to the Watergate at Landmark condominium complex where Boo-Boo's family rented two apartments.

As Boo-Boo had promised, a crowded party was in full swing when they arrived, with about thirty young people, all of them older than Kelly, as well as the two boys. Drinks were plentiful and the air was heavy with smoke of all kinds. But shortly after the teenagers arrived, everyone else left the apartment to spend the evening in Georgetown making the rounds of the trendy bars and popular night spots.

Kelly and her two escorts spent some time listening to music and dancing. Then Boo-Boo poured a large tumbler of neat Southern Comfort Whisky and the two boys suggested Kelly have a drink. She said no. They insisted. The situation was tense. Kelly wanted to leave. Feigning interest in the bric-a-brac, Kelly meandered around the L-shaped living room. She felt uncomfortable and ill at ease, but didn't see any easy way out of the situation. Should she just walk out? Could she call her parents' friends and ask them to pick her up? How much would a taxi cost? Surely her mother would expect her to know what to do, but somehow she just didn't. Quietly, she asked if she could be taken home. The answer came back abruptly: 'No.' Now she was really frightened.

She had never before drunk anything stronger than wine. But she accepted the tumbler of spirits the second time it was offered, afraid not to.

Unaccustomed to alcohol, she grew dizzy and subdued after a few minutes. She even thought of drinking so much of the awful tasting stuff that she would pass out. Then they would have to take her home.

Suddenly Boo-Boo was screaming as if he was really angry. Kelly was desperate to leave but didn't see how she could manage it. She was too scared to even talk. She just felt overwhelmed.

The two boys suddenly knocked Kelly to the floor. One held her head and shoulders down with his arm across her throat, nearly choking her. Boo-Boo stripped her from the waist down and then raped her. She couldn't believe what was happening. It was like a horrible dream. She felt sick and dizzy and frightened. Then the two changed places. Boo-Boo held her down forcibly while the other raped her. Head swimming, paralysed by fear, her mind and body froze.

Boo-Boo laughed and told her that she'd better not tell anyone what had happened. He even bragged that she was their third girl that day. Anyway, he boasted, it was pointless to tell anyone about it since they both had diplomatic immunity and they could do anything they wanted. There was nothing anyone could do to stop them.

Now the two boys said they would take her home. In the bathroom, Kelly cleaned up and got dressed.

In the car, as they drove her home, Boo-Boo again bragged that no one could do anything to them because they had diplomatic immunity. He was speeding, but when Kelly meekly suggested he slow down, he bragged that the cops couldn't even give him a ticket because of his immunity.

Back at her neighbour's house, Kelly tried to act as though nothing unusual had happened. What could she say? Who could she tell? She knew she would be in trouble. Her parents hadn't given her permission to go to the party. They would never understand. They would blame her. Vowing she would never tell anyone, she closed the door of her room where she lay awake most of the night. It was her fault, she thought, she should never have gone with them. If anyone ever found out, they would never believe her.

When her parents returned on Sunday night, she continued to try and act the same as she always had. She wasn't sure if she seemed normal to them, but she tried. On Monday at school, she spent the day staring at the floor, hoping not to see either of the boys or anyone else for that matter. Monday night she hardly slept at all. She kept waking up from nightmares, wanting to cry, but not knowing what to do. By Tuesday, she just couldn't take it any more. That night, Kelly haltingly told her mother what happened. Words like rape and intercourse and penis were hard for her to say. Between her sobs, she managed to get them out.

Her parents were sickened and angry. When you have a daughter, you pray you'll never hear those words. Her mother immediately called their family doctor and made an emergency appointment for Wednesday. The doctor confirmed that her daughter had been raped.

Her parents didn't know how to handle it. They didn't know what to say to Kelly, or even what to say to each other.

They went with Kelly to a lawyer. Then on Friday, Kelly had a private session with a psychiatrist. Together, they all decided a trial could traumatize Kelly further. Kelly and her parents decided not to prosecute. It seemed futile. The boys did have immunity and the thought of police reports and courtroom testimony and publicity was almost as horrible as the memory of the rape itself. She feared the kids at school. The psychiatrist felt that an ordeal like that would scar Kelly even further. When the family told police they would not prosecute, the matter was dropped, case closed.

In the following weeks, the boys bragged about the incident around the school. Lots of kids heard about it. Word spread fast. Kelly didn't know what to say, so she said nothing. Kids whispered to each other when she was nearby. Girls in the locker room stared at her. Her friends stopped talking to her. Other kids dropped notes inside Kelly's locker. 'Whore' was the nicest word they used. She threw the notes away but the awful words stuck in her mind.

About a week and a half after the rape, Boo-Boo called and invited Kelly out again. 'We had such a good time,' he told her.

Kelly confided in no one, just retreated into herself more and more over the next weeks. She continued to see the psychiatrist.

The transformation in Kelly's personality was all too obvious to her father. She was changing from a normal outgoing fifteen-year-old into a disturbed and deeply withdrawn child. Certain that facing the two boys day after day was unbearable for Kelly, as well as threatening to her long-term wellbeing, her father resolved to do something. He went to a neighbour who worked at the State Department. Couldn't *something* be done? There must be something?

The neighbour talked with consular officials at the State Department. He was told that State could pursue the matter only if it had been officially reported to the police. So Kelly and her parents, although they still did not want to prosecute, went to the local police. On March 28, 1983, an official police report, her doctor's statement of his examination findings, the psychiatrist's report and the parents' notarized statement were furnished to State.

Anxious to 'handle' the matter quietly, State Department officials had discussions with the Royal Embassy of Saudi Arabia and the father of the second boy. Though as a World Bank employee the Egyptian's immunity covered him only within the scope of employment and did not extend to his family, the State Department does not always make the distinction. The second boy's father, however, had already learned of the rape and had discreetly 'repatriated' his son to Cairo. Because of State Department pressure, Boo-Boo was on his way back to his homeland within eighteen hours, but the story does not end there.

Boo-Boo's parents were very upset. It seemed their son was not happy in Saudi Arabia, a strict Moslem country where the Koran is closely observed. It is not surprising that a rapist would be uneasy in a country where a hand is severed for robbery, a head is severed for murder and a penis is severed for rape. They feared that Saudi officials might try to extract Islamic justice for the boy's crime.

Since he had only two months left before his graduation, Boo-Boo's parents requested permission that he be allowed to return to the United States. Through the Saudi Embassy and the State Department, Kelly's parents were asked if they would agree that the boy could return to graduate. The Saudi Embassy assured them that it 'will undertake to ensure that the boy will in no way attempt to harass or harm the young lady'.

The State Department told Kelly's parents it was up to them. They decided that the episode had upset Kelly's life, her schooling and her family enough. They had no guarantee that their daughter would not be harassed by this boy – or even raped again. The mere assurances of the Saudi Embassy were surely insufficient. Ultimately, they reasoned, Kelly's safety was their responsibility. They flatly denied the bizarre request. They thought the matter was closed.

But in October, 1983, Kelly and her brother were jolted when they suddenly saw Boo-Boo across the carpark of a large shopping centre near their house. Kelly's parents immediately called their State Department contact. The State Department, in turn, sent an official letter to the Saudi Embassy inquiring whether the boy was back in the United States.

In its reply, the Saudis enclosed a copy of the diplomatic credentials of the family as a little reminder to the State Department that the family belonged to a protected class. The young lady was mistaken, they continued, she had seen Boo-Boo's brother who bears a close resemblance to Boo-Boo.

This explanation was absurd. 'Munster', as Boo-Boo's older brother was popularly known, wore a full beard. Telling them apart, even at a distance, was simple.

Again on December 19th, Kelly and a friend saw Boo-Boo, this time in a car at another local shopping centre. Again, her parents notified the State Department. And again, on January 11, her mother telephoned the State Department to say that Boo-Boo had been seen in Georgetown during Christmas week.

Ahmed Siraj, the Deputy Chief of Mission of the Saudi Embassy wrote a letter to the State Department on paper headed 'Office of the Ambassador' and dated January 19, 1984. Mr Siraj assured the State Department that Boo-Boo was not in the United States, and insisted that 'the complaining party continued to mistake his brother who is almost identical' to Boo-Boo. Anxious to alleviate the situation, Siraj reported that he had asked the family to consider moving and that they had agreed to move as soon as their sons' school terms were completed in June. Siraj was sure that would be acceptable 'since no one wants to have their childrens' education interrupted'.

At the Watergate at Landmark complex, Bill Albeck is the chief of security, having retired from the local police after twenty years on the beat. He too had seen Boo-Boo during the time he supposedly wasn't in the country, and he never had trouble telling the brothers apart. According to Albeck the boys had caused much trouble in the complex and were a sore point with the tenants association. The condominium board sometimes fined the apartment owners for their tenants' frequently drunk, rowdy behaviour. The Alexandria police were even investigating one of the older boys for using a stolen credit card. When the family's leases were up, they were not allowed to renew.

As Saudi officials at the embassy had promised, in August, Boo-Boo's family moved. They moved to a nice rented house. They now live just down the street from Kelly. If you stand on her front porch, you can easily see the house. Boo-Boo lives there too.

Former policeman Bill Albeck sighs with resignation. 'These kinds of problems with diplomats came up all the time. The law is clear that there is nothing you can do about it so you simply learn to live with it.'

Kelly's parents never realized American citizens were expected to learn to live with it until it happened to them. They are outraged as well as hurt by their daughter's traumatic ordeal. As for their daughter, she counted the days until she would graduate from high school and could leave the area to go away to college. Though she may move, she will take the nightmare called rape with her, knowing as she does that whenever she comes home, her assailant will be living down the street, totally free from fear of arrest.

The fact that the rapes discussed so far in this chapter all occurred in the United States does not mean that Britain has been free from diplomatic rapists. But because the Foreign Office steadfastly refuses to divulge either the names of diplomats who commit crimes or those of their victims, it is very difficult to piece together incidents in Britain involving diplomats.

In official figures released to the Foreign Affairs Committee, the Foreign Office admitted that twice in the last decade diplomats have committed rapes and that diplomats were guilty of indecent assaults on three other occasions.

These statistics go up to the end of 1983. On May 18, 1984, police in London were called to a flat where a woman said she had been assaulted by a man. He was identified and police were able to make a quick arrest.

The man was taken to the Southall Station in west London where he readily admitted, in fact almost bragged, of having had relations with the woman against her will. He was immediately charged with indecent assault.

Then he made his next announcement. He identified himself as an Algerian diplomat and demanded to be released. An all too familiar sequence took place. A call was made from the station to the duty officer at the Foreign Office who confirmed the man's immunity and out the front door he walked, a completely free man.

As with most of the diplomatic incidents in Britain, the Foreign Office has refused to identify either the diplomat involved or his victim. Police, acting on direct orders from the Foreign Office, also refuse to identify either party. But in this case, while refusing to identify either, one constable involved in investigating the case did tell us: 'When she learned that he had immunity and had been freed, the woman was terrified. She was certain he would return and attack her again.'

The identity of Britain's most serious diplomatic sex offender may never be known. In early 1984, London police knew they had a serial rapist on their hands, one who strikes again and again. His methods did not vary. He would lure women into his car, described as a dark Mercedes, and then drive to quiet, deserted alleys in west London where he would assault and rape the women, leaving them badly battered.

The only description police had of the attacker was that he was a large black man. Then, after an attack on April 19, police learned from an eyewitness that the car the rapist drove carried CD plates.

The Foreign Office was contacted and a circular letter was immediately sent to all embassies demanding their assistance in investigating these violent assaults. Immediately the rapes stopped. The rapist was never heard from again. Police speculate that either some embassy was able to identify the man and send him out of the country or the man himself knew how close he was to detection, and stopped his attacks.

CHAPTER FOUR

The Pakistani Connection – Drug Dealing Diplomats

IN LATE JULY, 1985, the British people were shocked by the death of Jason Fitzsimmons. The fourteen-year-old Liverpool schoolboy became the youngest victim in the wave of heroin addiction that has swept Britain in the last decade.

At a nationally publicized inquest, the county coroner spoke movingly of 'problems of the sort which were completely unknown in my boyhood', and said Jason's death was part of a drug abuse problem that could endanger 'the whole future of the nation'.

Historically, Britain has taken a *laissez-faire* attitude towards narcotics use. Until recently, addiction was considered a problem for the medical profession rather than law enforcement. For decades, the response to addiction was the 'British Heroin Maintenance Programme', under which addicts were registered and then maintained with government-supplied drugs. But no new addicts have been added to the programme since the early 1970s in an attempt to phase it out. Only addicts enrolled prior to the cut-off date are still being maintained.

As a result, an illegal black market grew up almost overnight. Since the mid-1970s illegal use of drugs in Britain has doubled and redoubled and then doubled again. It is a problem that a special parliamentary study called 'the most serious peacetime threat to our national well-being'.

What most concerns officials is that heroin is far and away the drug of choice in this new epidemic, especially among young people. By official government estimate, addiction to opiates, primarily heroin, has more than tripled just during the first half of the 1980s. This is especially true among those under the age of twenty who often heat the drug and inhale its vapours, a method called 'chasing the dragon', used in the mistaken belief that this is less addictive than injection.

In most of the western world, street heroin is of a low level of purity and is quite expensive. The cost alone results in a relatively limited market. In Britain, however, very pure heroin is actually cheaper than marijuana. A bag of forty percent pure heroin, that will last most addicts two days, usually costs only about ten pounds on the street. That figure has not changed for several years, a fact that officials attribute to the upsurge in smuggled supply.

Today there are over 12,000 officially registered heroin users in Britain, all remainders from the days of the official maintenance programme. The government puts the number of unregistered users at about five times the registered number or about 100,000 users. But experts outside the government believe the actual number is at least twice and possibly three times that number. This means that Britain, with a population of about fifty-six million, has almost half as many heroin addicts as the United States with a population almost four times greater.

At the same time that heroin use is reaching epidemic proportions, marijuana smoking, again a localized problem only a few years ago, is also on the upsurge. In addition, British officials are bracing themselves for an expected flood of cocaine as worldwide production surpasses demand in the US, its principal market.

For many years, most of the heroin reaching the West came from poppies grown in the notorious 'Golden Triangle' area of South-east Asia and then refined in the illegal laboratories of Marseilles – the famous 'French Connection' drug route. But in recent years, because of political upheaval in the cultivation region and police clampdowns at the laboratory sites, more and more of the West's heroin, and also marijuana, are coming from an area called the 'Golden Crescent'.

Huge crops of poppies are being grown in Pakistan, Afghanistan, parts of Iran and India. The opium from these poppies is being processed in labs within both Pakistan and

India and the resulting heroin is being shipped directly to the West with the United States and the growing market in Britain the main destinations.

According to drug enforcement officials, Pakistani farmers produced more than fifty tons of opium in 1984, yielding more than five tons of pure heroin. The estimates are that at least this much is also being produced in the other countries of the region. The fortune being made by the drug kings of these poor countries is so vast that corruption of local law enforcement officials is now the norm and the drug trade is running almost unchecked.

With supplies plentiful and local enforcement efforts almost non-existent, the only hurdle faced by the drug kings is how to transport their products to their markets in the West. They are looking for safe and effective means of transporting their goods and more and more the answer seems to be diplomats.

A diplomatic passport is usually the magic wand through customs. Usually diplomats are simply waved through with few formalities, their personal luggage almost never subjected to inspection. Diplomats can also carry larger containers into a country under diplomatic seal which, under the Vienna Convention, cannot be opened at all, only sent back to the originating country if suspected of containing contraband.

For most drug traffickers who are caught, the penalties are severe. But for those with diplomatic immunity, the worst that can happen is a loss of face and possible expulsion from their country's diplomatic service. More and more diplomats seem ready to take that risk, considering the potential rewards.

For more than six months, undercover officers from Scotland Yard's Drug Squad patiently built up their case against a group of Pakistani nationals living in Britain. On a number of occasions, undercover officers Neil Giles and Peter Hill, posing as drug dealers, had purchased heroin from the group. Finally, when enough evidence had been gathered, three men were arrested and brought to trial for drugs offences in the Wood Green Crown Court in early 1985.

During the trial, Philip Singer, the Crown prosecutor, made a startling revelation. He told the court that the two officers had been told by the Pakistanis that the heroin changing hands was coming into Britain in diplomatic bags from Pakistan. In fact, Mr Singer told the court, the three claimed that every flight from Pakistan to Britain during a six-month period contained a shipment of heroin in a diplomatic bag.

It is the policy of the Foreign Office not to reveal details of diplomatic transgressions. This makes it difficult to gather details about diplomatic drug couriers. But the Foreign Office did admit to the House of Commons Foreign Affairs Committee that a serious misuse of the diplomatic bag comes to light about once a year. Almost without exception, the prohibited import is drugs.

The Foreign Office mentioned one case in 1980 where by pleading immunity, a diplomat succeeded in avoiding prosecution for selling drugs. They admitted that in the last ten years there have been eight cases of possession of illegal drugs by diplomats who successfully asserted their immunity and avoided prosecution. Further, they reported that they're sometimes tipped off by the head of the mission who, anxious to prevent further abuse, aids the authorities. They declined, however, to name specific embassies or cases of drug smuggling abuses.

One known case occurred in July, 1980. A clerk stationed at the Moroccan Embassy in Pakistan went to the docks at the port of Harwich to identify several large crates marked 'diplomatic household effects' and addressed to him care of the Moroccan Embassy in London.

With him there to identify the crates, they quickly moved through customs without being opened and were placed on a lorry for the trip to London. Just when the man thought he was out of danger, bad luck struck. As the lorry pulled away, one of the crates toppled off and split open. There lying on the ground was a 600–pound slab of cannabis. The other crates contained the same cargo. After they were opened, customs officials had marijuana valued at more than £650,000 to add to their inventory.

Although the man was travelling on a diplomatic passport, he was not accredited to Britain, so his plea for diplomatic immunity was denied. He was placed on trial at Ipswich Crown Court and was subsequently sentenced to nine years in prison. At his trial, he told the Court he was working as a courier for a Pakistani drug ring that used only diplomats to ship its drugs, both heroin and marijuana, around the world under diplomatic seal. He revealed he was to have been paid £50,000 for delivering the shipment that had landed at Harwich docks.

Diplomatic couriers are also being used to ferry drugs into other countries, as in the following case of a Belgian diplomat:

It was early evening, Saturday, May 25, 1985, when a chancellor at the Belgian Embassy in New Delhi, India, entered a room at the Marriott Airport Inn across from New York's La Guardia Airport.

The short bespectacled man carried a large green canvas bag bearing the official seal of Belguim. It was an official diplomatic pouch he had carried off a plane from New Delhi which had landed two hours earlier at Kennedy Airport. His diplomatic passport had allowed him to move quickly through customs – no questions asked. The seal on the pouch guaranteed it would not be opened by customs inspectors.

He handed the pouch to the man waiting in the room. The man broke the seal and examined the bag's contents: a half dozen large manilla envelopes marked 'Ambassade van Belgie'. Inside the envelopes – 22 pounds of pure heroin with a street value in excess of forty million dollars.

Naturally the diplomat was in a hurry to leave. The other man instructed him to return to the same room the next night to receive the agreed upon $100,000 courier fee for delivering the shipment. The diplomat's last words to the man who took delivery were, 'Make sure you destroy the pouch.'

The following night the diplomat returned to the hotel room. There was no money waiting for him. The man to whom he had delivered the heroin was an agent of the Drug Enforcement Administration. He was the victim of the DEA 'sting' operation that was launched when agents, in March, has arrested an Indian as he allegedly delivered 4.5 pounds of heroin to four men, who were arrested. Prosecutors said the four were Sicilian organized crime figures. The Indian, as part of a plea bargain, told authorities how the drugs were getting into the country – by diplomatic pouch.

After his arrest, the diplomat tried to claim diplomatic immunity. But because he was not accredited the to the United States, he had no entitlement to immunity on US soil. He was arrested and entered a plea of not guilty. Later he changed that plea, and was sentenced to six years in a federal prison.

Eventually, acting on further information, the DEA agents arrested eight men, including two other non-diplomatic couriers and four distributors, and seized a total of forty-three pounds of heroin, including the twenty-two pounds that the diplomat delivered to the undercover agent at the airport hotel. Among those arrested was another Indian, the group's ringleader. He was arrested in Montreal, and was extradited to the US where he still awaits trial.

US Attorney Raymond J. Dearie, who prosecuted the diplomat, was visibly angered by the case. At a press conference he displayed the diplomatic bag that the diplomat had used to get his drugs into the United States. 'The world should know that there is a kind of certified way of entry for illicit drugs through the violation of diplomatic privileges,' Dearie said. 'If it's a diplomatic pouch it cannot be touched.'

Dearie called for a revision of accords prohibiting inspection of diplomatic pouches. 'It seems to me that we cannot allow the privileges and courtesies of diplomatic immunity to provide safe passage to drug couriers and their drugs,' he said.

Smugglers are frequently foiled at New York's Kennedy International Airport because cutoms and DEA officers make an especially strong effort there to stop the flow of drugs entering the US.

Article 36 of the Vienna Convention protects diplomats' luggage from inspection unless there are 'serious grounds' to presume it contains articles not intended for the personal use of the diplomat or his household, or that the contents are prohibited or controlled by law.

When the Vienna Convention was in the drafting stages, Sir Ian Sinclair, a member of the International Law Commission, told the House of Commons Foreign Affairs Committee there was an almost universal suspicion that diplomats were contemptuously flouting the laws of host nations. The many documented cases of abuse lent credence to the suspicion. Six or seven years prior to the drafting of the Vienna Convention, Sir Ian recalls, a diplomatic mission to a Scandinavian country was exposed for financing its operation by selling narcotics imported via diplomatic pouch. This and other similar cases led the drafting committee to include the 'serious grounds' clause in Article 36.

Financial support for a foreign mission may have been what was involved in the most serious breach of diplomatic immunity in Canada in recent years.

The third highest diplomat at the Nicaraguan Embassy in Ottawa, was charged with possession of cocaine for the purposes of trafficking and with carrying a restricted weapon, a .38 calibre Smith and Wesson. But he pleaded diplomatic immunity and slipped out of Canada, successfully avoiding prosecution for either offence.

On July 23, 1982, he went to an Ottawa car wash with his young son. While he was at the counter paying the bill, his son ran out of the door. The Nicaraguan diplomat chased after the boy, forgetting his purse on the counter.

Later that day, the management of the car wash discovered the purse. They opened it to see who had left it behind, and found thirty-five grams of cocaine with a street value of 100,000 Canadian dollars and a revolver. The manager of the car wash notified the police who collected the evidence and contacted the diplomat. He claimed diplomatic immunity.

Four days later, after investigating his right to immunity, police arrested him. He was arraigned before a Crown Magistrate. At the arraignment, Crown Attorney Graham Pinos objected to his demand for immunity. He explained to the court that Canada's Minister of External Affairs had received notification from the Nicaraguan Embassy on July 12 that he had been replaced. That was eleven days before he was caught with the illegal drug.

Pinos further argued that the man had left Canada after the 12th for a four-day holiday in the United States, and that his immunity had expired when he left the country. Pinos contended that the man re-entered Canada as a private citizen, not as a diplomat and, therefore, he should be subject to prosecution. Pinos asked the court to bind the Nicaraguan over for trial.

The man again asserted his diplomatic immunity and Provincial Judge Livius Sherwood ruled in his favour. The judge held that sixteen days was insufficient time for him to have packed his belongings and returned to Managua. The judge ruled that his immunity was in effect at the time of the discovery and the arrest, and, therefore, he could not be prosecuted.

The case didn't end there, however. Crown Attorney Pinos was resolved not to let diplomatic immunity prevent an indictment; he decided to appeal against the Crown Magistrate's decision. The appeal papers were with him in court, filled out and ready to be filed, when the decision was handed down. Pinos had the man's process papers at the ready and he planned to serve him to appear at the appeal before the diplomat left the courtroom. A legal service would have prohibited the diplomat from fleeing Canada until the appeal came before the courts.

The scene in the courtroom unfortunately developed into something of a farce. Just as Pinos made his move to serve the man for the Crown, an unidentified man stepped between them, preventing the service. The man took his cue and bolted out of the courtroom. The chase was on. Pinos dashed after him in hot pursuit, determined to hand him the summons. As he ran Pinos tripped, and the court papers went flying. By the time Pinos recovered his composure and his paperwork, the man had made good his escape.

He had fled to the inviolable Nicaraguan Embassy where, naturally, he could not be served. Some time within the next few days, he quietly slipped across the border. After his disappearing act at the court-house, he was declared an undesirable and was given forty-eight hours to leave Canada.

The Crown continued its appeal, despite the diplomat's absence and no reasonable expectation that justice would prevail since extradition wasn't likely. On February 11, 1984, the Court of Appeals upheld Judge Sherwood's ruling that his immunity was in force at the time of the arrest and dismissed the charges. The government succeeded in keeping thirty-five ounces of cocaine off the streets, but the smuggler went free, compliments of the Vienna Convention.

Later, Canadian officials speculated that the aid given the man by Nicaraguan officials indicated to them that the cocaine smuggling had been given a semi-official stamp of approval and perhaps was even being sanctioned by the cash-poor Nicaraguan government as a means of supporting its mission in Canada.

As a general policy, all incoming luggage on international flights at Kennedy is sniffed by drug detecting dogs. The DEA, keeping within widely accepted international practice, uses the 'serious grounds' clause to justify having dogs sniff the luggage. Because the bags are neither detained nor opened, both forbidden by the Vienna Convention, the sniff screening can be used on diplomatic baggage. When the dogs react to a particular piece of luggage, the diplomat who brought it in is asked to open it.

On April 10, 1984, a citizen of Bhutan arrived at Kennedy International on a Pan Am flight from New Delhi by way of Bombay and Frankfurt. A consul attached to the Foreign Service of Bhutan, a kingdom on the north-east border of India, he carried one of his country's diplomatic passports.

The man told customs officials he was going to the Bhutan Mission to the United Nations. Later a customs official was to say that he got curious because he had simply never met anyone carrying a Bhutan passport before and that the diplomat seemed unusually nervous to him. So he asked him to open his bags for inspection. The man refused, pleading immunity. Although he did have a diplomatic passport, he was travelling not on a diplomatic visa but on a business/visitor's visa. So, his two pieces of hand luggage were opened despite his shrill protests. Inside were found twenty-three bricks of heroin weighing fifty-six pounds. Because he was not accredited to the United States, he was prosecuted.

In Toyko, in 1984, Metropolitan Police raided a drug dealer and found fifty-eight kilos of 'Taiwan Root', a powerful type of heroin from the Golden Triangle that is processed in Taiwan. At the time of the bust, police said the drug ring might be the largest ever uncovered in Japan. They announced that they had apprehended two Japanese and were searching for two others.

Three weeks later, the police dropped a bombshell. Their investigation had uncovered evidence that the ring had smuggled over 181 kilos of heroin into Japan in the six months between October, 1983, and March, 1984. The drugs had a street value of 36.2 billion yen (about 145 million pounds). The ring involved Taiwanese, Japanese and Koreans, and was headquartered in Taiwan. A key man in the heroin smuggling ring was the Ambassador from a South American country.

Toyko police revealed that the Ambassador made frequent trips to Japan from Taiwan. On many of the trips, he carried considerable 'luggage' which escaped customs inspection because of his diplomatic status. Records showed that on five occasions within the six months, he had flown to Toyko or Osaka airports with between thirty and seventy kilos of luggage.

On July 19, the Taiwanese police announced that acting on information supplied by Toyko, they had raided a heroin processing factory and arrested four Taiwanese, six Koreans and two Japanese. Based on information compiled from the ring members' confessions, police detailed the operation's importation method.

A Taiwanese named Cho accompanied the Ambassador on all his trips to Japan. After he cleared customs, Cho took the heroin to a Toyko apartment. It was then sold to Japanese drug dealers. According to the police Cho and a Japanese who shared the Toyko apartment were the only two who knew him by name. The other ring members knew him only as 'the high nosed diplomat'.

Following the investigation, police realized that all the ring's heroin was brought into Japan under diplomatic seal. On his February, 1984, trip, the Ambassador had apparently secreted sixty-eight kilos in two trunks, both of which were under seal.

Because of diplomatic immunity, the Ambassador could not be arrested. At a press conference in Taiwan, he vigorously denied being involved in drug smuggling and called the charges 'a total fabrication'. He said that he had indeed made the trips to Japan but they had been a combination of business and pleasure. He said he was a physician and 'would never be involved in dealing drugs'. He also said he had not been to Japan in 1984.

Police had records of his trips to Japan, including those made in 1984. He was recalled home immediately and left the diplomatic corps. He spent no time in jail after his unimpeded smuggling career.

Between 1977 and 1979, a second secretary at the Nigerian Mission to the United Nations, smuggled more than ten million dollars' worth of cocaine and other drugs into the United States in his personal luggage. He was part of a well-organized syndicate that operated efficiently for two years and transported large quantities of drugs that filtered down to the playgrounds and streets of America.

When the ring was uncovered, members testified that the man's role was courier and he was paid on a commission basis. His confederates were prosecuted, but because he had immunity as a high ranking United Nations employee, he himself was not. He was recalled to Nigeria where he no doubt lives in high style on the profits of his smuggling activities.

In 1980, two Pakistanis were arrested at an apartment in Silver Spring, Maryland, and charged with possession of almost four and a half pounds of pure Golden Crescent heroin with a street value of twenty-eight million dollars. The trail of the crime led from the Golden Crescent to a Washington embassy.

During the investigation, it came to light that the two Pakistanis had several passports and many bank accounts containing large amounts of money. They had travelled extensively in the United States and told the court that they were gem dealers by trade.

Assistant US Attorney Daniel J. Bernstein asked that a high bail bond be posted for the pair, saying both men were 'working in connection with persons who have diplomatic immunity in this country'. Attorney Bernstein voiced his fear that the Pakistanis would seek asylum in a Washington embassy if they were freed on bail, and that an inviolable shelter would be provided.

Those 'persons who have diplomatic immunity' Bernstein referred to were a first secretary of the Chad Embassy, and a second secretary. Bernstein told the court that the two Chadian representatives used their positions 'to facilitate the import of heroin into the United States from the Khyber Pass region of Pakistan'.

Both men flew to Pakistan in July, 1980. One returned to the US with a false-bottomed suitcase containing six kilos of heroin.

The first secretary told the *Washington Post* the two Chadian diplomats had made the trip to Pakistan at the expense of the two Pakistanis, but he denied that it was a drug smuggling trip. He professed that he had met the two 'gem dealers', when they had stopped by his house the previous spring. The two young men told him they knew Chad was involved in a civil war and thought he might be in need of some cash. They persisted, the first secretary said, making several visits to the Chadians in what seems a blatant recruitment attempt. In the end, the lure was sufficient enough to win their complicity.

Later, when the first secretary got a letter from the father of one of them inviting him to Pakistan, he and the other man took the trip 'since we didn't have a lot of work to do'.

During the three-day visit, the elder man, who earned his living 'in the import and export business', showed the

Chadian diplomats around on sightseeing excursions. The first secretary said he only brought back a small rock and a letter to the other. After the first secretary returned to Washington, he was asked to make another trip within two weeks of the first, but he declined.

The two men were prosecuted, but the Chadian diplomats were not. They left the country shortly after learning they were under investigation. Chad later withdrew the diplomatic status of the pair, though they had already fled the States by that time.

All too often, corrupt diplomats are not simply couriers for faceless drug barons, but are drug dealers themselves. Their smuggling is not simply to earn a fee, but to gain all the considerable profit that can result from drug trafficking.

A shipment of two kilos (about four and a half pounds) of heroin was seized at Kennedy Airport in April, 1982. A man had concealed the heroin in a false-bottomed suitcase, and the drugs were found as part of a routine inspection. When he was caught he identified himself as a cultural attaché of the Dominican Republic and claimed diplomatic immunity.

The Dominican Mission to the United Nations admitted that the man, an unemployed car assembly worker and Dominican national who lived in North Tarrytown, New York, 'worked out of' their mission at 1270 Avenue of the Americas, but they also said the title was an honourary one and carried no diplomatic privileges.

When the man discovered his claim of immunity wouldn't work, he decided not to take the rap alone. He told what he knew and copped a plea. He informed police he had been recruited for his role in the illegal operation by a second secretary at the Dominican Republic's UN mission. He also revealed that a first secretary at the mission played a key part in the scheme. He telephoned him to arrange his flight to London.There he was to meet an Air India flight where 'the merchandise' would be transferred. He escorted him to the airport for the flight to London and assured him that when he returned with the baggage he would be met by the second secretary or himself.

The man was accompanied on the trip by another Dominican national, whose apparent function was as an enforcer. All he did was watch the man execute the pre-arranged plan.

At Heathrow, he met a man debarking from the Air India flight. The man, whose identity was unknown to him, gave him a claim ticket for the heroin-laden suitcase. Then he retrieved the case from the conveyor belt and checked it in as his own luggage on the flight back to Kennedy.

According to William Von Raab, Commissioner of the US Customs Service, the amateur 'is a sitting duck for the Customs Service if he's committing a crime because he gives himself away: he sweats a lot, he fidgets, he's nervous, he looks guilty. Professional smugglers are a different picture, and it takes investigation and intelligence to catch the guy.'

The man looked guilty, and that was his undoing. When the Customs inspector conducted his search, it wasn't long before he found the concealed narcotics. An investigation followed the bust, and the heroin was valued at three million dollars. The second secretary, who did not have full immunity, was prosecuted. The enforcer and co-conspirator was never found.

The first secretary, who ranked about seventh at the Dominican Mission to the United Nations, was to receive $100,000 for organizing the smuggling operation.

The United States requested that the Dominican Republic waive his immunity, which they did – after he was safely out of the country. The 35-year-old diplomat was said by a mission spokesman to have returned to Santo Domingo for the Caribbean nation's Presidential elections. He never returned to the United States.

Later, the Dominican Republic said that he had resigned his UN post. Efforts to extradite him proved futile. He was not prosecuted in the three million dollar heroin smuggling case. Whether he had been involved in other drug trafficking operations will probably never be discovered.

A Thai vice-consul stationed in Chicago was the kingpin of a drug ring that smuggled twenty million dollars' worth of heroin into the United States in diplomatic pouches. The investigation that led to the capture of the man began with an arrest in Baltimore on April 9, 1982. There, a Thai national arrested in a drug raid named him as his supplier.

The next pouch that came through Chicago's O'Hare International Airport addressed to the man was given to the sniffer dogs. DEA agents reported that the dogs 'went crazy' at the pouch. The federal agents did not open the pouch, but instead waited for it to be claimed. This is the DEA's standard operating procedure. To make a charge of trafficking stick, they pursue an airtight case – apprehension red-handed with the contraband.

The drug pouch was picked up from the airport. Over the next few weeks, the Thai vice-consul's movements were closely observed. In a restaurant near the consulate, the diplomat made two deliveries of three pounds of eighty-nine percent pure white heroin. Then agents moved in. He was arrested April 30.

Though the diplomatic pouches used in the scheme could not be opened, the man himself did not have full immunity because he was only a vice-consul. In his Chicago residence, police found another four and a half pounds of pure heroin, five pistols and a rifle. For each pound of heroin smuggled into the country, he received $10,000 cash commission. Bank records showed he smuggled up to fifteen pounds of heroin in total.

He said the government had no right to prosecute him because he had immunity. His attorney claimed in court that he was entitled to full immunity under the Vienna Convention. Though Thai officials in Chicago cooperated with the investigation, once he was arrested they too claimed he had immunity.

In Bangkok, however, the Thai Foreign Ministry waived immunity when they were presented with the evidence demonstrating the seriousness of the offence. This was not an isolated incident, this was a highly organized ring with distribution reaching half-way across the country. The vice-consul was charged in a Chicago Federal Court with seven counts of conspiracy, distribution of heroin and possession with intent to distribute heroin. He was convicted and the Thai 'Consul Connection' was closed.

As we have seen, some diplomats who are caught smuggling drugs are prosecuted. Though they think they have immunity, they don't. At Kennedy International Airport in May, 1982, a Bolivian cultural attaché stationed in Mexico City was arrested on charges of narcotics smuggling.

He had debarked an Aerolinas Argentinas flight from Buenos Aires where he had attended a meeting of the Organization of American States. Officers asked to search his luggage. He immediately asserted diplomatic immunity. Because he was not accredited to the United States, his claim was not honoured.

In the luggage, customs officials found eleven pounds of cocaine, gift-wrapped in brightly coloured paper. The cocaine had been sealed in plastic and put into twelve airtight plastic containers in case a drug sniffing dog was being used. The ruse didn't work. He was prosecuted.

Seventy pounds of marijuana were smuggled into New York's Kennedy Airport by employees of the Jamaican consulate during 1980, but no arrests were made. In one incident, two employees of the Jamaican consulate in New York were caught with a suitcase containing fifty pounds of Jamaican ganja, but they disavowed ownership.

Repudiating ownership of seized baggage is the usual first response of smugglers. Many professionals actually go to great lengths to made their denials seem plausible. One common ploy is to check in two identical suitcases, one packed with the contraband and clothes of the opposite sex of the smuggler. The other is free of illegal substances and packed with clothes that the smuggler might wear. If apprehended with the goods, the smuggler acts shocked. He says the suitcase wasn't his, then he walks back to the conveyor belt to retrieve the 'right' suitcase.

When a cardboard box apparently belonging to Jamaican Consul General Myrtle Johnson-Abrahams was discovered con taining twenty-two pounds of ganja, she too denied any know ledge of it. She told DEA officials that the box had been planted in her luggage. Although none of the three consular employees caught with smuggled marijuana was entitled to immunity from prosecution on a felony charge, none of them was arrested.

Normally, when that amount of contraband is discovered, the DEA alerts Port Authority police of the attempted smuggling. In the case of the Consul General, they did not. DEA officials notified the State Department, and the State Department arranged a meeting between themselves, Jamaican diplomats, the DEA and Jamaican drug officials.

Richard Gookin, Deputy Chief of Protocol for the State Department, told the media what the outcome would be for the Jamaican Consul General following the smuggling incident. 'She's not going to be prosecuted in the United States,' he said. 'Rather, the matter is being taken up, or being referred to, the Jamaican authorities.'

In the media uproar which followed the granting of immunity to someone not entitled to it, a Drug Enforcement Administration spokesman defended his department's actions by stating they had been restrained by the State Department. 'We were told "No press",' the DEA spokesman claimed, ' "Refer all calls to the State Department." '

Meanwhile, Myrtle Johnson-Abrahams maintained that someone had put the marijuana in her luggage on a flight from Jamaica and that she didn't know it was there. She remained the Consul General. The other two employees, who also avowed ignorance of the smuggled goods, were subsequently fired for 'unrelated reasons'.

Scandal erupted in Brussels in 1982 when seven Belgian police officers, including the former head of the anti-drug squad, were charged with drug dealing and corruption. A 45-year-old American DEA agent, Frank Eaton, was also accused of involvement in drug dealing.

When the case came to court the courtroom was under heavy guard. One of the investigating officers had been attacked in an apparent assassination attempt. In defending the Belgian officers, their lawyers contended that the police officers had infiltrated the drug underworld to catch the organizers. Their accusers maintained that they infiltrated the rings in order to control them for personal gain.

Frank Eaton didn't appear in court, however. The US Embassy sent a letter to the prosecution explaining that Eaton would not be appearing because he had diplomatic immunity. The letter also stated that Eaton had left Belgium and returned to the United States.

Though most governments do not scrutinize the charges for possible prosecution following a claim of immunity, the United States government did because Eaton's job was drug enforcement. Charges of corruption within the agency are a grave matter.

On his return, Eaton was put on paid leave while the government launched a full internal review of the charges. The DEA made a long and thorough investigation and found that Eaton was innocent. A spokesman said, 'A thorough investigation cleared Eaton completely and he was returned to active duty. We are absolutely sure that his accusers were lying in an attempt to discredit him and keep US drug agents and informers from testifying against them. We are sure he was absolutely innocent.'

Exonerated, Frank Eaton has returned to active duty in another post.

When it comes to smuggling drugs, diplomats are caught regularly, but the only cases that come to light are those that are reported in the press, and the State Department and the Foreign Office try their best to keep the public ignorant of the extent of the problem.

Because drug smuggling is such a grave offence, the State Department or the Foreign Office will generally ask the embassy in question to waive the diplomat's immunity. Foreign embassies often try to have it both ways. They comply with the waiver request, but *after* the diplomat is safely out of the country. That keeps them free from the charge of non-cooperation, while still allowing them to prevent their own nationals from being prosecuted.

CHAPTER FIVE

The Bag

In America it's known as the diplomatic pouch. In Britain it's the diplomatic bag. The French call it *la valise diplomatique*. Whatever its various titles, 143 nations have agreed, 'The diplomatic bag shall not be opened or detained', as stated in Article 27 (3) of the Vienna Convention.

Diplomatic bags and baggage are intended for the safe and confidential conveyance of articles intended for the official use of a mission or for a diplomat's personal use. Because of its inviolable status, the pouch, bag or valise has long been the diplomatic smuggler's best friend.

Most diplomatic bags are large canvas sacks which are sealed with wax or lead bearing the official stamp of the country and a tag or stick-on label identifying the contents as 'diplomatic'. The bag is intended for conveyance of classified documents, vital communiqués, encoding and decoding equipment, passports and government seals. The bags are generally carried by diplomatic couriers who must show authorized identification and cannot be detained. According to the Vienna Convention, Article 27 (5), a diplomatic courier should be provided with an official document declaring his status and indicating the number of packages constituting the bag on that particular trip. Not all diplomatic bags are accompanied by couriers. Some are conveyed by airline pilots and are picked up from the aircraft by a member of the diplomatic mission.

The bag must be clearly marked as diplomatic. If it doesn't have the diplomatic bag designation, it is considered ordinary air freight and has to go through customs clearance.

Article 27 (4) stipulates that the bag may only contain diplomatic documents or articles intended for official use. Articles for the official use of the mission are exempt from customs duties under Article 36 (1) of the Convention. Personal baggage, if suspicious, has to be inspected in the presence of the diplomat or his designated representative.

In July, 1984, the Soviets pushed the definition diplomatic bag to the limit when they proclaimed that a nine-ton tractor-trailer lorry was a diplomatic pouch. They refused to declare its contents to customs agents. The white Mercedes truck bearing blue Cyrillic letters reading 'Sovtransavto' across its side, tried to cross into Switzerland at Basel, bound for the Soviet Embassy in Geneva. The three Soviets driving the lorry put off a request for inspection proclaiming the entire truck was a diplomatic bag. Swiss customs inspectors, however, denied their claim.

Though the Vienna Convention does not specify any size limitation for the bag, Swiss officials said they considered 450 pounds to be the maximum allowable size. They sealed the lorry and told the Soviets it could not be unloaded. Then they allowed it to continue to Geneva.

In Geneva, the Sovicts still refused to reveal the lorry's contents for customs inspection. They announced that it contained sending and receiving radio equipment and equipment for coding communications, but would not permit an inspection. The Swiss wouldn't unseal the lorry. The resulting stalemate gave the Russians no choice but to return the lorry to Moscow.

On its way out of the country, the Swiss government removed their seals at Basel and the lorry rolled into West Germany.

West German customs officials demanded an inventory in Bonn, but the Soviets again refused. Eleven days passed with the lorry under heavy guard, prohibited from leaving. The Germans refused to accept it as a diplomatic bag, not because of its size, but because it was a motorized vehicle, capable of its own free movement.

Finally, Soviet officials allowed the West Germans to inspect the truck. The truck was opened on Soviet Embassy property in Bonn, legally considered to be inside Soviet territory.

The customs inspection lasted about twenty minutes. All the crates inside the truck bore Russian inscriptions and were photographed. The crates themselves were accepted by West Germany as diplomatic bags and therefore remained unopened. The inventory was registered as 207 diplomatic parcels. The truck was then allowed to proceed on its way back to Russia. A stand had been made – even the diplomatic bag had limits.

But the matter requires constant vigilance as another Soviet incident proved nearly a year later. In June, 1985, the Soviets shipped thirty-five tons of cargo marked 'household goods' out of Baltimore harbour. No customs agent examined the shipment. Later, Pentagon officials blamed the State Department for waving the shipment through without notifying customs.

Diplomats often import goods via the diplomatic bag to sell for personal profit. The Vienna Convention provides that receiving states shall grant exemption from 'customs duties, taxes and similar charges on articles for the official use of the mission and for personal use of the diplomatic agent or members of his family, including articles intended for his household'. This exemption on customs duties and other taxes was codified for the first time in the Havana Convention in 1928. Its abuses have been around nearly as long.

There are many well known cases, and the diplomats involved are sometimes even heads of missions. Charles W. Thayer, the respected diplomatic service veteran and author of *Diplomat*, reported that in 1930s Russia, many Western diplomats provided actresses and ballerinas with the latest Paris fashions which they had smuggled to Moscow in diplomatic pouches.

The post-war period, when restrictions, shortages and economic uncertainties made diplomatic smuggling a lucrative temptation, was rampant with such abuses. In 1953, Eduardo de Artega, Minister of Uruguay stationed in Brussels, was fined for attempting to smuggle diamonds with a value of $38,592 out of England in a diplomatic pouch.

In 1954, Don Luis F. de Almagro, the Cuban Minister to Egypt, Lebanon and Syria, was stopped and searched on his way out of Egypt. Customs officials there, who had for some time suspected him of smuggling, found large amounts of currency and jewels on his person. De Almagro pleaded ignorance. He told customs inspectors he didn't know it was illegal for him to take such things out of the country. In the scandal that followed, de Almagro was dismissed from Cuba's foreign service, but he wasn't charged.

After the war, there was an insatiable demand in England for good watches. The import quota on Swiss watches was much too low to satisfy the demand and a black market developed. Compared to diamonds, currency and narcotics, watches are heavy and bulky and therefore harder to smuggle, especially as you had to carry a lot of them before you could turn a respectable profit.

One post-war story illustrates some of the difficulties of watch smuggling. A Frenchman travelling on a diplomatic passport was overloaded with self-winding watches that had been sewn into the lining of his jacket and overcoat. On landing at Dover, the motion of the boat as it docked was sufficient to wind all the watches. When the diplomat arrived at the customs desk, he was whirring and ticking like a clock factory. Needless to say, he was caught.

His exploits, however, pale beside those of Georges Geoffroy, a French Consul who was stationed at Dusseldorf. On arriving at London airport he refused to be searched on the grounds that he had immunity. Customs officials insisted and found 2,190 watches sewn into the lining of his coat.

Cars, though even bulkier, can be an easier proposition. A car dealer in Recife, Brazil, had made a clandestine deal with two American employees of the Agency for International Development in 1964. The car dealer understood that they were to sell him their cars after two years when the cars were no longer subject to resale duty payment. The secret deal only surfaced when the Americans reneged and the car dealer filed suit.

To curb this corruption, the American Embassy imposed a restriction: US government employees could only sell their cars after receiving Embassy approval.

In another notorious case, an American Embassy employee imported five or six cars at the rate of one a week to sell through classified ads in the local paper. The following year, all overseas personnel were forbidden by the American government from selling their cars and personal possessions for a profit. By the early 1960s, the State Department had restricted diplomats' purchase of tax-free cars to no more than one a year.

The problem has existed for years in Canada. In the 1950s when Canadians were not allowed to import cars from the United States where they could be bought cheaper and chosen from a wider variety of models, Latin American diplomats stationed in Ottawa were regularly importing duty-free American cars, selling them, and realizing substantial profits.

More recently the problem has revolved around Canada's very high special sales tax on new automobile purchases. Diplomatic personnel are exempt from the tax and so can buy a car for much less than the average consumer. A number of diplomats have been accused of taking advantage of the exemption to buy cars cheaply for resale at a nice profit. In fact, several diplomats from small Third World countries were said to be supporting themselves by such activities – their countries being too poor to be able to pay them a living wage. Their ambassadorships are almost like a franchise. In order to survive, they must engage in reselling cars and smuggling spirits, which are also subject to high taxes and import duties, and which can be bought much more cheaply across the border in the US and then resold in Canada at a hefty profit.

The abuses have been so widespread that reform legislation was instituted all over the world. In France now, a diplomat cannot sell his car at all. When his tour of duty is over, he must export his car along with his other possessions. In Britain, a diplomat may import a car only within his first three months in his post and only if he owned it before he was assigned to Britain. He must also agree to export the car at the end of his posting or sooner. In Canada, importation of cars is permitted only when Canadian officials are provided with written certification of necessity signed by the chief of the mission, and they are carefully checked to insure that no one diplomat, or mission, is importing an excessive number of cars.

Though crackdowns stopped the profiteering on car sales, importation of other goods for resale was still common. A European envoy to one South American country imported eleven pianos in under two years. The Minister was out of the country on a leave of absence when the piano wholesaling came to light. He never returned.

In 1960, seven Marine guards at the US Embassy in London were caught selling large quantities of cigarettes and whisky that had been imported duty-free. A Dutch national who admitted buying from the Marine wholesalers was convicted in a London court. The Marines themselves were released after claiming diplomatic immunity, but they didn't escape military prosecution. Having been court-martialled and found guilty, they were fined, demoted and shipped out.

There are also diplomats abroad from countries where coups change the ruling class almost as frequently as the seasons. Corruption is a way of life and a consular post can be bought. Diplomatic status is conferred as a reward for favours, and the conferees know their licence to smuggle is good 'for a limited time only'.

North Korea's diplomatic corps has a well-deserved reputation for widespread use of diplomatic bags to import goods for sale on local black markets. In October, 1976, the entire North Korean delegation to Denmark, Norway and Sweden was expelled. Police said they were involved in large-scale trafficking of tax-free spirits, cigarettes and marijuana. The Vienna Convention stipulates that goods imported tax-free by diplomats are to be for personal consumption. When one of the North Korean diplomats was questioned by a customs official, he claimed that the two and a half million duty-free cigarettes he was importing were for his personal consumption.

India is a hotbed of illegal activity. Over the last five years, at least thirty-three diplomats have been caught smuggling duty-free goods into India in diplomatic pouches for resale. One of those caught and expelled was an American diplomat. A comptroller for the Agency for International Development, he used his diplomatic passport to smuggle contraband and other goods into India. Indian authorities found over two million dollars' worth of illegal goods in his home. In the illicit scheme, he imported the goods, then turned them over to an Indian, who sold them and paid him a commission. He pleaded diplomatic immunity to escape charges in India and was expelled.

Back at home, he was charged by the Internal Revenue Service for under-reporting his income. The IRS said he accepted $31,107 from the Indian in 1981, and a total of more than $100,000 from the same man between November, 1980, and November, 1982. Some of his smuggling commissions were deposited in a Hong Kong bank account to keep the income secret from the tax men.

He pleaded guilty in US federal court to charges of accepting bribes and filing a false income tax return for 1981. In exchange for the guilty plea, the government agreed not to prosecute him for other illegal activities he may have engaged in while stationed in India.

US customs officials estimate that, after drugs, art treasures are the single most lucrative illegal import. Art dealers capitalize on Third World poverty and ignorance to purloin antiquities, bringing them back to the West to market as expensive primitive art. One way these treasures have departed their homelands is via the diplomatic pouch.

John D. Cooney, Curator of Ancient Art at the Cleveland Museum, told a reporter than ninety-five percent of the ancient art in the United States has been smuggled in. 'Unless you're naïve or not very bright, you'd have to know that much ancient art is stolen,' Mr Cooney observed.

There is no way to determine how much has been stolen

or how many diplomatic bags have been used for the purpose. There is no inventory of mankind's cultural legacy, but at a time when a New York department store advertises for its pre-Columbian department by calling it 'a treasure-trove of over a thousand pieces', it is obvious that the pillage and smuggle cycle has gone on much too long. We face a future in which there may be no protection of the past.

The plunder of ancient artefacts is tragic in two ways: countries are robbed of their cultural heritage and one of their few natural resources; and, grave robbers and pillagers destroy irreplaceable archaeological sites that hold the secrets of lost civilizations.

Karl E. Meyer, in his comprehensive book, *The Plundered Past*, writes: 'The diplomat is an old and familiar friend; in the past, envoys were themselves frequently involved in archaeology or antiquities, as was the case with Sir Henry Layard, John Lloyd Stephens, Lord Elgin, and General Luigi Palma di Cesnola. Diplomats are often collectors, and sometimes they help other collectors or dealers by making accessible that invaluable privilege, the untouchable diplomatic pouch.'

Newsweek Magazine concurs. 'The real smugglers,' *Newsweek* pointed out, 'those who carry the artefacts across borders, are more often than not white-collar criminals – diplomats and journalists as well as art brokers. One time-honoured shipping route is the diplomatic pouch, generally immune from customs searches.'

Though many Third World countries have well-written patrimony laws, they do little to stop the constant flow of artefacts out of their native countries and into Western galleries and museums. Between 1977 and 1979, 3,000 cases of thefts of antiquities were reported in India. Only ten were solved. Since Nigeria passed its patrimony law in 1974, there have been only six convictions.

One of the most flagrant examples of the use of the diplomatic pouch to smuggle antiquities involved an American archaeologist. Edward Herbert Thompson recovered Mayan artefacts from Mexico during the 1900s from a sacred well at

Chichen Itza in the north of Central Yucatan, the political, cultural and religious centre of the Mayan and Mayan-Toltec civilizations from 800 AD to the mid-thirteenth century. Sacrifices were offered to the gods by plunging articles and even humans into the deep well, and Thompson managed to dredge gold, jade, copper, bones and textiles from the bottom.

Thompson was supported by wealthy and influential friends of Harvard University's Peabody Museum. These patrons funded his first trip to Mexico in 1885. They later used their influence to see that Thompson was appointed American Consul to Mexico so his excavating and exporting could be done under diplomatic cover.

Thompson purchased the land all around Chichen Itza and started a cattle ranch to obscure his true purpose. He began digging in 1904 and continued until 1911 when the Mexican Revolution exploded around him and he was forced to flee the country. His stolen collection included 30,000 items and has been declared 'the single most important archaeological treasure ever recovered in the Americas'.

Thompson sent the gold and bones to the Peabody via diplomatic pouch. He and his sponsors hid the purloined treasure at Harvard University. The valuable collection went unpublicized until 1926 when the Mexican government sued him in an attempt to recover the antiquities. A 1944 Mexican Supreme Court ruling declared that Thompson had not violated the law, since Mexico had no law to protect antiquities at the time of their removal. The Peabody Museum has since returned 'a representative portion' of the collection to Mexico.

The first director of the Metropolitan Museum of Art in New York was General Luigi Palma di Cesnola. After the American Civil War, the General was appointed US Consul to Cyprus. At the time, Cyprus was part of the Ottoman Empire. Without Turkish permission, di Cesnola excavated sites on the island between 1865 and 1876. He offered a 35,573 piece collection of the antiquities at silent auction to the West's major museums. The winning bid came from the recently founded Metropolitan Museum.

Turkish authorities learned of the imminent sale and issued orders forbidding export of the art treasures. But di Cesnola learned the order barring export was on its way, so he shipped his purloined treasure out of Cyprus before the written order arrived. This effectively ended his diplomatic career, but it ensured his next one. He was appointed director of the Metropolitan Museum of Art in 1879.

Controversy has surrounded the Elgin Marbles since shortly after their removal from Greece in the first decade of the 19th century. Their proper ownership has been debated ever since, and we are unlikely to resolve the matter here. The Marbles, however, bear mention because of their notoriety.

Thomas Bruce, the seventh Earl of Elgin, was appointed Britain's Ambassador to Greece in 1800. Disheartened by the Turkish neglect of the Acropolis, Elgin asked permission of the sultan to remove some of the ornaments. Because Nelson had just driven Napoleon's fleet from Egypt – also part of the Ottoman Empire – the sultan was in a generous mood when he met with the British Ambassador to discuss the proposal.

The sultan issued a permit for Elgin to excavate the Acropolis. However, the original permit in Turkish was subsequently lost and the only remaining document is an Italian translation that is subject to interpretation.

The British Museum booklet on the Marbles translates a phrase of the permit in Italian as 'any pieces of stone with inscriptions or figures'. Other scholarly translators contend the phrase reads, '*some* pieces of stone with inscriptions or figures'.

Whatever the original permit intended, Lord Elgin and his party removed seventeen figures from Parthenon pediments, fifteen metopes, fifty-six slabs of the temple's friezes, the Caryatid column, thirteen marble heads and a large assortment of vases, pillars and carvings. The Ambassador personally funded the removal of the Acropolis collection which was shipped via the Royal Navy. He sold most of the collection to Britain for £35,000 in 1815, and the Elgin Marbles have resided in the British Museum ever since.

It is arguable that the collection is better preserved in the Museum than in Greece where air pollution is disfiguring what is left of the Acropolis. However, Elgin undoubtedly took liberal advantage of the sultan's permit, a privilege only conferred upon him by virtue of his ambassadorship.

South Africa House in London has apparently used the diplomatic bag to smuggle out articles which they hired professional criminals to steal. At the trial of Edward Aspinall, a professional burglar with twenty convictions to his name, evidence revealed that he had been hired by South African Warrant Officer Klue to steal documents from the offices of organizations on which the South Africans wanted to spy. In a programme broadcast on the South African national television network, some of the stolen papers were shown on film. Aspinall testified that he had given these papers to Klue.

The papers, evidence in the case against Aspinall at the Old Bailey in 1982, were presumably transmitted to South Africa in a diplomatic bag.

Klue was barred from returning to England, and the Home Secretary said they 'had good reason to believe that he had been engaged in activities incompatible with his official status in this country. He will not be allowed to return.'

Perhaps the most outrageous exploitation of the diplomatic freedom from search of luggage and bags is the case of Umaru Dikko, the former Nigerian Minister of Transportation, who was drugged, manacled and dumped in a crate addressed 'To Ministry of External Affairs, Federal Republic of Nigeria, Lagos, From the High Commission London.'

Dikko was the brother-in-law of deposed Nigerian President Shagari who was overthrown in a military coup in December, 1983. Within days of the takeover, Dikko was among those on a 'most wanted' list. He was alleged to have been an 'economic saboteur' who helped bring his country to the brink of bankruptcy by his corruption while in office. He was accused of amassing a huge personal fortune while Minister of Transportation.

Immediately after news of the overthrow reached Dikko, he went into hiding in Lagos for two days. Then he drove to a border town where he abandoned his car and fled Nigeria on foot through the bush. Safely out of the country, he flew to Amsterdam then to London where he took up residence in a £400,000 house at 49 Porchester Terrace, Bayswater.

Shortly after midday on July 5, 1984, Dikko walked out of the house planning to meet a journalist friend. Outside he met up with a gang of kidnappers who were supposed to return him to Nigeria for a state trial.

The abduction team, who revealed themselves as bungling amateurs at each step of the operation, staked out Porchester Terrace that morning in a beige Vauxhall Cavalier and a yellow van. The previous evening they had also been observed in the conspicuous yellow van with the rear door windows masked with orange paint. Because the van cruised the street slowly, then parked, then cruised again, the neighbours couldn't help noticing it.

That afternoon, the abductors grabbed Dikko and hurled him into the back of the van right in front of his house as pedestrians watched. Witnesses said Dikko put up a desperate struggle while being forced into the van. The struggle continued as the yellow van disappeared down the street before the back doors were even closed. Dikko let out a yell and then he was silenced.

Elizabeth Hayes, the 25-year-old personal assistant who fled Nigeria with Dikko, was inside the house. She heard the commotion.

'I heard a loud bang and a scream,' Ms Hayes recalls. 'I saw a van going off. I was looking to see if Dr Dikko was still around. It was like a photograph: people were just standing there. No one would say anything or talk to me. "Oh my God," I thought. "Think, think", I said to myself, "There's no point in crying." '

Dikko remembers his abduction quite vividly. 'They grabbed me and held me. They took hold and banged me against the van. I hurt my back. God, the pain.'

Elizabeth Hayes acted immediately. She telephoned police

who responded within minutes. 'The police were fantastic,' Ms Hayes continues. 'They were here like a shot. They said that Hucklesby would get Dr Dikko back.'

Commander William Hucklesby is head of C–13, the anti-terrorist squad. He and Commander Frank Carter, head of Scotland Yard's Serious Crimes Squad, were in charge of the manhunt. They swung into action without delay. Hucklesby guessed that the kidnappers would try to smuggle Dikko out of the country. All planes bound for Nigeria from Heathrow and Gatwick were to be searched for the missing man. The smaller airports of Stansted and Luton were alerted to be on the lookout for suspicious 'cargo'.

Inside the van, Dikko was injected with drugs, blindfolded, and manacled. His shirt was stripped off. A drip tube was placed in his arm and a rubber tube was forced down his throat to prevent choking.

Meanwhile, at Stansted Airport, a Nigerian Airways Boeing 707 cargo plane waited on the runway. This part of the operation was also poorly managed. The plane had flown in empty from Nigeria the night before and was scheduled for a 9.00 a.m. departure. The delay of the white plane with the Nigerian flag on its tailfin was not explained to airport officials. The manifest stated the plane had been flown in just to transport four and half tons of catering equipment back to Lagos, but the plane was capable of a forty-ton payload.

In the middle of the afternoon, freight agents at Servisair, who were to load the cargo, received a phone call saying that two crates of 'extra cargo' were on their way. The crates arrived at 4.00 p.m. in a white rented van, accompanied by two black Mercedes saloon cars bearing diplomatic licence plates of the Nigerian High Commission. The convoy went to the Servisair hangar and the two crates were unloaded by forklift trucks.

Both crates were handmade. One was four feet high by four feet wide and four feet two inches long. The other was four feet high by four feet long but only two and a half feet wide. There were air holes in the crates.

As the crates were on pallets waiting to be loaded onto the

plane, word came to the freight handlers to delay boarding the crates. Customs wanted to have a look. The forklift wheeled the crates next door to the customs shed.

Workers at Stansted reported that the first thing that aroused their suspicion was the 'medicinal-type smell' coming from one of the crates. An employee of Servisair said, 'There was a feeling something fishy was about all afternoon because we had to wait specially for these crates and that was unusual. You don't normally hold an aircraft up for just another ton.'

The labels on the crate were handwritten in amateurish scrawl and the crates were accompanied by Mr Okon Edet. When customs officers checked the diplomatic list they found Edet listed as an attaché at the high commission, not a courier. Customs officers stalled the Nigerians while they telephoned the Foreign Office to inquire what the crates' diplomatic status was.

The Foreign Office asked whether they were marked 'diplomatic'. Since the crates had no official seal and were unmarked, they were not considered diplomatic bags. Foreign Office personnel told customs to open them in the presence of an official Nigerian representative.

Article 27 of the Vienna Convention requires that the diplomatic courier bear 'an official document indicating his status'. Mr Edet could produce no credentials to prove that he was a diplomatic courier, nor any documents to prove the crates were diplomatic bags.

Police surrounded the airport and sealed it off. Mr Edet was asked to serve as the embassy's witness when the crates were opened. He did not object. Between 5.00 and 6.00 p.m, customs officers prised open the crates with a hammer and crowbar.

One crate contained Umaru Dikko, still shirtless, drugged, blindfolded and bound, with a tube leading into one of his arms from a bottle clamped to the side wall of the container. A rubber mat padded the bottom of the crate which was littered with empty brown ampules giving off a medicinal smell.

One of the loaders later reported that Dikko had 'a small

hypodermic needle in his cheek. A small electrolysis type of pad was on his chest and his wrist was bandaged. There was another hypodermic needle sticking through the bandage into his hand.'

In the same crate was Dr Lev-Aire Shapiro, a Russian-born Israeli citizen. The other, smaller crate also contained two people – an Israeli and a Nigerian. The three were immediately arrested and Dikko was rushed to York Ward of Herts and Essex General Hospital.

Mr Edet, the plane's four-man crew, the Nigerian ground crew and Mohammed Yusufu were also arrested. Yusufu, who worked at the Nigerian High Commission, pleaded immunity, but his claim was denied. Although he carried a diplomatic passport, he was not accredited to the United Kingdom. Mr Edet was released because of diplomatic immunity but was ordered to leave the country within seven days.

A British Caledonian 747, already forty-five minutes into its flight from Lagos, was ordered back to Nigeria in retaliation for the arrests. The plane's 222 passengers and twenty-two crew members were detained by orders of the military junta. Later, they were released.

Dikko later said had his kidnappers been successful, he would have faced 'torture, a show trial and possibly a firing squad'. He was naturally grateful to police for his rescue.

'I cannot praise the police highly enough,' he said after his recovery. 'If this had happened anywhere else in the world the outcome could easily have been different.'

The Nigerian High Commission had a staff of 122, the largest of any London mission. They disavowed any knowledge of the kidnapping. The Government had evidence which implicated some staff members, but the Nigerian government refused to let police question any of the emissaries.

Britain expelled two members of the high commission. The High Commissioner himself, who had gone to Lagos to confer with his government on the kidnapping, was not allowed to return to London. Reciprocal measures were taken by Nigeria against British diplomats in Lagos.

Britain stopped short of breaking relations with Nigeria, largely because of its importance as an export market. Even though Nigeria's oil revenue dropped by forty percent when world oil prices fell in 1984, the country remained the world's ninth largest importer of British products.

Nigeria responded to the Dikko affair less diplomatically. It effectively kidnapped and held under appalling conditions three British citizens who happened to be in the wrong place at the wrong time.

On September 18, 1984, British businessman Graham Coveyduck, thirty-seven, the father of two young sons, flew to Lagos on what was supposed to be a two-day business trip. Coveyduck, a management consultant, grew up in Nigeria where his father was a former chief superintendent of police during the days of British rule.

Shortly after his arrival, Coveyduck was arrested and charged with 'stealing £100,000 from the Nigerian government'. According to his family, the first ten days of his captivity were spent in an apartment near the Lagos airport where he was subjected to round-the-clock interrogation. From there, he was taken to a medium security cell with five other inmates. Finally, six weeks after his arrest, he was allowed to see a representative of the British government.

In November, Coveyduck was arraigned before a Nigerian court. A request for bail was denied and he was returned to his cell. But then, suddenly, all charges against him were dropped.

This did not mean, however, that he was a free man. In fact, his troubles were only beginning. The Nigerian government announced that he would continue to be held under the 'security decree' that has ruled the country since the 1984 military coup.

Coveyduck was placed in a ten foot by eight foot cell in Lagos' notorious Kiri-Kiri prison. Fourteen other men shared the tiny cell where the sanitary facilities consisted of a bucket which was emptied only occasionally. He and his fellow inmates were allowed outside the cell for only one hour a week for a shower and exercise. Coveyduck's health began to fail. He suffered a huge weight loss and contracted malaria, before he was finally returned to the UK in September 1985.

Two other British citizens, Kenneth Clarke and Angus Paterson, pilots who had gone to Nigeria to fly a plane back to Britain, were also held long after the trumped up charges brought against them had been dropped.

The Nigerian government had made its position very clear – the day Dikko is expelled from Britain and those being held for his kidnapping are freed, so will the two British citizens. But the two were returned.

Sir Geoffrey Howe, while before the House of Commons Foreign Affairs Committee investigating the kidnapping, stated the British government's position: 'The inviolability of the diplomatic bag cannot take precedence over a human life. If the Customs and Excise or any other authority had reason to suspect that the crate contained a human being, they would consult the Foreign Office who would, in such circumstances, whatever the labelling, authorize such action as was necessary in the circumstances. This is what actually happened in this case.'

There are two other known cases where diplomatic bags were used to transport people. Neither instance was successful.

A rescue as dramatic as Dikko's occurred at Rome's Fiumicino Airport on November 17, 1964. Italian customs officials were startled to hear human cries coming from a trunk marked 'Diplomatic Mail'. The trunk was on the tarmac being transferred to the cargo bay of a plane bound for Egypt. It was addressed to 'The Foreign Ministry, Cairo', and was accompanied by Abdel Maneim El-Naklawy and Selim Osman El-Sayed, both First Secretaries at the Rome Embassy.

On hearing the cries, customs officials insisted they open the trunk. Inside, they discovered a man who was bound, gagged and drugged. After freeing him, the man first identified himself as Joseph Daham, a Moroccan linguist. Two days later, though, the abductee admitted he was thirty-year-old Mordecai Luk, an Israeli citizen who had been an interpreter at the Egyptian Embassy in Rome. Luk had been

No sign of remorse as Syrian diplomat Ahmed Rajab finally leaves Britain in disgrace, after his refusal to vacate the Chaffeys' Kensington flat with his family became headline news in March 1985. *S & G*

Umaru Dikko, the former Nigerian Minister of Transportation, was discovered in a crate at Stansted Airport drugged, bound and blindfolded in July 1984. The crate was about to be loaded onto a Nigerian Airways plane bound for Lagos, but luckily for Dikko it was not deemed to be a diplomatic bag. *Express Newspapers*

Above: As she lay fatally wounded in St James's Square, WPC Yvonne Fletcher's last words to her colleagues were those of a true professional: 'Keep calm.' *Express Newspapers*

Below: For days after her shooting on April 17, 1984, WPC Yvonne Fletcher's black and white uniform hat lay abandoned in St James's Square. At her funeral it was placed on her coffin. *Express Newspapers*

On April 27, 1984, the occupants of the Libyan Embassy were finally evacuated, taking with them back to Libya four large canvas bags, each closed with a diplomatic seal. One of the bags contained the rifle used to shoot Yvonne Fletcher. *Express Newspapers*

kidnapped from a Rome café on November 16, but he had good reason to conceal his identity.

In 1961, Luk had crossed into Egypt where he broadcast anti-Israeli propaganda by radio from Cairo. After the kidnapping, Luk was deported to Israel where he was wanted for spying for the United Arab Republic.

In the meantime, the two diplomats, El-Naklawy and El-Sayed, were arrested and charged with kidnapping. They claimed diplomatic immunity and were released. The Italian government declared them *persona non grata* and expelled them. A spokesman for the United Arab Republic Embassy claimed, 'We know nothing about this situation.' The reason for this container abduction was never elucidated.

In Britain, over the last ten years, there have been five cases of illegal possession of firearms by diplomats who claimed immunity to avoid prosecution, in addition to the tragic Yvonne Fletcher incident. The Foreign Office sends regular circulars to remind the diplomatic community of the restrictions on firearms in Great Britain. These circulars describe the procedure for declaring firearms and ammunition for importation into the country:

Foreign envoys are to declare their weapons to Her Majesty's Customs and Excise Officers at the time of importation. A police permit or letter of authority must be presented at that time. If the certificate is not granted for legal possession of the weapon, the applicant may make arrangements for the weapon or ammunition to be exported.

It goes without saying that those who wish to import firearms for terrorist purposes are hardly likely to declare them. Metropolitan Police Commander Neal Brittan said in a recent BBC interview, 'As a policeman, I'd guess there are weapons inside most diplomatic premises in London.' Most of these weapons have been smuggled in via diplomatic pouch.

John Cartwright, MP for Woolwich, has been investigating the subject of diplomatic abuses of the pouch. 'There have been a number of extremely violent incidents in London,' he has said, 'where there is at least the suspicion that the weapons came in through the diplomatic bag. Now it does seem to be that that's a very vulnerable area. We really need to move towards some sensible modern method of electronic surveillance of diplomatic bags, a quick examination to ensure that they are not being totally misused.'

Sir Ian Sinclair, in reporting to the Foreign Affairs Committee on the proceedings of the 1984 session of the International Law Commission, said many of its delegates shared the same feeling. 'Preliminary debate on Article 36 at this year's session of the Commission revealed widespread concern about recent flagrant abuses of the protection given to the diplomatic bag,' Sir Ian told the Committee. 'The vast majority of those who spoke were sympathetic to the notion that some steps should be taken to minimize such abuses. Various ideas were put forward. For example, it was suggested that bags might be divided into two categories – one containing official correspondence only and protected against even remote examination, and one containing articles intended for official use which would be subject to remote [X-ray] examination.'

But another draft article under ILC consideration would specifically add an exemption 'from any kind of examination directly or through electronic or mechanical devices' to the Vienna Convention.

Does an X-ray examination of a diplomatic bag, or for that matter, having a sniffer dog work it over, constitute an 'opening' of the bag which is forbidden by the Geneva Convention? The 1979 Edition of Satow's *Guide to Diplomatic Practice* says, 'The receiving state may subject a bag to detector devices designed to show the presence of explosives, metal or drugs, since this does not involve opening or detaining it.'

The Thatcher government noted in its White Paper on diplomatic abuses: 'There is no reference to scanning in the Vienna Convention. In our view, this does not rule it out though it is arguable that any method of finding out the contents of a bag is tantamount to opening it, which is illegal. Since, however, we do not regard scanning as unlawful, we have had to consider whether it would prove an effective and practical solution to the problem of abuse of diplomatic bags.'

Whether or not to X-ray diplomatic bags has become the subject of a bitter debate between Parliament and Whitehall. Following the events in St James's Square and the admission that the weapons had probably entered Britain in diplomatic bags, there was both a political and public outcry for the scanning of bags. But Whitehall is resisting.

The whole argument is a difficult, even embarrassing, one for Whitehall because it was already on record within the international diplomatic community as opposing scanning, at least where it pertains to *British* diplomatic bags.

In mid-1984, when the government of Kuwait started scanning bags after a series of bombings blamed on Iranian extremists, it was Britain that led the international protest against the practice. In fact, on two occasions, British couriers returned to England with diplomatic bags rather than permit them to be scanned.

When there was public pressure for Britain itself to initiate a practice it had bitterly opposed in Kuwait, a way around the problem had to be found. The government declared it would not scan, arguing that it would do little to prevent abuses and it was potentially bad for British diplomacy.

As the government wrote in its White Paper, 'Scanning would be of only limited practical value.' Weapons could be disassembled and shipped in over a period of time or could be hidden within bundles of paper to prevent X-ray detection. Even if a weapon was found in a bag, the paper argued, the most Britain could do would be to refuse admittance and return it to the sending state.

'A major disadvantage to scanning,' said the government, 'is that it would make our own bags vulnerable to generalized and indiscriminate challenge. The element of uncertainty and the potential disruption that could be caused either by retaliatory action or by widespread introduction of such a practice could seriously undermine our freedom of communication.'

The Government therefore decided against routine screening, but it did not totally rule it out in extreme instances.

'We will be ready to scan any bag on specific occasions where the grounds for suspicion are sufficiently strong.'

Another question, that of limiting the size or weight of a diplomatic bag, is also before the International Law Commission. Currently, a bag cannot be rejected for size or weight alone. The Foreign Affairs Committee recommended that the government keep records of the size and weight of diplomatic bags entering the country. Patterns would then be a matter of record and could be assessed. The government came out against this recommendation also, saying it would have no real effect on the problems that the Committee was trying to eliminate.

While the export of the murder weapon of Yvonne Fletcher out of Britain in a diplomatic bag was still fresh in people's minds, the International Law Commission was asked by Bulgaria, with the support of other Eastern Bloc countries to extend to consular bags the total freedom from inspection or detention afforded diplomatic bags.

Under Article 30 of the Vienna Convention on Consular Immunity, consular bags can be opened and searched in the presence of a consular representative if the receiving state suspects they are being used for illegal transport of contraband, weapons or other controlled or illegal substances. If the request for search is refused, the bag may be denied entry and returned to its country of origin. With consulates in every major city, one can only begin to imagine the increase in abuses passage of such a measure would allow.

CHAPTER SIX

Licensed to Kill

IN THE AUTUMN of 1982, one young man was a regular customer at The Godfather, a discreet Washington nightclub where nude dancers were the main attraction. A curly haired, bearded, 23-year-old, he dressed neatly when he came to drink and watch the girls. Though he was a student at American University, he lived in his parents' plush home. His father, was the Ambassador of a South American country.

On Monday, November 29, Kenneth W. Skeen was working as the bouncer at The Godfather club. He was a small quiet guy who stood in the club – just in case there was trouble. There seldom was. Everyone called him Kenny; he was a carpenter by trade and like the young man he was twenty-three years old.

After graduating from high school in Massachusetts, Skeen enlisted in the Army. It was during his military days that he had a large lion's head and the word Freedom tattooed on his biceps. When he got his discharge, he settled in the Washington area because he'd heard there were good opportunities for work. He found that he liked the area quite a bit. He worked a construction job during the day; and, to earn extra money, he moonlighted at night as a bouncer at The Godfather.

Skeen was a conservative, no-nonsense type. At five foot nine his upper body was more developed than most and he was even stronger then he looked. Though his attitude was to live and let live Skeen knew how to take care of himself.

The previous night, the young South American's father jetted down to his country's capital to help his government prepare for President Reagan's first stop on a four-country

South American tour. The visit was an important one for his country's precarious economy. While there, Reagan would announce the United States Treasury's 1.2 billion dollar 'bridge loan', a series of short-term loans to help the country out of its current, and critical, cash shortage.

With his father out of town, the young man decided to spend Monday evening at The Godfather. At 10.50 p.m., he got into a disagreement with the club's manager, Harry Taylor. The young man got louder, and Taylor suggested he leave. He agreed to go, but first he wanted to use the men's room.

When he came out he was brandishing a 6.35 millimetre Beretta automatic pistol.

'I'm with the Mafia,' the young man shouted at Taylor, 'and I'm going to kill you.'

Kenny Skeen saw the commotion but not the gun, so he casually went over to throw the troublemaker out. The young man pointed the Beretta at him and pulled the trigger.

'He was pulling the trigger but the gun wasn't going off,' Kenny later explained. 'It was just clicking. Naturally, I wasn't going to stand around, so I went towards him and he moved towards the back door.'

While covering his position, the young man edged out of the back door and made a run for it down the short flight of stairs and into the alley.

Kenny grabbed a piece of piping and followed him out of the back door. Harry Taylor followed close behind.

The young man concealed himself in the shadows between two houses. Pulling a second gun, a .32 calibre revolver, from inside his coat, he began firing at his two pursuers. Charging towards the flying bullets, Kenny bolted around the corner of a house and rugby-tackled him.

He discharged another round, hitting Kenny in the stomach. Kenny grabbed the gunman's hand to aim the gun away from his chest. The young man continued to fire, however, emptying the entire chamber. Two more bullets penetrated Kenny's flesh, one through the hand, the other through his leg.

Kenny smashed his assailant on the head with the length

of pipe. Then he realized he had been shot. 'I went over by the side of the alley and waited for the police to come,' Kenny recounts.

When the police arrived, Kenny was taken to Georgetown University Hospital. The young man was arrested and taken to Second District Police Headquarters. Since he refused to give his name and address, he was booked under the name 'John Doe'. The arresting officer entered the charge: 'Assault with a deadly weapon, gun.'

Then the gunman was taken to DC General Hospital where he was treated for a minor cut on the mouth. He told a nurse in the hospital his name was Sanchez, but when police asked his name once he left the hospital, he again refused to give it.

Kenny Skeen spent Monday night in intensive care. Doctors operated to remove the bullet in his stomach. Fortunately, it hadn't penetrated the intestinal wall. Another bullet was removed from his thigh, and his hand was put in plaster after the bullet in it was removed. Hospital costs were piling up at an alarming rate.

On Tuesday, 'Frank Sanchez' was arraigned and held over on a $2,000 bond. At 8.00 pm Tuesday, not having posted bail, he was transferred to the central cell block at Police Headquarters to await trial.

On Tuesday evening, the embassy involved reported to the FBI and the State Department that the Ambassador's son was missing. The FBI passed his description on to the police asking if there was any chance they might have such a person in custody. The young man finally revealed his true name that night. A short time later, an embassy representative and a State Department official arrived at police headquarters. They formally identified the young man as the Ambassador's missing son. He was released around 10.00 pm and all charges against the armed assailant were dropped because he had diplomatic immunity.

Kenny got a phone call the next morning while he lay in his hospital bed recuperating from the three bullet wounds. 'While I was in the hospital, I got a phone call telling me that the guy had diplomatic immunity and that he had been cut loose,' Kenny remembers. 'That really made me mad, for him to hurt me like that and then simply walk away. It wouldn't have mattered if I lived or died.'

When the police found out the young man had diplomatic immunity, they eliminated all records of the incident. In the arrest book, even the entry 'John Doe' and the charge of assault with a deadly weapon were erased.

Off the record, police sources confessed that Second District police were 'mad as hell' when diplomatic immunity was invoked. But angry as they may have been, they refused to give Kenny any further information about his assailant. Kenny was even unable to get back the clothes he was wearing that night at work. Police told him his clothes had been destroyed.

When reports of the shooting came out, a police spokesman explained the situation to the media: 'Since he had diplomatic immunity, he is considered not to have been arrested. That's international law – it's the law that governs diplomats everywhere. They are considered not to be responsible for criminal acts that come under our criminal code.'

Kenny couldn't believe what was happening to him. Like most people, diplomatic immunity was an expression he had heard without attaching any particular meaning to it. Now he was painfully aware of what it was and that it meant a criminal could walk free, and he resented the diplomats' special treatment.

'You know, it's like they're an angel,' he says, 'like they're upper class. And they aren't. That's what I can't understand. The point is they can get away with so much more than we can – in our own country.

'Where he's guilty, I say he should be punished for it. I mean, you're talking about sombody's life. You're not talking about a traffic ticket. If my own country won't back me up when I'm in the right, you know, who will? Who can I turn to?'

The embassy issued its own statement to the press:

> The Ambassador's son was having a beer at a Wisconsin Avenue bar on the evening of November 29 when, for

some trivial matter connected with a pack of cigarettes, he was ordered by a bartender to leave the premises.

He argued that he wanted to finish his beer, but in view of the threatening attitude of the bartender, he stepped back, stumbled and fell down, at which time he was kicked in the mouth.

He then attempted to leave, but was followed by five or six people who began to attack him, hitting him with a stone, striking him with sticks. Not being able to withstand the aggression any longer, he pulled a gun and, though lying down, fired some shots at random. He then lost consciousness and only came to at the police station.

The Ambassador's wife insisted her son was innocent. 'It's not true,' she asserted, 'he was not at the club.'

On December 3, the Ambassador's wife and son fled home to South America. The Ambassador told United Press International his son had been a victim of brutality.

The embassy could have waived immunity and allowed the prosecution of the young man, but did not. It's likely that he withheld his identity from police officers because he had been charged with assault before and was fearful of what discovery of a previous charge might have meant to prosecutors. He needn't have worried. Just as prosecution on the previous charge had been blocked by the claim of immunity, so was this one.

The State Department was deluged by calls from the press inflamed over the incident. Memoranda labelled 'Press Guidance' were circulated to staff members, should they be asked to comment on the case.

The official State Department line stated: 'Mediation procedures to settle disputes between diplomats and American citizens begin with the aggrieved citizen's filing of a written claim with supporting details to the Office of Protocol. We use our good offices, when appropriate, to bring the matter to the attention of the diplomat's embassy with a request that it use its best efforts to promote a just settlement of the dispute.'

Such a bland admission of impotence satisfied no one.

Senate Minority Leader, Democrat Robert Byrd of West Virginia, said it seemed 'inconceivable to me that the relative of a diplomat can carry a gun in this country and shoot an American citizen and cannot be arrested; cannot be brought to trial; can just be turned loose on the street.'

Kenny Skeen's hospital stay resulted in a bill of more than $10,000 for which the US government would not reimburse him. He was unable to work and his only income was a weekly $100 unemployment cheque.

Feeling helpless, he hired a lawyer, John Coale, who called the State Department. 'I was told there was really nothing they could do. I was hoping maybe they'd act as a go-between with [the country concerned] and help us out in some way, to see if [they] would be willing to compensate and do something, but they told us they wouldn't do that,' he recalls.

The police wouldn't help either. Mr Coale says, 'As soon as they found out he had immunity, the whole thing became a non-event. It was as if it hadn't happened.'

On December 9, Kenny Skeen filed a ten million dollar suit in US District Court. Asking one million in compensatory damages and nine million in punitive damages, the suit was filed under the Foreign Sovereign Immunities Act.

The Foreign Sovereign Immunities Act of 1976 authorizes suits against foreign governments under some circumstances – assault and battery is one – and leaves it to the court to determine whether there is jurisdiction in the case. Mr Coale felt it could be used to get some justice for Kenny.

Coale filed his suit directly against the government of the country concerned. He argued that everyone who has diplomatic immunity is an 'employee' of a foreign government, as 'employee' is defined in the Act. And since immunity is in force twenty-four hours a day, he further argued, then employment must also be a twenty-four-hour a day situation. Under the Foreign Sovereign Immunities Act, a foreign government is responsible for the official actions of its employees and agents. Thus Coale argued, the fact that the young man had immunity made him an 'employee' and the twenty-four-hour nature of immunity made everything he did an 'official act' and thus subject to the Act.

The Godfather nightclub had insurance, but their worker's compensation scheme denied the claim because the injuries were sustained outside the club. Creditors hounded Kenny, but with his hand in a cast he couldn't get work. Without work, he couldn't pay his bills.

'The State Department wasn't very helpful,' Kenny remembers, 'they even gave my lawyer a bad time. It was like, "He has diplomatic immunity – too bad. You lose, he wins." I wrote President Reagan a letter but he didn't reply.'

Kenny's letter to the President was forwarded to the Department of State for an answer. On a covering form, a White House Secretary summarized the letter: 'The writer, who was shot by the son of [a South American] Ambassador, is confused over and protests the diplomatic laws that permit immunity in these kinds of cases.'

The lawsuit against the government concerned remained in the courts. No amount of protest or publicity seemed able to produce the money to cover Kenny's hospital bills, let alone his loss of income during his three to four months recuperation period.

A confidential State Department memo points out that had his assailant been an ordinary person, Skeen would have had no problem obtaining a judgment worth between two and three hundred thousand dollars. The State Department continued to meet secretly with the embassy in an effort to get Skeen compensation, but the diplomats remained firm in their resolve not to pay Kenny's medical bills.

In March, 1983, the ambassador returned home permanently. No new ambassador was named and nothing was resolved. A summary of an April 25 secret meeting between the Deputy Chief of Mission and the State Department noted that the DCM remained adamantly unsympathetic with Skeen's complaint because 'he should not have pursued [the man] out of the bar, but should have called police.'

A US District Court Judge dismissed Kenny's lawsuit on July 6, 1983, saying the court had no jurisdiction in the case, in essence upholding the defence of diplomatic immunity. Kenny and his lawyer took their case to the Court of Appeals.

In September, a new ambassador was finally appointed to the US. About a week before oral arguments were to be presented in the appeal, the State Department came to Kenny's attorney to represent an offer by the new Ambassador of cash in return for withdrawal of the appeal.

'They were very careful not to connect the payment with the legal proceedings,' John Coale says. 'They did not even use their lawyers to make the offer. They said they wanted to make a voluntary payment of Kenny's bills. It was an inadequate settlement if we could have got into court to sue, but given the circumstances we didn't have much of a shot. We had to take what they offered. It was better than nothing, but not much.'

Through his lawyer, Kenny received a payment almost equal to his medical bills. One condition of the settlement was that he should not publicly discuss its terms. Kenny and his lawyer both feel that had it not been for the publicity and lawsuits, he never would have received a cent.

Kenny Skeen's assailant is enjoying his freedom in luxury. Kenny Skeen still has a twenty percent disability in his hand as a souvenir of his encounter with diplomatic immunity.

'I'm lucky,' says Kenny pointedly, 'I'm still alive.'

Cecelia McNeil wasn't so lucky. Her encounter with a diplomat's son left her dead on arrival at New York's Bellevue Hospital.

Twenty-two-year-old Cecelia of Morris Avenue, the Bronx, was walking near the corner of 26th Street that late Thanksgiving afternoon. Because of the holiday there wasn't much traffic. Nearly everyone was at home.

The black Cadillac belonging to the North Yemeni Ambassador to the United Nations was hurtling down Park Avenue South at frightening speed when Cecelia McNeil stepped into the street at the corner and started across. The 18-year-old son of the North Yemeni Arab Republic's Ambassador slammed on the brakes. At 4.40 pm, his car ploughed into Cecelia with lethal force.

It wasn't that he didn't try to stop. The thirty-foot skid mark attested to his attempt. It was simply that he was driving too fast to stop in time.

Police arrived at the scene to investigate the accident. At 5.08 p.m., an ambulance rushed Cecelia to nearby Bellevue Hospital, but it was too late; she was dead.

The man was taken to the police station. Not long afterwards, he was released. No charges were brought because he had diplomatic immunity. Detective Robert Znaniecki, who investigated the case, said charges were not discussed 'because he has diplomatic status and there's nothing we can do anyway'.

Later, police admitted the preliminary investigation of the accident indicated the young man was unquestionably speeding. Znaniecki told me, 'All you had to do was look at the scene and you knew the kid was guilty of a criminal offence. But he has diplomatic status so what can you do? Working as a New York cop you get real used to this fact very early and if you let it bother you, you'll go nuts. You see or hear of abuses every day.'

The file of New York Police Case Number 181–66, 'Cecelia McNeil – Deceased', was closed.

The State Department tries to keep quiet cases of acts of violence committed by the children of diplomats. By and large they are successful, but occasionally incidents do become public, such as the case of the fifteen-year-old son of a high-ranking diplomat at the Washington Embassy of Gabon who started two fires which caused thirty-one thousand dollars' worth of damage to his school in 1979. Police were unable to arrest him on two counts of arson and one count of burglary, because of his immunity.

The boy's only reason for starting the fires was that his cassette player had been confiscated as a disciplinary action by his gym teacher. When the gym teacher locked the tape player in the office, the boy argued heatedly. The next night, after a dance in the school gym, the teacher's office mysteriously caught fire and the flames spread to the nearby girls' locker room. After the blaze was extinguished, the gym teacher noticed the cassette player was gone. He told arson investigators of his argument with the boy and how the cassette player had disappeared.

A few days later, the cassette player turned up again – in the boy's possession. School officials reclaimed it and locked it in the principal's office.

The same night, when a police officer was driving by the school at 2.37 a.m., he noticed smoke coming from inside the building. He went inside and ran into the boy in a corridor. In the confusion of the spreading flames and smoke, the boy escaped.

When the fire department arrived, they discovered six separate fires around the main school office, including one on top of the principal's desk.

In the morning, the policeman who had interrupted the boy's flight from the scene of the fire went to the diplomat's house to see if he could identify the obvious suspect. He positively identified the boy as the arsonist, though the charge was adamantly denied.

Despite the seriousness of the damage, diplomatic immunity ensured that the only punishment meted out to the boy was a suspension from school.

If you imagine that cases of assault by those with diplomatic immunity are rare events in the US, that is the impression the State Department tries to give. But these instances are not as isolated as they pretend. Despite the conspiracy of silence, reports involving the abuses of diplomatic immunity are coming in all the time from all over the country. What follows is a selection of incidents involving bodily harm.

In Washington DC a Guatemalan was charged with assault, disorderly conduct and carrying a concealed weapon, but his diplomatic immunity liberated him. Though he left the country not long after the charges were dropped in February, 1983, the State Department fears he has re-entered the country.

In October, 1977, the Metro-Dade County Police in Miami called the State Department to verify the diplomatic immunity claim of a Nicaraguan national who was employed as a messenger at the Washington Embassy. The Nicaraguan was visiting his mother when he had a dispute with her neighbours over the boundaries of her property. To stake his claim, he fired several rounds directly at the neighbour and his wife. He was released immediately upon confirmation of his diplomatic status. (Because of the 1978 Diplomatic Relations Act, today a messenger would have immunity only when acting in his official capacity.)

The husband of a Colombian Embassy official, was involved in a scuffle outside a restaurant in Aspen, Colorado, on December 29, 1980. A fight broke out during a dispute over the bill. Though another restaurant employee and a neighbour witnessed the man hit the restaurant owner several times in the face, the assault charges were promptly dropped when his immunity was confirmed.

In New York City, a chauffeur-driven grey limousine was blocking the intersection of 33rd Street and Fifth Avenue on Monday, May 12, 1980. Manhattan's mid-afternoon traffic was barely moving as it was, so Patrolman Owen Reiter ordered the limo to pull over onto 33rd Street and began to write out a ticket. When Sherif Meguid, a Fordham University student and son of the Egyptian Ambassador to the United Nations, saw this, he got out of the car and went to a public telephone on the corner. Two more officers happened along in their squad car. The three officers later claimed none of them noticed that the limo had diplomatic licence plates.

Meguid returned from the phone and, according to the officers, punched Officer Touth in the stomach and began swearing at him. The officers subdued him and were putting handcuffs on him when someone jumped on Officer Reiter's back. Turning quickly and leading with his fist, Reiter hit the person in the face, then realized it was a young woman. In fact it was 25-year-old Omnia Meguid, the Ambassador's daughter-in-law.

The two Egyptians were taken to Midtown South Station where they were identified as having diplomatic immunity and released. Officers Touth and Reiter went to St Clare's Hospital for medical treatment.

The Egyptian Ambassador registered a formal protest to Donald McHenry, US Ambassador to the United Nations. The next day, Mayor Ed Koch and the New York Police Commissioner personally appeared at the Egyptian mission to deliver a formal written apology. The apology, signed by the Mayor, stated, in part, 'I extend a personal and deeply felt apology on behalf of the City of New York and its Police Department.'

The three officers were brought up on departmental charges. Reiter was given a four-month suspension, and the other two were given written reprimands for their 'disrespect' towards the two Egyptians and for taking them into custody.

At about 2.30 am Monday, June 24, 1985, David Caldwell and a couple of friends were walking along a street in Georgetown, Washington DC, when they saw a young woman running towards them. She quickly explained that she had been standing on the corner of 34th and M Streets when a man pulled up alongside her and attempted to pick her up. When she declined and started to walk away, the man got out of his car and started to follow her.

Caldwell accompanied the woman back in the direction of the car. By that time, the man had got back into the car and locked the door. Caldwell gave the man a piece of his mind and, he admits, kicked the car.

Then the man backed the car up about a hundred feet, aimed it at Caldwell, and stepped on the accelerator. As the police report noted, the man attempted to run over Caldwell 'by chasing him across the street and up some stairs with the vehicle'. When Caldwell fled 'north on 34th Street, the car attempted to drive down the sidewalk after him'.

The episode was witnessed by DC Police Officer Ronald M. Shroeder, who drew his service revolver and gave chase on foot. The driver was unable to mount the sidewalk, and Shroeder caught up with him. Pointing the gun at the man, he ordered him out of the car and placed him under arrest.

The driver was taken to the Second District station and was booked for assault with a deadly weapon – the car.

Claiming he had only used the car 'to defend himself after

he was threatened', the man identified himself as an employee of the Italian Embassy. He claimed diplomatic immunity. The State Department confirmed that he had full immunity. He was then released.

A spokesman for the embassy, Ludovico Ortona, claimed that the man 'had no intention of injuring the youngster and he didn't'. He claimed that he 'had tried to contact the girl and there were some youngsters in the area who threatened him'.

Later it came to light that at the time of the incident, the man was serving as 'a secretary to the Italian military attaché', which raised the question of whether he was entitled to immunity. His job seemed to fall somewhere between 'technical staff', entitled to full criminal immunity, and 'service staff', entitled only to immunity for official acts.

The State Department, by identifying him to the police as technical staff, gave the man considerable benefit of the doubt.

Steven Goldstein is a 25-year-old real estate salesman in New York. Residential properties are his speciality. On Wednesday, April 3, 1985, he had been to see a new client who wanted to sell an apartment on East 72nd Street near Third Avenue. Absent-mindedly, Steve had left his umbrella behind. The next night after work, around 9.30 pm, he went back to East 72nd Street to retrieve the umbrella before heading home to Scarsdale.

Steve pulled his 1985 Oldsmobile up in front of number 178. As is usual for Manhattan, parking was at a premium. Though most New York City streets are one-way, East 72nd is a wide, busy two-way street. Steve finally found a place to park, at least for long enough to run across the street and pick up his umbrella. He noticed a sign stating some kind of parking restriction but, he admits he didn't read it closely. He thought it was a common notice that restricts parking during the 4.00 to 7.00 p.m. rush hour, but the sign actually read: 'No Parking except Consul C and Diplomatic A & D.' Only cars with those specified diplomatic plates could park there.

Since he'd be there no more than five minutes at the most,

Steve pulled his car all the way forward, till it nearly touched the car in front of him. The Oldsmobile was only a foot and a half into the restricted parking zone.

The house Steve parked in front of, 178 East 72nd Street, is a six-storey building occupied by a Central American representative to the United Nations, the Ambassador Extraordinary and Plenipotentiary.

In the building across the street, two doormen were on duty. Steve told one of the doormen he'd left his umbrella upstairs.

'I doubt if you're going to try and rob us,' the doorman joked, recognizing him from the previous night.

The lift attendant went to the flat to bring down the umbrella. Steve waited in the lobby for about three minutes, chatting with the doormen. Every once in a while, he glanced over at his car across the street.

Once he had the umbrella safely in his hand, Steve headed back to his car. As he started to cross the street, a blue Mercedes pulled up, swinging into the restricted parking zone, right behind Steve's car. Dodging through the traffic as he crossed the street, Steve saw his car being pinned in by the driver of the Mercedes.

He motioned to the driver to back up so he could get his car out, but the driver jumped out of the car in a rage. Pointing to the sign, he shouted, 'This is my spot. This is my spot. This is my spot.' The driver's eyes bulged and his face became ashen. The man was extremely upset.

'Fine,' said Steve. Even though he knew the city of New York didn't 'assign' individuals specific parking spaces, he shrugged off the angry outburst as the behaviour of just another New Yorker whom urban survival had pushed too close to the edge.

'Move your car back,' said Steve. 'I'll leave and you can have your spot.' There was a hint of sarcasm in his voice.

Steve says he wasn't scared. He was a little taken aback by the driver's fury, but not really surprised. In New York, you're never surprised.

The screaming started again. Steve was getting a little impatient. 'All the driver had to do was back up eight inches and Steve could pull out and the whole thing would be over with.

'Move your car,' Steve shouted to the driver. 'Move your God-damned car, and I'll leave and you can have your spot.'

Suddenly the driver ran into the house, leaving his Mercedes parked with Steve still blocked in. The doormen at 180 East 72nd noticed the commotion and were looking over. The doormen across the street, where Steve had picked up the umbrella, were staring too.

Steve assumed that the driver had just parked his Mercedes there to trap his car, and wasn't coming back. He'd have a job getting the car out but he had no alternative. Jumping into his car, Steve locked the doors and started it up.

Inch forward – stop. Inch backward – stop. After a couple of minutes Steve was nearly out.

When he looked up, Steve saw the Ambassador standing at the kerb by the passenger side. But this time he had a gun in his hand.

Steve, a Marine veteran, recognized it as a semi-automatic pistol. It was pointed at him through the window.

The Ambassador smacked the passenger window of Steve's car with the butt of the pistol. Glass flew in every direction. It was all over the inside of the car, all over Steve. Fortunately, Steve was wearing glasses which protected his eyes from the fragments as they showered him.

Then the diplomat stuck the pistol through the window and pointed it right at Steve. 'I thought I was dead,' he says.

Then unexpectedly, the Ambassador ran back into the house. He had cut his hand when the glass went flying.

Steve jumped out of his car and ran for help. The doormen were standing there mesmerized by the scene.

'Call the cops,' Steve screamed.

Steve ran to the corner of Third Avenue, which was about a hundred yards away, hoping to flag down a police car. He saw a Metro Transit Authority cop and got him to pull over.

'Do you have a radio?'

'Yeah.'

'Could you call the cops 'cos some guy's got a gun.'

The transit cop radioed for police assistance. Steve ran back to his car in time to see the police cruisers coming east across 72nd Street. Standing next to his car, he flagged them down.

Then the Mercedes' driver reappeared, this time without the pistol in his hand. Seeming calm now, the Ambassador produced a little black booklet from his pocket. Jet black, with a silver insignia on the front, it said 'United Nations' and bore the UN symbol.

'I am an ambassador.'

The police, having surveyed the damage, begin to question the Ambassador.

'I don't like the tone of your voice,' he said regally. He turned on his heels and went back inside his inviolable residence.

When an incident involves a diplomat, New York police can't just fill out a report and leave. They must wait until the ranking officer comes down to make sure everything has been handled properly. A sergeant arrived at the scene and took down some information. 'Oh, boy,' was all the sergeant said.

He got on the radio and called for a captain to come down. He was going to let the captain handle this. If the Ambassador had not had immunity, he could have been charged with assault, brandishing a dangerous weapon, possession of a deadly weapon and disturbing the peace.

'I went down to the Nineteenth Precinct house while two officers confirmed his immunity,' Steve recalls. 'If he didn't have it, they were going to go back and arrest him. But after about an hour, they found out he did. They told me you can't sue, you can't do anything.'

The NYPD notified the State Department who called the Ambassador's residence. Whoever answered the phone said the Ambassador was not in but that Goldstein had rammed into the Ambassador's car and had attacked him. By the next morning the story had changed: now the Ambassador had not even been at the scene of the attack. The country's mission later told the press it was the Ambassador's chauffeur who was involved; Goldstein had attacked the chauffeur with a lead pipe, and the Ambassador had not even been in town.

'When I found out he was an ambassador,' Steve said later, 'I thought, how does a guy like this get to be an ambassador? All this for a tight parking spot? This guy was a lunatic. I was in the Marines. I know guns. It was a semi-automatic and it was loaded. At the bottom of the gun the clip was protruding. For all I know, he did pull the trigger and it misfired.'

The *New York Post* printed the mission's allegation that Steve had attacked the chauffeur with a lead pipe. The US government lodged formal protests with the UN and with the government concerned. But he just went about his business, unencumbered.

Within a month, Steve Goldstein got a cash settlement of an undisclosed amount from the foreign government. The terms of the settlement prevented him from further discussing the case publicly. He never received an apology from the Ambassador, and the Central American government continues to insist that it was the chauffeur who was involved.

Diplomats have long been willing to fight for their honour. In London, in 1661, the French Ambassador felt his coach should procede that of his rival, the Ambassador from Spain. The Frenchman tried to manoeuvre his coach in front of the Spanish Ambassador's. When the Spaniard offered resistance, the Frenchman drew his sword. The rivals and their coachmen then fought a pitched battle with swords and pistols. After two horses had been hamstrung and a man mortally wounded, the French assumed their place of honour.

Offending those with diplomatic immunity has always been a risky business. A Biblical story records that King David eliminated the Ammonites for insulting his ambassadors. The most notorious example in more recent history of punishment meted out for daring to offend a diplomat is the Affaire Mattueoff, which prompted Parliament to pass its first diplomatic law in 1709. Monsieur de Mattueoff, Russia's

Ambassador to England, was arrested on a London street for not paying his debts and carted off to prison. His creditors had obtained a warrant, and the constables were well within their bounds. De Mattueoff was detained for a short period. He considered the whole ordeal an abusive affront to his dignity, even though the creditors had a just claim.

A vitriolic Peter the Great also took enormous offence when he learned what had befallen his Ambassador and, in retaliation, the Czar demanded the death penalty for those who dared insult the dignity of his representative. Peter settled, however, for a personal apology from the Crown and the passage of the Diplomatic Privilege Act of 1709, sometimes known as the Act of Anne. This Act of Parliament is the first recognition of diplomatic immunity in English law and was the basis for America's statute of 1790 which contained similar provisions for the guarantee of a diplomat's privileges and immunities.

Another classic case of 'Diplomatic Justice' demonstrates what you can expect if you pursue diplomatic personages to point out their violation of the law. In November, 1935, Iranian Ambassador Ghaffar Khan Djalal and his chauffeur were speeding through Elkton, Maryland. The officers on duty were unable to get them to pull over. The two policemen had to resort to jumping onto the running board of the Ambassador's car to get the attention of the occupants. The Ambassador protested and resisted arrest. The two officers took him and the chauffeur to the police station where they were released after paying seventy-five cents in costs. The Ambassador took umbrage and made a formal protest. Both Secretary of State Cordell Hull and the Governor of Maryland came forward with formal apologies. The arresting officers were fired, tried for assault, and received substantial fines.

As a final illustration of how justice has historically tipped her scales in favour of the diplomat, there is the 1959 case of Jean Mezière, the former French Consul-General in Genoa, Italy. He filed a lawsuit against a local transport firm claiming that in a traffic accident with one of the company's lorries about three years earlier, he had suffered a fractured finger. Mezière's lawyer asserted that because shaking hands is 'an important act of diplomatic life', the injury had been detrimental to his client's chosen career because he had been unable to participate in social and public events. Mezière won the case, and the Italian court ordered the transport company to pay him damages of four million lira (about $6,500 at the time).

Those with diplomatic immunity have been known to inflict bodily harm and even death on each other. When they do, police are again helpless to arrest them.

District of Columbia police were called to the Soviet Embassy January 6, 1984, to remove the body of Evgeniy Gavrilov. Soviet diplomats suspended the inviolability of the mission long enough for police to retrieve the body for embalming but denied them access to the room where the body was found and refused to answer their questioning. After an autopsy had been performed, medical examiner Douglas Dixon rulled that the 32-year-old secretary died of asphyxia caused by compression on the neck. Law enforcement officials were prohibited from investigating further, but even if they had, diplomatic immunity would have made an inquiry pointless. The file was closed.

On a Sunday evening in April, 1982, Washington police were called by the wife of a Thai embassy employee who had been beaten by her husband. It was the second time in a week the battered wife had requested police assistance. The woman told police her husband had kicked her during an argument.

Police went to the Thai's apartment building, and discovered that neighbours had seen the embassy employee running out of the apartment wielding a large kitchen knife. There was nothing they or the police could do. Since this was the third distress call from the wife, the police notified the State Department. The Department wrote a letter to the Thai Ambassador informing him of his employee's violent behaviour. That was the extent of action that could be taken to safeguard the woman.

In cases where a diplomat leaves the host country following

an assault on a fellow countryman, it is doubtful that the diplomat will be prosecuted at home. Even if he is, the sending state often does no more than put on a show trial. In one notorious case from the late 1950s, André Toussaint, the First Secretary at the Haitian Embassy in Washington, was charged with fatally shooting the Minister Counsellor of his mission. He was released from custody, shielded by diplomatic immunity. He returned to Port-au-Prince and stood trial there two years later. Unsurprisingly, the two-day trial resulted in an acquittal.

Consuls, which are plentiful in every major city of the US and Europe, are entitled by the Vienna Convention on Consular Immunity to protection from prosecution if they are accused of a crime while working in an official capacity. But guidelines for police officers in New York City give consuls full diplomatic immunity as a matter of course. Because it is so problematical to determine when a consul is on duty the police prefer to err on the side of expediency.

Diplomatic immunity is such a useful gambit, many try to claim it when they're not entitled. In some cases they succeed and in others they fail. But in either case, the unsuspecting citizens of the host country pay the price. When law enforcement and State Department officials assist those who are not entitled to get more than they deserve, the injustice is compounded with insult.

Paul J. Coombs, aged forty-five, the owner of a carpet cleaning business, was driving home in his van to Fort Pierce, Florida, on June 4, 1984. He approached the intersection of Thornhill Drive and Airosa Boulevard in Port St Lucie and, since he had the right of way, continued on. Suddenly, from out of nowhere, he was hit by a 1983 Oldsmobile rental car driven by a Bahamian. The man, the Chief Executive Officer of his country's National Car Rental, had sped through a stop sign without hesitation. He collided with Paul Coombs' van with such force that Coombs was flung from the van and died at the scene of the accident. The other man himself spent two days in intensive care at Port St Lucie Hospital.

Though Paul's moment of suffering was mercifully brief, his family's was not. Paul Coombs was survived by his wife, Brenda, and their three children, Paula, Benita and Paul Jr.

The wife of the Bahamian appeared in court the next day and told the court her husband had diplomatic immunity and could not be charged over the accident. Though he held a diplomatic passport, he had no diplomatic function in the United States. He was not an accredited diplomat.

But though the court did not honour his claim of immunity, he was charged not with vehicular homocide as the seriousness of the accident might have indicated, but with a minor traffic violation. Sergeant Peggy Barcelona, the police officer in charge of the case, denied that the lesser charge was filed because he had raised a defence of diplomatic immunity. It was her contention that a charge of vehicular homocide was not made because there were no witnesses. Therefore, she claimed, she could not prove recklessness or wilful and wanton neglect.

In October, 1984, at his criminal court appearance, he dropped the claim of diplomatic immunity. He pleaded no contest to the reduced charge and was fined $500.

The Coombs family's lawyer, Christian Searcy, is angered by the fact that the police said they couldn't find a witness and so reduced the charge from vehicular homocide. He himself had no trouble finding a witness to the accident.

Brenda Coombs was disappointed but not surprised that he was only fined. 'Since the beginning,' she says 'It seems like he's had all the breaks. And neither he nor his attorney has made any attempt to contact our family. I feel, as a human being, he could have at least said he was sorry.'

Brenda Coombs and her three young children, faced with no means of support, no savings and inadequate life insurance, filed a wrongful death suit against the man about a month after the accident. Not surprisingly, he filed to bar the suit; he claimed diplomatic immunity. Because the claim had succeeded in getting a reduced charge, he probably assumed that a claim of diplomatic immunity could help him with the civil suit as well.

The family's law firm got an affidavit from the State Department indicating that he had no claim to either civil or criminal immunity from prosecution in the United States. Though the affidavit was filed in court in August, 1984, the court issued a continuance in the case to January, 1985. In January, 1985 he attempted to sustain his claim of diplomatic immunity but the court refused to dismiss the case and set a date for trial. Faced with the possibility of a verdict against him, he settled with Mrs Coombs for a substantial sum.

Another Florida incident, an unprecedented case involving a Saudi Prince, proves that you don't have to have diplomatic immunity to get the benefit of it – if you can pull the right strings.

Prince Turki Bin Abdul Aziz of Saudi Arabia, his wife, Princess Hend, and his sizeable entourage stopped at a Miami Beach Hotel in 1980 on their way to Disney World in Orlando, Florida. They liked what they saw, so they stayed in Miami for eighteen months. The group included the Prince's four wealthy brothers-in-law, the Sheiks al-Fassi, along with their individual retinues. The Prince had enough money to make himself comfortable anywhere in the world, and he made himself opulently at home in Miami. He purchased a luxury penthouse condominium at the exclusive Cricket Club as well as a $3.2 million estate on Indian Creek Island formerly owned by the Woolworth family.

As soon as the Prince, one of the 5,000 member Saudi royal family, and several sheiks who were related to his wife had taken up residence, it seemed as if their sole mission in life was to make everyone in Miami aware of their royal presence. If it was, they certainly succeeded.

Not long after their arrival, reports of the Saudis' extravagant lifestyle became popular gossip around town. Newspapers frequently detailed the immoderate shopping sprees, the fleets of limousines shuttling relatives around south Florida, the yacht parties, the helicopter jaunts and the hotel bills that ran into the millions.

Time passed pleasantly for Prince Turki and his Princess, but on Sunday, February 26, 1982, the paradisal calm of their existence was shattered.

It all started with newspaper accounts stating that the Prince's servants were not allowed to communicate with the outside world, were forced to work twenty hours a day, seven days a week, and were paid slave wages. A police investigation into the charges received inside information from an informer which was confirmed by other sources. The police checked with the State Department several times to make sure the Prince did not have immunity. They were told he did not, so they took the next step.

Lawyers for the Prince had told the Assistant State Attorney for Dade County that several interviews with servants would be arranged to assess whether they were prevented from leaving their employment. But no interviews were forthcoming. 'After several weeks,' Assistant State Attorney Tom Peterson reports, 'when we realized they were simply stalling, we started out on our own investigation.'

The investigation uncovered enough for a judge to issue a warrant to search the Prince's premises.

At 5.00 that Sunday afternoon, twelve Miami police officers and an Arabic interpreter arrived at the Cricket Club condominium. The search warrant named an Egyptian nanny sources said was being held against her will in a state close to slavery.

Neither the warrant not the police uniforms were sufficient credentials for the French bodyguard stationed outside the apartment who tried to prevent them from entering. Police arrested him. Having made their way through the first line of defence, they went to the door and rang the bell. Once they had been admitted to the penthouse a further struggle ensued.

The police carried a portable tape recorder to record the questioning of the servants, and it was running from the time they entered. A voice identified as the Princess's shrieked, 'Out! Out of my house! I will break your nose!' The Princess spat at several police officers, hurled obscenities, threw a chair at them and bit a detective on the hand.

Police also wrestled with four more French bodyguards, the Prince himself and his mother-in-law. One officer was felled by a kick in the groin. The Prince's voice on the tape recording said, 'Nobody is leaving here! No! No! No! I have immunity. I challenge you.' When a policewoman handed a bathrobe through the bathroom door to the Prince's mother-in-law, the door slammed shut, smashing the officer's arm. As a result of the embarrassing row, five of Miami's finest sustained injuires.

The Egyptian nanny was not there. The interpreter interviewed two maids, who avowed they were not enslaved by their employers. Many of the charges, including one of a former valet who said servants were required to surrender their passports, had been corroborated by former employees, but the two maids had no complaints. Later, Abdelmejid Daifi, the Moroccan former servant who supplied police with information, failed a lie detector test concerning the allegations of slavery. But that was not the end of the matter.

After the police left, they considered whether the Saudis could be charged with assault for their conduct during the search. But the State Department, who heard of the incident shortly after it occurred, asked Florida State Attorney Janet Reno not to prosecute.

The outraged Prince Turki filed two lawsuits accusing Dade County law enforcement officials of 'abusive, disgusting and violent conduct'. He sought 210 million dollars in damages. When police learned of the lawsuits, they were furious. Four police officers filed countersuit.

In the mid–1970s, Prince Turki had been one of Saudi Arabia's Deputy Defence Ministers. Though he had resigned in 1978, he was well connected. The Saudi government has been likened to a family business, and Turki was family. Wheels started turning, and in less than three weeks the State Deparment received a formal request from the Saudi government asking that Prince Turki be granted diplomatic immunity. Two days later, on March 19, the State Deparment's Associate Chief of Protocol, Richard Gookin, and a former US Ambassador to Saudi Arabia, John West, were dispatched to Miami to smooth things over.

West met with the Prince and concluded that he had been 'treated outrageously', though he hadn't met with law enforcement officials, nor heard the tape, before his pronouncement. On April 2, the State Department granted Prince Turki full diplomatic immunity *retroactively*. They informed the State's Attorney that the Prince could not be charged for his conduct in the raid. The news was not taken lightly.

Sergeant John Collins, who headed the expedition to the Cricket Club condominium, said, 'We're sitting here getting rolled over by a crime wave that won't quit and we've got a Prince buying his way out of a crime. Something has got to be done to protect Americans in this country from their own State Department.'

In answer to media queries, the State Department admitted it didn't know the diplomatic title of Prince Turki. But, a spokesman continued, the Saudi government said the couple did have a diplomatic function in the United States, though he could not reveal what that function was.

Janet Reno, the Florida State Attorney, was asked by Deputy Secretary of State Joseph W. Twinam to stop all criminal proceedings against Prince Turki and his family. Reno called their retroactive immunity 'a sham' and was so outraged, she wrote a letter of protest to the State Department. Her letter said, in part: 'All the evidence indicates that the State Department took that action in response to pressure from the Saudi government which wanted to keep one of the members of the royal family from being embarrassed.'

In the month following the granting of immunity, former Ambassador West returned to Miami and met with the Prince. 'He asked me to come down,' West announced, 'and discuss how to change his image, make some peace.'

The Prince and his equally free-spending brothers-in-law, the Sheiks al-Fassi, who also lived in the area, inaugurated a two-month gift-giving spree in order to purchase some good will. Donations of half a million dollars went to hospitals, universities and cultural institutions. Public television, a theatre-group and the University of Miami were some of the beneficiaries of the Saudis' largesse.

In May, the Prince offered the four police officers involved in the counter-claim $100,000 in exchange for dropping their suit. They rejected the Prince's offer.

At the end of the month, Prince Turki travelled to Washington to attend a party in his honour hosted by the image-conscious former Ambassador West. Top ranking State Department officials attended, as did Defence Secretary Caspar Weinberger, diplomats, Congressmen and Senators, retired admirals and generals. Following cocktails, raw oysters and prime beef sandwiches, the Prince made a speech praising US–Saudi relations. After polite applause, the Prince shook hands and departed.

On June 7, the Prince's 210 million dollar lawsuits were dropped.

With the death of King Khaled less than a week later, the Prince, his family and his entourage left in their personal chocolate brown Boeing 707 to return to Saudi Arabia. Before boarding their jet, the Prince and Princess talked to the press.

'People are not used to this type of life,' said Princess Hend. 'It's not because we are behaving wrong, it's just different. It guess you don't have many royal families living here.' She concluded her interviews by saying, 'We love Miami, and we'll always be coming here. And nothing will change our minds.'

CHAPTER SEVEN

A Question Of Morality

Though rape is undoubtedly the worst form of sexual assault, diplomats have been known to commit sexual offences of all kinds, many of them no less horrifying for the victims. Cases of indecent assault and gross indecency involving diplomats are all too common, as many women have found out to their cost.

One such unsuspecting victim was Lynn Reynolds, a 28-year-old mother of two small boys living in Kensington. Her husband, Robert, was a Royal Parks constable, assigned to Kensington Gardens. Consequently, their small home was no more than fifty yards away. Quite literally, Kensington Gardens was the Reynolds' back yard and on one Thursday afternoon in March, 1984, Lynn decided to take advantage of the good weather to let her two young children play in the park.

Four-month-old Darren was sitting in his push-chair as he and his mum watched Robert playing a few feet away. The children were clearly enjoying themselves, the sun was shining and all was peaceful and pleasant.

Then she noticed a man, a foreign-looking man, watching her very intently:

> He was about five foot ten, with dark hair and he wore beige trousers and a blue anorak. He just kept staring at us for several minutes. Then he came across to where I was standing with Darren and he asked if I was the boys' mother. When I said I was he said that I was too young-looking to be a mother. Then he leaned over and kissed

> Darren on the forehead – which I thought was a very strange thing for a man to do.
>
> Then he stood up and without a word grabbed me by the arm. He pulled me towards him and then he touched my breast. He said, 'I would love to kiss and caress you.' I was terrified. I broke away from him, grabbed Robert into my arms and ran off pushing Darren in the pram. I ran home where Robert was and told him what had happened. He called the station and then ran out to help his mates. Within a couple of minutes they had captured the man who was still in the park.

When the park constables first approached the man he pretended not to speak English. But when they got him to the station he suddenly found that he could in fact speak the language. The first thing he said was 'diplomatic immunity'.

He identified himself as a member of the communications section of the Jordanian Embassy which is located in nearby Upper Phillimore Gardens. He produced his identification which satisfied the constables that he was who he claimed to be, and a call was made to the Foreign Office.

The answer was immediate. The man was entitled to immunity. So instead of being charged with indecent assault, a charge that could have resulted in several years' imprisonment, the man was simply sent on his way.

Then a series of strange things began to happen. A spokesman for the Jordanian Embassy said the mission 'knows nothing about an incident like this but we are making inquiries'. Later, they said, 'We have no idea who this man is. He is not a member of our mission. He is not a Jordanian diplomat.'

It must be remembered that the park constables had positively identified the man, that the Foreign Office had confirmed he was entitled to immunity and that later Mrs Reynolds had picked out his photograph. Yet the Jordanians said he was not one of theirs and had no immunity.

The police tried to find the man again, intending to reintroduce the charges. But by this time he had left the country – back to Jordan according to immigration records.

Mrs Reynolds was naturally outraged by the release of her assailant. 'This man must not be allowed to get away with this,' she insisted. 'I was terrified, and other women might be in danger.'

Actually, the spring of 1984 saw a series of sex offences committed by diplomats. On April 8, police in Soho came upon a man committing a sex act with a 17-year-old youth. The man was arrested and taken to the station to be charged with gross indecency. There he identified himself as a Jordanian attaché, and claimed diplomatic immunity. A call to the Foreign Office confirmed the immunity so he was released. At the request of the Foreign Office he was returned to Jordan.

Then less than a week later, this case was repeated almost exactly. Police in Hyde Park came upon an older man committing a sex act with another youth, aged nineteen. He was arrested and charged with gross indecency. Taken to the station, the sixty-year-old man identified himself as a clerk in the French Embassy and claimed immunity. Another call to the Foreign Office confirmed the immunity and the man, who was never identified, was released. As in the Jordanian case, the man was sent home at the request of the Foreign Office.

In England between 1974 and 1984, there were sixteen *reported* incidents where perpetrators of indecent assault, gross indecency, attempted gross indecency, rape and even incest were not prosecuted because of diplomatic immunity.

In May, 1984, less than a year before Mrs Reynolds' assault, another young married woman was attacked and molested by a London embassy official. In that case, a 49-year-old Egyptian Embassy official manhandled a 21-year-old woman who had tried to be a good samaritan.

The young woman later reported how the incident occurred. In Clapham, south London, a man approached her in the street. He asked if she would be kind enough to help him with his shopping bags. Because he was walking with a cane and seemed sincere in his request for assistance, she decided to help him.

The young woman helped the man up the stairs to just outside of his flat. There, in the corridor, she decided her mission of mercy was completed. She was about to leave the bags and go when he begged her to help him take the bags inside. She went in first, and put the shopping bags down. He followed her and then locked the door behind them.

'I got very scared,' the young woman said, recalling her ordeal, 'and he pushed me onto a sofa. Then he sat down beside me and asked me to take off my coat. I got up and pushed him away from me, but he kissed me on the cheek. Then he kissed me on the lips. By then I was crying and he placed his hands inside my coat and got hold of my breasts.'

The telephone rang just then and interrupted the man's advances. A ringing telephone had never been such a welcome sound to the young woman. The narrowness of her escape terrified her. She ran to a house where a friend was working and phoned the police.

The Egyptian was apprehended and questioned by the police, but he was released almost immediately. Scotland Yard had confirmed his diplomatic immunity.

A spokesman for the Egyptian Embassy, Mr Said Refaat, denied the young woman's report. 'It is sheer fabrication,' he stated indignantly. 'This man could not harm a butterfly. He did not invite her inside his flat or harm her in any way.'

Refaat alleged that there had been a caretaker working in the bathroom the whole time. He claimed the caretaker heard the Egyptian talking to a woman in the hallway, but that he never saw her.

The young woman's account didn't rule out the possibility of an unseen person. If he was working in the bathroom, as he might very well have been, he never came forward to make a statement, probably because he was unaware of the entire incident. But the case never came to trial. The young woman had no legal redress because of diplomatic immunity.

Another Egyptian, this one a security guard at his country's Washington embassy, committed indecent exposure on several occasions at the Landmark Shopping Centre in Alexandria, Virginia.

September 25, 1982, was a Saturday, the most crowded time at the shopping mall. There, the Egyptian revealed himself to a young woman going about her Saturday shopping. Two of the store's security staff were alerted by the victim of the indecent act. They searched the floor for the suspect.

They found a man answering the woman's description. Any doubt that this was the perpetrator was removed when the envoy exposed himself again, this time for the benefit of the guards. Whisking the exhibitionist away from shoppers, they detained him in the security office.

In keeping with normal procedure, the Alexandria Police were called in to make the arrest. The store's Chief of Security had turned up other complaint reports from his file. Other victims described this same man from his previous indecent acts.

The Egyptian Embassy security guard had fourteen years' experience with their military office before coming to the United States in 1979, and he was a married man. Because he had diplomatic immunity, he was released from police custody, with no summons issued.

As a result of his frequent, repeated offences, the exhibitionist was transferred back to Cairo. He left Washington about a month after the double exposure.

A more disturbing incident occurred near the end of February, 1983. An eleven-year-old girl had gone shopping with her mother at the post exchange at Fort McNair, Virginia. The little girl's father was a Latin American military attaché stationed in Washington.

While her mother went shopping, the little girl, armed with a handful of small change, went to play some video games in one area of the exchange. Preoccupied with Space Invaders and far-away galaxies, the girl became a target for a perverted Pakistani military attaché. The envoy closed in on the girl while the games distracted her. He then fondled her.

When her mother had finished shopping and was ready

to go, she found out what the Pakistani attaché had done to her daughter. She alerted post police immediately.

'I went into the store,' the mother told them, 'grabbed the man by the hand, and started to pull him out of the store. He was very nervous and shaking. We took him to the military police and the Criminal Investigation Department.'

According to the military police report, this is how the girl described the incident: 'This man started to touch me all over on my waist and bust and put his body close to me.'

Naturally, delicacy is required in questioning a young victim of sexual abuse. The police have to verify what happened without traumatizing the victim further. They didn't ask the girl to get more specific.

The Criminal Investigation Department were about to charge the Pakistani officer with assault against a minor when headquarters contacted the State Department. The Pakistani child molester was listed in the State Department 'white book' and had full diplomatic immunity.

When the Pakistani Ambassador was informed of the incident, he judiciously decided to send the girl's molester home. It was the Ambassador's view, according to a State Department document, that to either pursue the case or attempt to develop a defence for the man would serve little constructive purpose. Of that there is no question. The man was sent home and the State Department closed the case. Again, he was neither charged nor punished for his crime. Though the Ambassador will forget, and the State Department will forget, the little girl will never forget.

Some who are not entitled to full immunity have managed to get it anyway, even when the crime is attempted rape. Nineteen-year-old Carol Goff was followed into the lobby of her Brooklyn apartment building by a 23-year-old Ethiopian living in New York. He attacked her, but Carol valiantly fought him off. She succeeded in avoiding rape and alerting the police. The Ethiopian was taken into custody.

The man claimed diplomatic immunity. New York police checked his assertion and found his name on the United Nations diplomatic list for the Ethiopian mission. They consequently released him. Almost immediately he left the country.

Later, it was discovered that he wasn't entitled to immunity of any kind. He was the brother-in-law of the head of the mission, and that was how he ended up on the diplomatic list. He wasn't even employed by the mission, and his claim of immunity was a total fraud, but by the time it was discovered, he was on safe soil, having escaped prosecution.

In another, more complicated case, a member of a United Nations delegation escaped prosecution on a charge of attempted rape although he, too, was not eligible for diplomatic immunity. This time, the crime took place on Labour Day weekend, 1982.

North of New York City, in suburban Westchester county, several groups were scattered randomly around a large park for family picnics and barbeques. But the pleasant holiday atmosphere was destroyed for a 43-year-old woman who was walking in the park when a foreigner began chasing her. Following her down a bridle path, the man started to gain on her. She tried to run faster, but so dogged was the man's pursuit that he was soon at her heels. He then tackled her from behind. The woman struggled so fiercely that the North Korean threatened to hit her with a rock. He then attempted to rape her.

The woman continued to fight back; she would not give in. She managed to rise to her feet and slip out of his grasp. She ran for help and then returned to the scene with the police, but the man had disappeared. Together, the victim and the police officers patrolled the area searching for the attacker, until they came upon a group of North Korean picnickers.

The North Korean group was from the Observer Mission to the United Nations. Scanning the faces of the group for her assailant was unnerving for the victim following such a violent assault. She was still too shaken by the encounter to isolate one face from among many.

Later, after she had recovered from the attack, and with an assortment of photographs of mission members, the woman was able to identify her assailant. On September 21, 1982, a warrant was issued for the arrest of 0 Nam Chol, thirty-eight.

Initially, the North Korean mission appeared to cooperate with police efforts. But suddenly, mission officials denounced the charge as a lie and invoked immunity for Mr Nam. Because North Korea is not a member nation of the United Nations, but only an observer mission, UN treaties don't guarantee its employees full immunity.

But the warrant for Nam's arrest could not be served. Nam had retreated to the 'safe house' of his inviolable mission.

The Manhattan mission for North Korea incorporates residential quarters and administrative offices. It occupies a penthouse in an elegant twenty-five-storey modern building on East 80th Street and Madison Avenue. The safety it provided was a luxury Nam took advantage of; he refused to come out.

Reasoning that Nam couldn't remain in the building forever, Westchester County police instituted round-the-clock shifts outside the building. Whenever he emerged, they were prepared to arrest him for his crime.

Westchester law enforcement officials felt it was vital to take a stand. Their vigil was neither obstinacy nor harassment. County District Attorney Carl Vergeri asserted, 'In Nam's case, I thought it critical to establish that our court had jurisdiction, which we did. Otherwise, these people will just laugh at our laws and that can't be allowed to happen.'

Unfortunately, Nam's protection from the law couldn't be prevented, because the safety of missions can't be violated. The State Department and the UN took over for Westchester county officials and began negotiations with the North Koreans. Weeks passed but Nam still hadn't emerged.

After six weeks of the stand-off, Joan Dicket, a spokeswoman for the US Mission to the UN, observed, 'Both sides are at loggerheads. They refuse to surrender Mr Nam, and we believe it would be unseemly for the State Department to devise a way for him to escape the law.'

Weeks turned into months. Thanksgiving, Christmas and the New Year came and went. Nam still hadn't emerged from 40 East 80th Street. Valentine's Day passed and Easter was just around the corner. Many observers began to wonder how long this could go on.

Inviolable premises had provided refuge for as long as fifteen years in previous cases. In 1956, the US Embassy in Budapest had provided shelter for Cardinal Jozsef Mindszenty to protect him from execution on a charge of treason because he spoke out against the Russian takeover of Hungary.

In Santiago, Chile, in 1984, the Papal Nuncio had provided shelter within the walls of the Vatican Embassy for four armed guerrilla rebels. Those cases were primarily ideological, not criminal, but they set a precedent.

For O Nam Chol, the mission could provide shelter from the law indefinitely. In February, the United States tried to force the situation by applying some pressure. They prohibited re-entry visas for North Korean members of the mission who had returned home on leave. The pressure was felt, but it didn't yield results. Nam still hadn't emerged.

Finally, in July, the State Department threatened to expel the First Secretary of the mission unless Nam came out and faced the charges against him. The North Koreans had few options, but they succeeded in reducing the charge against Nam. In exchange for pleading guilty to a lesser complaint of sexual abuse, Nam would walk free. Then, he would have forty-eight hours in which to leave the country.

On July 26, over ten months after the attempted rape, Nam surrendered himself, pleaded guilty and departed as had been negotiated. Though he hadn't been entitled to immunity, the net result was the same. He avoided paying for his crime.

After Nam fled, North Korea changed its stance. The official North Korean news agency, KCNA, accused the United States of violating the United Nations charter. They denounced the indictment as a trumped-up charge designed to force the expulsion of their innocent representative.

The KCNA release read:

They took the measure of expulsion because our secretary

> had really committed a crime. But this is a sheer lie, which is totally unfounded. Our secretary has committed no crime.
>
> That the US side forced the secretary . . . to leave the United States is an open infringement upon the sovereignty of the Democratic Peoples Republic of Korea and a crude violation of the UN charter . . .
>
> This 'case' is part of the open hostile policy towards the DPRK and is a 'case' cooked up by the US side deliberately out of the political purpose of totally paralysing the function of the permanent observer office of our country at the United Nations and blocking its activities.

There were other allegations that 'Comrade Nam' suffered harassment and that his health was impaired. In a letter to UN Secretary General Javier Perez de Cuellar, North Korean Ambassador Han Si Hae wrote, 'Owing to such unlawful acts of the authorities of the host country, the health of Comrade Nam has deteriorated.'

Nam was later interviewed back in North Korea by an American television crew. He again proclaimed his innocence and said the charges were 'politically motivated'. He also said that when he returned home 'I was accorded a hero's welcome.'

Even though the North Koreans later repudiated the charges, the compromise that led to the release of the would-be rapist allowed everybody to save face: the State Department, the North Koreans, the United Nations – and most of all, O Nam Chol. No one lost; no one, that is, except the victim of the crime.

A situation very embarrassing to the Soviet Union occurred in February, 1981. Yurily Osipov, who was listed on the diplomatic rolls as a first secretary at the Soviet Cultural Office, apparently had too much to drink at a late-night embassy party in Washington. He left the party and headed for a local park known as a homosexual cruising area.

At 5.20 a.m., a District police officer observed Osipov speeding and pulled him over. Osipov identified himself in perfect English as a Soviet diplomat, but would say nothing more until a representative of the Soviet Embassy arrived. By the time Vladimir Vikulov, a political officer, arrived at the stopped car, Detective James Pawlik had also been dispatched to head the inquiry.

Osipov and Vikulov consulted in rapid Russian. Then Vikulov told Detective Pawlik that Osipov had been robbed and was speeding because he feared the two black men who robbed him might be on his trail. The Russian was released into Vikulov's custody.

Meanwhile, a very different version of events was being related at a nearby police station. Sammie Smith, nineteen, complained that he had been accosted by a man with a thick foreign accent whom he had tried to help a few minutes earlier in the park. Smith told police he was walking through the park on his way home from his girlfriend's house when he noticed a man ardently importuning a well-known local homosexual. Smith then observed two black men interrupt and start jostling the white man. Smith assumed it was a robbery in progress, so he rushed up and convinced the two to leave the man alone.

After the blacks left, the man with the accent said he had lost some papers. Smith offered to help him find them. Returning to the car, the man offered Smith a ride home. As soon as they got into the car, Smith revealed, the man 'tried to grab my privates'. When Smith resisted, the man started to choke him. Smith jumped out of the car and fled on foot to the police station.

The next morning, police officers put the two cases together and called Smith back to the station. He was shown a photograph of Osipov, and Smith immediately identified him as the man who had tried to molest him.

When confronted with the facts, the Soviets quickly claimed immunity for Osipov. Within days, they notified the State Department that Osipov and his wife had departed for the Soviet Union.

Law enforcement authorities have uniformly agreed that sex offences are the least reported crimes. How many cases go unreported to the police cannot be guessed, neither can the number of cases which go unreported to the public.

In the light of the rampant abuses of privilege and the variety of criminal activities diplomats have recently been involved in, closer scrutiny of applicants' moral character would seem in order. For too many countries, it is simply too easy to become a diplomat and be eligible for that coveted salve so soothing to every legal malady – diplomatic immunity.

They don't always get away with it, however, and in one case, a Hong Kong judge felt diplomatic status had been pushed past its limits so he put his gavel down. In October, 1983, Raymonde Montague Sacklyn appeared in a Hong Kong court wearing a morning coat and a cream-coloured brocade sash. He had been ticketed for jaywalking, but didn't want to pay the fine. Sacklyn's attorneys informed the court that Sacklyn was 'an ambassador' of the Hutt River Principality in Australia and was thereby entitled to diplomatic immunity.

The Hutt River Principality is an area of twenty-nine square miles in Western Australia with a population of 2,000. It was 'founded' in 1970 by a farmer, Leonard Casley, who proclaimed the land a principality in order to dodge taxes. Needless to say, the move was never endorsed by the Australian government.

Sacklyn's lawyers asserted that Sacklyn could not be tried by the court. They proposed that the matter of Sacklyn's jaywalking be taken up by the International Court of Justice in The Hague. The Hong Kong court rejected Sacklyn's ludicrous claim of immunity and found him guilty. The 'diplomat' was ordered to pay his fine.

Frequently, the diplomatic lists submitted to governments are padded with wealthy foreign nationals living abroad who have gained favour with embassy officials or with the government of the day. They enjoy the status and privileges that come with being on the diplomatic list. The fact that they have no actual duties with the embassy, save hosting and attending receptions and parties, has little to do with it.

San Marino, a country with a population of 23,000,

occupies twenty-four square miles in the Appennines. San Marino regularly bestows diplomatic and consular status on wealthy men and women around the world who serve only a decorative function in the conduct of world politics.

In 1983, San Marino's Consul-General in Washington was Enrico di Portanova, a Texan oil millionaire of Italian descent. Twice a year, he joins the hundreds of consuls-general appointed by San Marino to appear in cutaways, pearl-grey trousers and ceremonial medals at San Marino's Palazzo Valloni to witness the inauguration of the two new captains-regent. Their diplomatic passports give them at least 'functional' immunity and consular corps licence plates around the world.

John Kenneth Galbraith, who served as US Ambassador to India, commented, 'In India, during my time, there were some fifty ambassadors . . . [who] were a spectacular example of what economists call "disguised unemployment". The ambassadors from Argentina and Brazil could not have done more than a day's serious work in a month. The more deeply engaged diplomats from Scandinavia, Holland, Belgium or Spain could discharge their essential duties in one day a week.'

Harry Wriston, the former president of Brown University who headed a committee to review State Department practices in 1954, reported, 'In 1914, in the ten nations where Britain was represented abroad, its chiefs of mission had an average of thirty-three years of professional experience; the French chiefs of mission in the ten capitals had over thirty-four; the American ambassadors and ministers had a little less than one year of service in the field of diplomacy.'

In an average year, thirty percent of American ambassadors are political appointees. The patronage system in ambassadorial appointments is so accepted a practice that the proportion reached as high as forty-nine percent at one point recently.

The American passion for giving political allies comfortable appointments in pleasant world capitals dates back to the birth of the nation. Four of the first six American Presidents served as foreign ministers before their party's nomination to presidential candidacy.

The spoils system appointees were not always the picture of decorum one might expect. John Randolph, a career politician, was appointed as United States Minister to Russia in 1830 by President Andrew Jackson. When Randolph presented his credentials to the Czar, his somewhat inappropriate opening line was, 'Howaya, Emperor? And how's the madam?'

Half a century later, General Daniel Sicles was US Minister to Spain. For part of his tenure, which lasted from 1869 to 1875, the Civil War hero carried on a very public affair in Paris with the exiled Queen of Spain – a gesture not likely to enhance his country's relations with the new ruling class in Madrid. Even before this breach of etiquette, the most naïve judge of character might have suspected that Sicles was less than an ideal candidate for the diplomatic service. Ten years prior to his appointment to Spain, Sicles had shot and killed Philip Barton Key for what he considered to be undue attentions towards Mrs Sicles, though Sicles was acquitted on a defence of temporary insanity.

Then there is the saga of Franklin Roosevelt's appointment of Ed Flynn as Ambassador to Australia. The Democratic boss of Bronx County, New York, was involved in a scandal because it had been discovered that the paving blocks used in his personal driveway had been paid for by the city. Speculation was rife that Flynn had not paved his way to Australia merely with good intentions. The press commented angrily and Roosevelt withdrew the appointment.

Political patronage is bound to have repercussions. Abba Eban, in his book, *The New Diplomats*, commented, 'When the strongest nation in the world appoints a tycoon or a wealthy hostess to head an embassy, the discredit and frustration spread throughout the entire diplomatic corps in the country concerned.' Ambassadorial appointments of the wealthy and influential have long needed reform. In 1980, Congress passed the Foreign Service Act to control such abuses as the spoils system. The Act states: 'Contributions to political campaigns should not be a factor in the appointment of an individual as a chief of mission.' Despite the new law, Reagan's 1981 ambassadorial appointments included more than one wealthy campaign contributor.

Patronage appointments may be an American tradition, but we can be sure that what goes on in the USA goes on around the globe. Foreign service postings of wealthy or well connected individuals occur world-wide, most commonly in countries where bribery is an institutionalized practice.

Patronage encourages diplomatic corruption, but there are other factors which may also contribute. Ambrose Bierce, in *The Devil's Dictionary*, called diplomacy 'the patriotic art of lying for one's country.' The definition is apt, and may prove useful in a discussion of why diplomats are so frequently involved in criminal activity.

Lying, cheating, stealing and even murder are considered acceptable when undertaken for one's country. Some diplomats may become so used to the little deceptions necessary for national security and international intercourse that they lose any sense of personal morality. They cease applying a moral standard to their personal conduct, reasoning that if it is acceptable behaviour for nations, it is acceptable for them. Duplicity becomes second nature.

Machiavelli, whose very name has become synonymous with expediency and deceit, offers another clue. He himself was a diplomat for the Florentine court when he wrote, 'The world has always been inhabited by human beings who have always had the same passions.'

When the temptations of those passions are unchecked by fear of prosecution, the weak find it easier to yield to their baser instincts. Diplomatic immunity, in its present form, may polish the apple of temptation, making it difficult for a wavering diplomat to resist indulging himself.

Another contributor to the problem can be found in the increasing number of diplomats dispatched to world capitals. When the diplomatic community was more modest in size, those who became known for their unreliable or immoral behaviour would find it impossible to shake off their bad reputation, wherever they might be posted. Today's proliferation of embassy workers creates an atmosphere of anonymity which may encourage the flouting of a host country's laws. The feeling that they won't be caught or that no one will notice an indiscretion may motivate some. It's certainly easier to get lost in a crowd, and today's diplomats unquestionably are too numerous to know by name or reputation.

Though the foreign service is a respected profession, and many applicants are their country's brightest and most gifted young people, some have suggested the quality of applicants has declined over the last twenty years. The best and the brightest are sought by increasingly competitive employers, both in the government and in the private sector.

Eric Clark, in his book, *Diplomat, The World of International Diplomacy*, notes, 'In Germany, foreign ministry officials concede it [the foreign service] has lost some of its appeal'. . . In Spain, in 1971, there were less than eighty candidates for admission where twelve years before there had been four hundred . . . Some recruiters say the standard of those attracted has begun to fall.'

With the increased salaries and rewards offered in other fields, the foreign services of the world may today be accepting candidates whose overall abilities would have been considered insufficient just a few years ago.

Perhaps an arrogance that comes with the job contributes to diplomats' widespread disregard for the law. Diplomats are used to living the good life, and many have come to expect special treatment. Living in foreign capitals, in daily contact with the world of power, pampered by limousines, state dinners and receptions, and a jet-set lifestyle that few ordinary citizens could afford, they begin to feel they belong to a privileged class. Some of them even assume that they are above the law.

CHAPTER EIGHT

Diplomatic Slavers

BEHIND THE CLOSED doors of some of the world's seemingly most respectable homes dwell hundreds bound by the invisible chains of domestic slavery. Deprived of their basic human rights and cowed into submission by often violent threats, these victims live in deplorable conditions. Generally women, they almost never see the outside world. They work interminable hours every day, seven days a week, for little or no wages. They may be made to sleep on floors and eat table scraps; sometimes they are beaten or sexually abused. Their passports are withheld by their masters as insurance against escape. In many cases their masters are diplomats operating under the protection of diplomatic immunity.

In London, late one afternoon, a very frightened woman stumbled into the small West End food shop of Selvan Lingham. 'The woman was almost starving but had no money,' said Lingham, 'so I gave her some biscuits to eat.' Concerned about the woman's condition, Lingham called the police. When they arrived and began talking to the woman she told them a tale of horror that is almost unbelievable in the 20th century.

The woman identified herself as Laxmi Swami and said she was being kept as a slave by Princess Faria Alsabah, a member of the Kuwaiti Royal family, in a £500,000 home nearby.

'I was whipped, kicked, beaten and starved,' the woman told police. 'I had my clothes torn from my body and have been covered with blood and bruises.'

She told tales of being beaten with a riding crop if she did anything to displease her mistress. 'If I did not get up the stairs quickly enough when I was called, I was beaten. If I cried out during the beating, I was beaten harder.' She told of working twenty-hour days and of being beaten if the Princess found so much as a speck of dust around the house.

'The Princess would go out until after midnight and when she returned I was expected to massage her for hours. But I still had to be up and working by 6.00 a.m. while the Princess slept until the afternoon.'

She told of never being fed a complete meal. 'The Princess would show me scraps left over from the children's lunch and tell me I could eat them if I did my work well. Then she would lock them up.' She said that her bondage had continued for over three years and that another woman, Samsui Asiffa from Sri Lanka, was being held under the same conditions.

When the Princess was confronted with the charges she denied nothing. Instead she said it was a private matter and as a member of the Kuwaiti Royal Family she was entitled to immunity.

However, on February 4, 1985, Princess Faria was sentenced to six months in prison, suspended for two years, and also ordered to pay £2,000 in fines, costs and compensation to the maids.

Diplomats abusing their servants and then hiding behind diplomatic immunity is not a new story in Britain. Wing Commander Trevenen James tells a chilling tale which unfolded before him several years ago when he was living in Harley Street: 'A Kuwaiti diplomat, his wife and a young servant girl were living in a flat opposite us. One day the servant girl was talking to our housekeeper. Although she could barely speak English, she told about beatings she took. She rolled up her sleeve and showed a bite mark on her upper arm. Then she parted her hair and the imprint of a stiletto heel was clearly visible on her head. My housekeeper was very concerned and called the police but they said they could do nothing because he was a diplomat. On several other occasions we heard the girl screaming, but there was nothing we could do to help.'

Then one day he personally witnessed a chilling scene. The

young servant girl was being dragged, crying and screaming, down the flat's stairs by the diplomat and another man. She was resisting with all her might, but to no avail. She was thrown into the back of a car with CD plates and it went roaring off into the night.

'Finally we decided to talk with the man who owned the flat to let him know what was happening in it. Shortly thereafter the Kuwaiti moved out but I believe he simply moved on to another flat in London taking the servant girl with him. For all I know he is still here.'

Then there is the experience of the man who sold his large house to an Asian diplomat. The seller had moved out and the Asian had started to move in, even before all the final legal documents had been signed, and before money had changed hands.

Several days before the final closing on the house, the seller remembered he had forgotten some things that had been stored in his former basement, so he went back to the house to collect them. In the basement he saw some workers installing something along one of the walls. Upon closer inspection he saw they were installing sets of shackles and leg clamps. He immediately called off the impending sale.

In an expensive London clinic, a diplomat was undergoing treatment. He had with him a young female servant whom he insisted sleep across the threshold of his room at night. The young woman was clearly in a state of near exhaustion. The hospital staff was concerned, and pointing out that there were many hospital staff members available to see to the patient's needs, suggested that the girl be sent home for some much-needed rest. In answer to protests, the diplomat callously replied, 'She stays here at my pleasure. There are plenty more where she comes from.'

Victims of domestic slavery are defenceless. Deportation is a threat constantly hanging over their heads. Ignorance of the English language, lack of money and fear of reprisals stop them from running away. Their masters have no such fear, for even if they are caught, they can't be prosecuted. They belong to that privileged class called diplomats.

The Vienna Convention on Diplomatic Relations permits each diplomat to bring one personal servant with him or her. Because this is a privilege specified by the Convention, too many diplomats wantonly ignore their reponsibility to accord their servants with their full rights. But Article 41 of the Convention directly states the diplomat must respect the laws and the regulations of the receiving state. Too often these laws are ignored by diplomats who unilaterally deprive their servants of dignity, freedom, decent working conditions and fair wages.

This arbitrary contempt for human rights is a world-wide problem. Peter Davies, secretary of the Anti-Slavery Society, the world's oldest human rights organization, reports instances of diplomats in London, Washington, New York and Geneva who keep slaves but are protected from prosecution by diplomatic immunity.

Several London-based social service groups have encountered cases of this kind. Colonel Patrick Montgomery, the Anti-Slavery Society's former secretary, says, 'What evidence we have has been discovered purely by chance. It is probably no more than the tip of the iceberg.' Father Jack Dennehy, an Irish priest who runs a social and religious centre for London's Filipino community, has discovered similar situations with domestic workers. Over the course of a year, he may hear stories of this kind of abuse from a dozen women.

Octavio Lendon, acting director of the Spanish Catholic Centre, an outreach programme of the Washington DC archdiocese of the Catholic Church aimed at newly arrived Hispanics in the Washington area, concurs. 'I have to stress that we see these cases all the time,' he says, 'perhaps a new one every couple of weeks, about twenty-five to thirty cases a year.'

'It's a fact of life,' says Peter Davies sadly. 'These people move around in private aircraft and they bring in hordes of young people . . . as chattels brought in as part of the baggage. It's not an unfamiliar situation with diplomats from Middle Eastern countries who are used at home to having these sorts of servants that they bring with them.'

*

Lawyers who specialize in the problems of immigrants, like Vernon Gutjahr of Washington, often see the persecution which exists inside diplomatic residences.

In one particularly shocking case, which Gutjahr handled and remembers vividly, an Egyptian diplomat who had been stationed in Bolivia was reassigned to the United States. He brought a Bolivian servant named Rosalba to his new post. She was permitted entry to the United States as a domestic on a diplomatic visa. But in the land of the free, Rosalba was kept as a virtual prisoner. The only time she was allowed out of the house was to take the family's children to the local playground. She never received even a penny for her seven-day a week servitude. As is usual in these cases, the diplomat kept her passport to make sure she wouldn't try to escape.

Rosalba lived with the diplomat and his family for over a year under these conditions. During this time, she developed a severe gum disease that necessitated emergency oral surgery. Despite very obvious bleeding and infection, she was denied any medical treatment. At the age of twenty-two, Rosalba faced the probability that she would lose all her teeth and have to wear dentures for the rest of her life. The diplomat didn't care.

One day at the playground, Rosalba met another housekeeper from Bolivia who happened to be a client of Gutjahr's. Rosalba related her deprivations to her new-found friend and the woman managed to arrange for Rosalba to sneak away from her employer. The woman took Rosalba to see Mr Gutjahr and ask for his help.

When Attorney Gutjahr called the Egyptian, the diplomat refused to discuss the matter.

Because the case involved three governments (Bolivia, Egypt and the United States), it was more than usually complicated. Officials at the Bolivian Embassy were extremely upset, and wanted reparation for their national. Mr Gutjahr managed to interest a local television station in the case. When the story was broadcast, more pressure came to bear on the Egyptian Embassy and a meeting was finally arranged to include the Bolivian Embassy, the Egyptian diplomat, the State Department, Mr Gutjahr and Rosalba.

The diplomat admitted he had agreed to pay Rosalba $100 a month but had paid her nothing. For one year's work, she was given $1,200 in back wages. She also got back her personal effects and her passport.

The Egyptian viewed Rosalba's requests for justice as a mere nuisance and was indignant. Mr Gutjahr is certain the employer would have invoked his diplomatic immunity and done nothing had there not been so much pressure from his ambassador.

'This is one of those times that I wanted to step out of my lawyer's role and punch the SOB in the nose,' remembers the attorney. 'I figured if we can't sue diplomats they shouldn't be able to sue us for assault and battery. But of course, they can, so I let the urge pass and watched the guy storm out of the Embassy and into his car with those diplomatic plates.

'What was going on here was nothing short of slavery, pure and simple,' he explains, 'under the protection of diplomatic immunity.'

The more he thought about Rosalba and the inhumane treatment she received at the hands of this diplomat, the more outraged he became:

> What happens is that you give these types a title and you send them here as diplomats and they think that they're some kind of a god. In their countries you can often treat a servant like a dog and they don't see why they can't treat their servants here just the same way. I'm sure you wouldn't find this happening in the British Embassy or the French Embassy, but if you look into the embassies of the Third World I think you'd be shocked at how common it is. And there is little you can do because of that damned diplomatic immunity.
>
> They run roughshod over these people, most of whom don't have any education whatsoever or who don't realize they have any rights. Many of these servants don't speak English and don't even know how to use the telephone. Often it is only by accident they find somebody who they trust enough to tell how they are being abused and then

it is luck if that person is intelligent and concerned enough to help.

The cases that have surfaced almost do so by accident. I would venture to guess that for every case that hits the State Department, there are probably fifteen to twenty others that are never discovered. This is most definitely a common problem. It is not a question of lack of sophistication on the part of these diplomats – that they don't understand our customs. They are very sophisticated. They know exactly what they are doing and how they are protected by diplomatic immunity. The problem is that some of these guys are Nazis who couldn't give a damn.

Diplomats frequently use their official positions to retaliate against those who dare to rebel. Mr Gutjahr remembers another case which illustrates the price a servant can pay at the hands of a diplomat who abuses his position.

'A Pakistani woman was being held in virtual servitude,' he related. 'She worked seven days a week, eighteen hours a day, taking care of the diplomat's two or three children. She could never leave the house – not to go to church, not even to go to the doctor. She was literally *never* allowed out the front door.'

Her son was brought over at the same time she was, to work as a maintenance person at the Pakistani Embassy. He lived in a separate residence from her with some other Pakistanis. Mother and son were never allowed to see each other. The son had a friend whose father was a client of Mr Gutjahr.

'My first recommendation was to get the mother out of the house,' remembers Gutjahr. 'So the two young men went to the house and waited outside until both the husband and wife were gone. In this case, the husband was the number two man at the Embassy.'

The two men followed Gutjahr's plan and rescued the woman. Then Mr Gutjahr tried to obtain the release of her belongings and her passport which were being held by the diplomat. Mr Gutjahr was brushed off and his requests for his client's wages and passport were ignored so he took the case to the State Department. Through the State Department, he was able to obtain the woman's clothing and personal effects, but the diplomat still retained her passport.

Inside the passport was the visa needed to prove to the Immigration and Naturalization Service that she had made a legal entry into the US. Aliens in the US are required to prove their immigration status, but without her passport and visa, the woman could neither prove her Pakistani citizenship nor that she had entered the country legally. Without a passport, she could not return home. She became a person without a country, without any official record of her identity.

'The woman was terrified,' says Mr Gutjahr. 'She had very little, if any, education. Here she was going up against the second in command at the Embassy. She had no bargaining chips, no leverage whatsoever.'

She was completely at his mercy and so was her son. The Pakistani diplomat was delighted to use the power of his position to humiliate them further. Once she abandoned the post, her son was immediately fired from his job at the Embassy and they also retained his passport.

'At the time,' he continues, 'the situation in Pakistan was sensitive, so the State Department was not willing to anger the Embassy here over an incident involving a domestic servant. In fact, at the time, Pakistan President Zia was just about to make an official visit here and diplomatic relations between the US and Pakistan were in a state of flux.'

Finally, after a very long wait, her passport was turned over to the Embassy. The Pakistani diplomat was off the hook as far as the State Department was concerned. But he continued to wield his power to subjugate the woman. Embassy workers were instructed not to return her passport unless she flew back to Pakistan immediately. They told her they'd hand over the passport only when she came in with a confirmed reservation and a plane ticket for her departure.

'She got back her clothes but never got her back wages,' Mr Gutjahr says, 'and still does not have that passport.'

The story of Gabina Camacho Lopez is another typical tale of domestic slavery – except for its surprising conclusion.

Gabina was brought to Washington DC from Bolivia in October, 1976, by Señor and Señora Martinez. Manuel Martinez worked as a travel agent for an American company. Rosa Martinez was an employee of the Pan American Health Organization. Like most foreign diplomats, the international treaty which brought her to the United States allowed her to bring one domestic servant from her native country on an A–3 diplomatic visa.

Gabina was nineteen, an uneducated girl from a poverty-stricken background. Like the impoverished everywhere, the young woman hoped for a miracle that would lift her out of poverty and give her a brighter future. When she was recruited by the Martinez family, their offer seemed like just such a miracle. They were going to live in America, land of opportunity, and had offered to take her along as a maid. In exchange for taking care of their three children and looking after the house, Gabina was to have a salary, round-trip transportation and free room and board.

Rosa Martinez notified the Pan American Health Organization of her domestic's name. Since the organization's full-time staff are considered diplomats, the State Department quickly relayed the young girl's name to the American Embassy in La Paz, and a diplomatic servant's visa was issued for Gabina to enter the United States.

When she arrived in Washington DC, the exciting new life she had envisioned didn't materialize. For ten to twelve hours a day, she worked. She never had a single day off. Worst of all, she was never permitted to leave the house unless accompanied by a member of the Martinez family or one of their friends. Gabina was strictly prohibited from rest and leisure, from making friends, from having any life of her own whatsoever. The most you could say was that she had a roof over her head.

For nearly three years, her working conditions didn't change. But what could she do? A stranger in a strange land, she didn't speak any English. She knew no one. The Martinezes held her passport. If she ran away, where would she go? She didn't have the money to return home; they hadn't paid her. She didn't have any money for food, let alone shelter. If she left, she wouldn't get very far.

Gabina didn't have her passport, so she couldn't prove she was in the country legally. Because she knew little of the world beyond the door of her private prison, she didn't know that there was help. She didn't know there were *laws* governing minimum wages and minimum working conditions. She didn't even know that her treatment was criminal.

In the spring of 1979, Gabina was desperate. By a stroke of luck, Gabina met Kenneth Weckstein, another attorney specializing in problems of foreigners in the United States. When he heard of her situation, he planned a getaway. Gabina had asked the couple for her back wages when she knew she was leaving. They refused to pay her a cent. In June, Gabina left the Martinezes home for good.

Finding a job as a housekeeper in another Washington area home was not too difficult, and with Mr Weckstein's help, Gabina was soon happily settled.

Shortly after Gabina escaped, Attorney Weckstein filed suit against Señor and Señora Martinez for her back wages. Though Rosa Martinez' job provided her with many of the perks of diplomatic life, including the ability to bring a servant into the country, she was not immune from civil suit in this case because as a lower echelon employee of an international organization, her immunity was limited to her official actions. The Martinezes were shocked at Gabina's suit. They were even more shocked when a US District Court judge said they were obliged to pay her the minimum wage. He awarded Gabina $56,000 in back wages for the three years of her employment.

In the September, 1980, judgment, Judge Aubrey E. Robinson Jr found that the Martinezes 'exploited for their own purposes a young, poorly educated naïve alien who was completely at their whim and mercy.'

The Martinezes were shocked at the judgment against them. 'We won't be able to pay that. No way. I earn about $12,000 a year and my husband earns about $10,000,' said

Rosa Martinez. But for three years, Gabina was paid absolutely nothing.

'She was part of our family,' claimed Rosa. 'We brought her here so she could come to the United States and have the chance to better herself. It's just hard for me to believe this has happened.'

'We have three children and a house we just bought,' protested Manuel Martinez. 'I can hardly make ends meet trying to pay for our family expenses right now.'

The Martinezes' condescending attitude towards 'one of their family' is typical of these diplomatic employers. A servant should be *grateful* to be held a virtual prisoner in their home. Mrs Martinez said as much when she considered Gabina's free servitude as 'bettering herself'.

This case provided a deterrent to others who don't have complete immunity, but for those who do, the Martinez judgment is ignored as if it had never happened. Even though the ruling means diplomats can't flaunt the minimum wage law, the number of cases of servants being paid nothing or next to nothing has not diminished.

The case of Gabina Lopez is rare only in that it came to trial. Hundreds of similar cases will never come to trial because the diplomatic slavers have complete immunity from criminal prosecution and from civil suits.

Octavio Lendon, the acting director of Washington's Spanish Catholic Centre, is doing something to help the victims of diplomatic slavemasters.

A well-dressed, dark-haired man in his late thirties, Lendon's heartfelt concern is obvious as he speaks of the many people he and the agency have helped. Sitting at the cluttered desk in his modest but functional headquarters in the Adams-Morgan section of Washington, Mr Lendon relates his experience with helping abused servants escape from exploitative diplomatic employers.

First, he appeals to whatever remaining sense of decency they have, because he finds guilt often gets the best results. If that doesn't work, he and his staff might take the case to the ambassador or the State Department. If that effort is futile, they may take their case to the press. Sometimes, though, the uneducated labourer is too frightened and would rather drop the case rather than launch an all-out fight for his or her rights.

The following are only a handful of recent case histories from Mr Lendon's diplomatic abuse files. At the request of the agency, the names have been changed.

A nineteen-year-old girl we will call 'Guadalupe' was working for a diplomat's family from a South American country. The family had complete immunity. Guadalupe hadn't been paid for months. As is so often the case, she had to work all the time, with no time off. Guadalupe's passport had been confiscated to prevent her escape. Her unhappy complaints were met with threats of deportation. She called the Spanish Catholic Centre for help.

Mr Lendon went to the house to escort the girl away. The lady of the house was furious when she saw Mr Lendon because she knew it could mean only one thing. She knew he worked for the Catholic Centre and assumed he was a priest. The undiplomatic wife yelled at him in Spanish, 'So you are the well-known priest who butts into other people's business.' Then she threw the girl's clothing out onto the street and slammed the door.

When Mr Lendon approached the diplomat a short time later, he found him cooperative. A military attaché, he was embarrassed by the whole incident. The tables were turned. Now he was the one who was afraid – afraid the story of abuse would leak out into the diplomatic community or to the press. He knew he risked losing his appointment. Quickly, he returned the girl's passport and gave her some of her back pay.

The Centre secured Guadalupe another job with a good family.

Even though he encounters between twenty-five and thirty cases a year, Mr Lendon's clients are limited to those from Spanish-speaking countries living in Washington. The cases he sees are just those servants who found their way to him and were brave enough to seek help. It is hard to guess how many other cases of domestic slavery there are per year.

Mr Lendon, who has headed the Catholic Centre for eight years, continues:

> You have to remember there are two kinds of people with immunity employing foreign domestics. The first are the regular diplomats and embassies which have immunity. Then there are the employees of international organizations such as the World Bank or the Inter-American Bank who are also allowed to bring in a domestic if they want. But while they can be very harsh employers, these cases tend not to be as severe as the others because they have immunity only as it relates to their official duties and they are very well aware that they can be taken to court.

Esperanza worked for a Latin American family as a household maid. For a year and a half, Esperanza toiled eighteen hours a day, seven days a week with no free time for herself and no days off. She hardly had time to eat. She was strictly prohibited from leaving the house. The family paid her fifty dollars a week, when they paid her, which was very irregularly.

One day when the washing machine broke down, Esperanza was ordered to take the dirty clothes down the block to a friend of the family's house to do the wash. While she was waiting for the machines to finish their cycles, she took a walk, her first in eighteen months.

When she saw a Hispanic face walking towards her, she anxiously rattled off her troubles in Spanish. The sympathetic woman suggested Esperanza call the Spanish Catholic Centre. She gave her the telephone number and assured her whoever answered the phone would also speak Spanish.

The young domestic called at her first opportunity. With the organization's help she was able to flee her employers.

Because the head of the household worked for an international organization and did not have complete immunity, by using the threat of a lawsuit the Centre was able to recover her passport and her possessions and they succeeded in pressuring the employer into paying Esperanza some of her back wages.

The young domestic started her life in America over again, this time with a good family who respected her rights and paid her decent wages.

Ambassadorial residences are the most lavish and elegant homes many of these domestics have seen. The idea that they are to take up residence in one of these homes must seem like a fairy tale, even though they will probably end up in a much more ordinary house. They are told they will become a member of the family. When the manservant or maid is issued his or her diplomatic passport, with its fine paper, elegant writing and impressive seals, and a plane ticket to a foreign land, their happiness is complete.

What really happens in many of these situations comes as a terrible awakening. When workers from the Centre go on their rescue missions to a diplomat's home, they frequently bring a patrol car to sit outside in case there is trouble. The employers almost always get angry and scream that their servant is 'being taken away'. They feel unfairly persecuted and some become violent. The home of a member of the diplomatic corps is not inviolable, as is the embassy or the ambassador's residence, so police could assist if required.

A Peruvian domestic named Juana was working for an employee of the Inter-American Development Bank. Juana wanted to get a better job. The employers held her passport and wouldn't release it, an attempt to force Juana to stay with them. Eventually, it was the husband, the diplomat, who returned the passport. Typically, the diplomat's wife, who supervises the domestic and has the most to lose by her servant's departure, becomes the most abusive and vitriolic.

Mr Lendon also reports a pervasive attitude that a domestic is the God-given right of diplomatic status. In one case, he received a call from a woman who screamed at him for 'taking her servant away'. The woman told him she was now divorced from her diplomat husband, and she was paying the servant what she could afford in her reduced circumstances – which, of course was next to nothing. She said she really needed the housekeeper.

'How could you do this to me?' the woman wailed according to Lendon. 'How can you take my housekeeper?'

'Give me a break, lady,' Lendon says he replied. 'If you need a housekeeper, pay her a decent wage. There are actually some people in the United States who can't afford a housekeeper and do their own cleaning.'

But the diplomatic divorcee felt somehow it was her God-given right to have a servant and that it was Lendon's fault that the girl left. 'She thought I was a priest and repeatedly kept telling me how good a Catholic she was.'

Characteristically, these employers do not allow their servants to go to church, yet another deprivation for those of them who are Catholics. The diplomats know that at church their servants will meet concerned priests or others who know about minimum wage laws, kidnapping and false imprisonment, and who know of the services offered by the Centre. If the employers do allow their chattels to go to church, they warn them to stay away from the Spanish language chapels, insisting that they are run by Communists.

Occasionally, a diplomat will even deny he has the servant's passport. In this case, little can be done. If the alien tries to get a replacement, often the employer, who is well connected at the embassy, will block the passport re-issue.

Once a distraught maid came to the Centre after taking flight from a diplomatic family. She had been trying to get her passport back for a year. When the Centre interceded on her behalf, the housewife disavowed any knowledge of it. She repeatedly claimed the girl had lost it herself. Unfortunately, there was nothing the social worker could do. The embassy wouldn't re-issue it and the maid had no proof of citizenship.

In a sad reversal of the usual situation, there is the case of a young woman who was abandoned at the Centre with all her personal possessions. The woman, later discovered to be a domestic imported by a diplomatic family, was mentally incompetent. She was nearly catatonic and was unable to recall for whom she had worked or how she had got into the country.

Workers from the Centre took the girl to a mental health

facility for treatment. After considerable effort to determine where the girl had come from, social workers traced her to her former employers. Though it took some effort, they convinced the diplomat it was inhumane to bring someone into the country then simply desert her like an unwanted animal when she required medical attention. Eventually, the diplomat reluctantly furnished the severely disturbed woman with a ticket home.

Remedy for the injustice done to household workers is hard to come by, because receiving states place low priority on these cases. What is a critical problem for the domestic, who lives on the receiving end of this abuse, is less pressing to the bureaucrat who is supposed to be doing something about it. The person whose day to day existence may depend on back wages and whose future depends on reclamation of his or her passport has survival at stake. Bureaucrats have nothing at stake, so feel no discomfort if the problem is shuffled around via correspondence for months, and in some cases, years.

What follows is the anatomy of an exploitation case that got log-jammed in the sluggish bureaucratic papermill. Even with a social service organization lobbying for the woman's rights, her problem was not considered urgent enough for a prompt settlement. For two and a half years, the correspondence piled up between social agency, assorted bureaucrats, politicians and embassy employees without anything actually being done.

Concepcion G., a Bolivian national, came to the United States on June 8, 1979, as a housekeeper for Mrs A., a clerical worker at the Bolivian Embassy. For the first nine months of her employment, Concepcion received regular payment for her work. Then, the family stopped paying her. Concepcion continued to work, believing her wages would be forthcoming. Near the end of July, after not having been paid for three and a half months, Concepcion quit. Before Concepcion left Mrs A.'s employ, the cost of a round-trip ticket from Washington to La Paz had been deducted from her pay.

But Concepcion never received the ticket she'd paid for. Whenever she asked for it, her requests were shrugged off.

Before she left the house for good, Concepcion asked for a letter of recommendation so she could find another job. Mrs A. obliged, writing the recommendation in Spanish. 'To whom it may concern: I certify that Concepcion G. has been employed as a domestic for one year, having performed her work very well. This statement is sworn on my honour to be true.' The letter, which was headed 'Certificate of Employment', was signed by Mrs A. on July 30, 1980.

After Concepcion had left the household, she tried unsuccessfully to collect her back wages. Then she turned to a social service organization for assistance. The social service agency wrote and telephoned Mrs A., but the former employer refused to discuss the matter. After months of fruitless communications, the social worker tried another tactic. He took Concepcion's case to her congressman.

In a letter dated December 30, 1980, the social worker outlined the case to Congressman Michael Barnes and asked to be directed to the proper federal department to secure payment on Concepcion's behalf. The paper chase was on.

Mr Barnes was concerned and wrote to Attorney General William French Smith to find out the appropriate course of redress for Concepcion.

The Attorney General, the highest law enforcement official in the United States and head of the Department of Justice, replied that because the matter involved an embassy employee, the proper channels were through the Department of State.

By mid-March, the State Department's Assistant Secretary for Congressional Relations assured Congressman Barnes the matter would be taken up with the Bolivian Embassy.

The Protocol section of the State Department wrote to the Bolivian Embassy politely inquiring if Concepcion's case was valid. Mrs A. answered the State Department, alleging that Concepcion had never worked as a domestic for her. She took offence at the charge that she owed back wages and instead claimed that Concepcion owed her room and board for the time spent in her house.

By the beginning of June, Protocol section had referred the letter back to the Congressional Relations Department and Congressman Barnes learned of Mrs A.'s response.

The exchange of phone calls and letters continued at a snail's pace throughout 1981 and by the turn of the new year had ground to a complete halt. Nothing was any further than it had been when Concepcion left the household.

On May 24, 1982, Concepcion renewed her quest for the money she was owed. The agency felt a first person plea might be more effective, so they wrote the letter under Concepcion's signature. It recapped her story to the State Department. As supporting evidence, a photocopy of the 'Certificate of Employment' signed by Mrs A. was attached.

In August, the Department of State again made inquiries at the Bolivian Embassy. Time passed without response. Eventually, the State Department wrote directly to Ambassador Julio Sanjines Goitia, but the Ambassador replied that he had personally reviewed the case and dismissed the claim out of hand.

There remained, though, the sticky, unexplained matter of the signed 'Certificate of Employment'. The sceptical State Department even went so far as to compare the signature of Mrs A. on the document against her signature on their file documents; it matched.

Months passed without explanation by Embassy officials of the signed certificate. The Ambassador was reassigned elsewhere, replaced by a chargé d'affaires *ad interim*. Still, the State Department wanted an explanation of the certificate.

On January 11, 1983, Mrs A. wrote to the State Department reiterating her story. No mention of the 'Certificate of Employment' was made. Though various Embassy officials denied the existence of a 'Certificate of Employment', none of their denials were put in writing. In a letter dated January 31, 1983, the State Department again asked for clarification of this discrepancy.

For two and a half years, Concepcion's plight was the subject of innumerable phone conversations and sincere letters. The matter never was resolved. Concepcion never received her back wages nor the round-trip ticket to La Paz which had been deducted from her pay. The matter died of clogged bureaucratic arteries, but only because it wasn't considered important enough to resolve.

To these charges, the State Department responds that all the Vienna Convention permits them to do is expel the diplomat, which would have a deleterious effect on US relations with the country involved.

Octavio Lendon relates his own experience:

> We used to try to work through the State Department in these matters but we have stopped. You would be sent from one office to another and they were always polite, but nothing would ever happen. They really dislike getting involved in these kinds of cases, so we have stopped calling them except in the truly extraordinary case. We try to use our own resources and deal directly with the embassy involved.
>
> What really concerns me is that I don't see any movement on the part of the State Department to do anything about this problem. Civil rights and human rights are being violated every day. I think they could put a lot more pressure on diplomats stationed here to stop these abuses. They could simply say that if you want to bring an employee into this country, you are to pay them and treat them to the standards of this country. If you don't abide by certain rules we will deny you the right to bring an employee over. That might stop a lot of the problem and it could be done without changing in any way the concept of diplomatic immunity.

According to the Vienna Convention, diplomats are obliged to honour the laws of the receiving state. It's just that no one, including the State Department, pays much attention to that provision. While this obligation certainly includes minimum wage laws and minimum working conditions, efforts to put a stop to diplomats' domestic abuse are non-existent.

The problem of domestic slavery is encountered as regularly in other countries as in London and Washington. Similar reports have also come from Geneva and Paris. Bureaucratic indifference is equally common. As in the American cases, the cases which have come to light in Britain were only exposed when the servants involved could no longer stand their mistreatment and sought help. It is unusual that those who enslave their workers are brought to justice. Most servants who do escape never contact the authorities because they fear deportation. When the authorities are notified, they are rendered helpless by diplomatic immunity.

The countries who are members of the United Nations have already pledged to honour the UN Universal Declaration of Human Rights. Article 4 of the declaration, states: 'No one shall be held in slavery or servitude; slavery and the slave trade shall be prohibited in all their forms.' The Declaration also specifically mentions 'just and favourable conditions of work and pay . . . adequate health and well being . . . the right to rest and leisure . . . the right to participate in the cultural life of the community . . . and to enjoy the arts.'

The United Nations even sponsored a Supplementary Convention on the Abolition of Slavery, the Slave Trade and Institutions and Practices Similar to Slavery which included domestic slavery by name. All signatory states agreed to 'take all practicable and necessary legislative and other measures to bring about progressively and as soon as possible [their] complete abolition or abandonment'.

Domestic slavery is one instance where citizens must demand that moral considerations unequivocally transcend political considerations. Abraham Lincoln proclaimed, 'Those who deny freedom to others deserve it not for themselves.' Diplomats are no exception.

CHAPTER NINE

Daylight Robbery

THEFT, PRIMARILY SHOPLIFTING, represents a major category of crime for which diplomats claim immunity. According to official British Foreign Office statistics, in the ten-year period from 1974 to 1984, diplomats and their dependants claimed immunity 240 times to avoid prosecution on shoplifting charges.

According to the Foreign Office, it is by and large diplomatic dependants – wives and children – who commit these offences. During the period between 1981 and 1983, for instance, forty-two diplomatic wives were accused of shoplifting and claimed immunity. In 1984, there were sixteen cases of diplomatic shoplifting, and of this number, thirteen of the crimes were committed by diplomats' dependants.

The case of the wife of a Yugoslavian counsellor, is typical. The woman was stopped outside Liberty's for taking a girl's dress worth ten pounds without paying. She identified herself as having diplomatic immunity and she was released on the spot. Later it was revealed that the police and the Foreign Office thought the matter 'so minor' that neither the embassy nor her husband were ever notified.

In July, 1984, the seventeen-year-old son of an Algerian attaché, was caught coming out of Boots on Kensington High Street with six pendants worth seventeen pounds for which he had neglected to pay. When he was stopped by the store's security guards, his reaction was the same as most diplomatic dependants. He told one of the guards, 'I have immunity. You can't do anything to me.'

One case of shoplifting, the kind of case which the Foreign Office always calls 'minor', had major repercussions.

The Indian High Commissioner lives in one of the grandest ambassadorial residences in London, a two million pound mansion located in the shadow of Kensington Palace. In November, 1984, Prakash Mehrotra, a highly esteemed career diplomat, resigned his post and moved from his lavish surroundings after invoking immunity to keep his son from facing trial for theft.

Twenty-one-year-old Ravi Mehrotra was browsing in Dillon's, the bookshop next to London University. There, under the eyes of a store detective, the young man secreted fourteen pounds' worth of stationery and pens in his bag and left the store. When confronted on the street by the young, female detective, Mehrotra tried to flee. He was caught, however, and when police arrived he declared that he was the son of a diplomat, claimed immunity and demanded to be released. He was, and his father stood by him, insisting the charges be dropped because of his immunity. Like most countries, India maintains that immunity must always be demanded as a matter of principle.

Prakash Mehrotra, however, was a man of honour. Shortly after his son was released, he tendered his resignation and returned to India. In his resignation, he stated simply, 'People in public life should set high standards.'

In the United States, there is even less excuse for shoplifting by diplomats than there is in Britain. In the US, diplomats and their families are accorded a shopping privilege most would envy. They are issued cards which exempt them from paying sales tax, which is normally added to the bill when a sale is rung up. Presentation of the card at the cash register can save them up to nine percent sales tax on all merchandise. Yet despite this privilege denied ordinary citizens, diplomatic shoplifting is rampant.

In the US, the Eastern Bloc and Third World countries' representatives are the most frequent shoplifters. The plundering of top retail shops by Soviet diplomats and their dependants is so frequent that it borders on harassment. The State Department circulates regular memos on the subject to the Soviet Embassy.

In one incident in 1983, a police officer was in the security office of a large suburban Washington store. Staff detectives spotted a shoplifting incident in progress on the closed-circuit television monitors. An on-duty police officer happened to be in the security office and observed the Soviet shoplifter, 'Comrade X', take several items. Closed-circuit cameras in different positions recorded the thief at work as he progressed from department to department. In his clothing, he secreted two belts, a woman's swimsuit and a small vase. Then store security men moved in. As he was escorted to the security office, Comrade X struggled unsuccessfully to jettison the booty from his well-laden pockets.

At the office, when Comrade X identified himself as a foreign diplomat, the security officer called in the waiting policeman. After verification of his diplomatic status, Comrade X was released.

The call to the State Department for verification of status struck a familiar chord. This was not the first time Comrade X had been caught in the act. The State Department forwarded this memo to the Soviet Embassy:

> The Department of State considers the act of shoplifting unacceptable behaviour for a diplomat. The Department wishes to point out that this is only the latest in a long series of such incidents involving Soviet diplomats. It urges the Embassy of the USSR to take whatever steps are necessary to ensure that its diplomats desist from the reprehensible and illegal behaviour. The Department's patience in the face of such provocation is not inexhaustible. The Department of State wishes to inform the Embassy that it intends to observe closely the conduct of [Comrade X] and gives notice that should he engage in any further acts not in keeping with his diplomatic status, concrete steps will be taken.

Though the memos are regular, they have no perceptible effect. No 'concrete steps' seem ever to have been taken.

Wives of Soviet diplomats shoplift even more often than their husbands. Two weeks after the incident with Comrade

X, the wife of a Soviet diplomat was leaving a Saks Fifth Avenue store with a thirty-dollar pair of men's Bermuda shorts hidden under her jacket.

She was caught by the store's security guards and taken to the security office behind the scenes where these matters are 'straightened out' with minimum embarrassment to the offender.

Earlier, the Soviet woman had been observed secreting the price tag in her purse. When asked to take it out again, the woman did so and then promptly swallowed it.

The woman hadn't told her inquisitors that she was the wife of a diplomat, but while she was being questioned, the guards noticed a diplomatic ID in her now open handbag. It wasn't that they had such keen eyesight, just that they had seen diplomatic identification papers so many times before.

The woman was released when the store confirmed her immune status and the State Department sent the standard Soviet shoplifting memo to the Embassy. Dated May 3, 1983, it read, in part:

> The Department of State wishes to point out that this is yet another in a long series of unacceptable acts of shoplifting engaged in by Soviet diplomats and their dependants. It urges the Embassy of the USSR to take strong measures to ensure that its diplomatic personnel desist from such reprehensible and illegal behaviour. Provocative incidents of shoplifting not only exhaust the patience of the Department of State, but reflect poorly on the Soviet Embassy.

The letter resulted in an informal protest by the Soviets. Their response implied that the State Department had refused to meet with Soviet representatives who wanted to voice objections over the shoplifting memos. The State Department responded that the meeting had merely not been scheduled yet, but that the facts in the case were indisputable. Both cases were backed up with the store detectives' eyewitness accounts.

Soviet protests are as common as the shoplifting incidents themselves. Even when they are clearly in the wrong, the

Soviets like to work up a sense of indignation. In December, 1982, Yelena Tarasova, the wife of a Soviet diplomat assigned to the United Nations, was caught stealing a pair of children's tights in a Paramus, New Jersey, discount store. Since she had no diplomatic papers with her, Mrs Tarasova was detained in the store's security office for fifteen minutes while her immunity was verified by a local policeman. The action was both legal and standard operating procedure.

A few days later, angry Soviet diplomat Nikita Matkovsky demanded an apology for the detention from the Paramus Police Chief Joseph Delaney. Delaney stood his ground, insisting his officer was in the right.

'The Third Secretary to the USSR came out here and demanded an apology,' Delaney recalls. 'I told him we did everything right. We were professional, we were courteous, and that we certainly were not going to apologize. It lasted about 25 minutes and became very argumentative at one point. And I finally told him it would be a hot day in Siberia before I apologized for this department's actions, which I considered to be very professional. He still persists and at that point, I guess, being born and raised in New York City, I had had enough of him and I said, "Hey, you can go pound salt." '

The incident received wide media coverage and as a result, Delaney achieved folk-hero status for standing his ground under diplomatic pressure. Two hundred and fifty fan letters, hundreds of congratulatory calls, telegrams and citations, a ceramic eagle and thirteen pounds of salt arrived at the station. Delaney also got vociferous support from other police stations.

'The most interesting one was from the New York City Police Department that covers the UN area,' says Delaney. 'They called me and said, "Chief, we want you to hear what went on at morning roll call." And the guy holds the phone away and there's cheering and hooting and hollering. And he said, "You gave us the best Christmas present we could ever want," because they go crazy over there with all the problems with the diplomats.'

New York City police would never have been able to

handle a diplomat in that manner, no matter how much he was in the wrong. Delaney relates what New York's finest told him. 'He said they would probably have to apologize, which surprised me, frankly. But he said, in order to maintain their status in that area, they would have to apologize.'

As for the Russian, Delaney confesses he must have caught him off guard.

'I'm sure he thought he was coming here to talk to some Podunk police chief,' says Delaney, 'and because he represented the Soviet Union I would do a back flip.'

Delaney was an equal adversary though. The 47-year-old veteran undercover cop and former head of an organized crime strike force said, 'If you're a diplomat, our government says you have a right to speed, to steal, to be a public drunk and I guess to kill. If you're a diplomat, you can get away with it all. They might be able to get away with it but I sure as hell am not going to apologize to anyone for upholding the law. That's my job.'

Shoplifting diplomats come from all over the globe. Because of immunity none of them are answerable to the shops or the police.

In 1980, the wife of a Japanese diplomat took a shoplifting expedition to Bloomingdale's in Tysons Corner Centre in McLean, Virginia. A woman store detective watched the diplomatic wife slip a thirty-five dollar sweater in her handbag, zip it closed and leave the store. Outside, about forty feet from the door, two security personnel stopped her, unzipped the handbag and produced the sweater. But the Japanese woman insisted it was all a mistake, that she had merely wanted to look at the sweater in the sunlight. They invited the woman to accompany them to the store's security office.

Officer Brett Reistad of the Fairfax County Police Department was called to the store. The woman denied the allegation of shoplifting. She told the officer she had diplomatic immunity and couldn't be held. Then she called her husband who worked for the Ambassador of Japan. Officer Reistad called the State Department who verified her status. She was free to go.

The woman had been told by her husband to wait for him in the security office. When he arrived, the diplomat demanded he see the head of security to clear up 'the misunderstanding'.

Jo Ann Junk, the regional security manager, happened to be in the store that day so she conferred with the Japanese diplomat. He stated he had been married for fifteen years and his wife had never done anything like this before. He insisted not only that she had not done it, she was not capable of doing it. It was all a terrible mistake. The sweater had been lying over her arm, and it 'fell into her handbag'. Then he attempted to demonstrate how this had occurred. He took his wife's handbag and draped the sweater over his arm. He walked across the room and shook his arm to make the sweater fall into the bag. It fell on the floor. The demonstration had failed.

Officer Reistad informed the husband that his explanation was unbelievable.

Ms Junk asked the Japanese if his wife wanted to see the sunlight, why did she continue to walk down the sidewalk forty feet towards the parking lot? If it was an accident, why was her handbag zipped closed?

Because the State Department had verified her diplomatic immunity and therefore knew about the episode, the Japanese couple were invited in for 'a discussion'. The husband told Protocol Officers that the police and security people were lying. He denied his wife had taken the sweater. Though the State Department knew the security report was correct, they warned the wife not to return to Bloomingdale's again and dismissed the matter.

Diplomats and their wives are not the only ones entitled by diplomatic immunity to pillage the host country at will. The children of diplomats are sometimes even worse offenders.

In Washington, the son of a high-ranking Pakistani Embassy official was taken to juvenile court for car theft and larceny. He was charged with two counts of car theft and one count of petty larceny for shoplifting in a hardware store. The charges were dismissed after the youth's defence of immunity was entered.

Diplomats have been known to steal in many ways. But two of the most unusual cases on record involved the daughters of diplomats, one the daughter of a Thai diplomat stationed in London, and the second the daughter of a French diplomat stationed in Washington.

In the spring of 1983, Secret Service agents arrested the daughter of an administrative worker at the French Embassy in Washington for passing counterfeit currency. She signed a confession stating that she had bought $900 in fake currency then spent it in various shops around the area.

The young woman had lived in the country for seven and a half years and was engaged to marry an American citizen. Her mother had been reassigned and had returned to France on March 4. Although her arrest took place ten days after her mother left the country, the State Department decided that since the arrest occurred within a month of her mother's departure, she was still entitled to full immunity.

The French Embassy asked the State Department for a thirty-day 'grace period' so that it could investigate the matter. The State Department agreed it would take no action for thirty days. Then, without notifing US officials, she departed for France on the twenty-ninth day of the thirty-day grace period.

But that didn't end the matter. The young lady was still engaged and wanted to live in the US. But the government was not willing to forgive and forget. So a deal was struck.

In October, she returned to the United States. In exchange for making restitution to the stores she cheated, waiving her immunity and telling the Secret Service what she knew about the source of the phoney money, she was allowed to enter a plea of 'no-contest' to the charges in a Federal Court where she was given a suspended sentence and was allowed to remain in the US. Her wedding went off according to plan.

As well as the more direct forms of stealing, diplomats are often guilty of refusing to pay bills they have incurred and repudiating contracts, knowing that their immunity will allow them to get away with it.

No case better illustrates the use of diplomatic immunity to avoid obligations totally unrelated to a diplomatic function than the saga of the redecoration of one Saudi Arabian diplomat's luxurious London flat.

The diplomat, who has lived in Britain for thirteen years and reportedly has substantial private business interests, is officially listed as an assistant attaché at the Saudi Arabian Embassy. In late 1983, he wanted his £400 a week flat in the ultra-fashionable Water Gardens block of Bayswater completely refurbished, and so he hired the husband and wife professional interior design and decorating team of Georgina and Raouf Fahmy. It was to become a job the Fahmys would never forget.

The Fahmys believe the way to work is to completely understand a client's wishes before beginning. So they held a series of meetings to discuss the renovation with the diplomat and a woman identified as his girlfriend.

Georgina Fahmy remembers these conferences. 'From the start he asked for only the most expensive materials and methods. He asked for very, very high quality decorations to be put in the flat – wallpaper, tiling, bathroom suites. Everything had to be first class for him . . . We spent many nights together with him and his girlfriend deciding on which wallpaper to choose, which bathroom tiles to choose, until finally he was satisfied.'

Now that their client had decided on what he wanted the work could begin. Since he wanted only the best it was a very expensive job. But when it was finished, Mrs Fahmy says, 'he told us how happy he was with the job, how beautiful the flat was.'

But then came the matter of paying the bill. The Fahmys invoiced the diplomat for £3,877 and waited for the cheque to arrive in the post. They waited and waited but nothing happened. Each month they patiently rebilled him but no payment was ever received.

Finally and, as Mrs Fahmy says, 'very reluctantly' the Fahmys took the dispute to court. They brought suit in the

Westminister County Court asking the court to order the diplomat to pay his debt.

At first he maintained that he had already paid the bill, but he could offer no proof. Then he started to talk about damages that had been done during the renovation and started talking about a counterclaim against the Fahmys. Finally, though, his defence was simple. As put forward by his solicitor, he challenged the court's jurisdiction to hear the case. As a diplomat, he claimed, he was entitled to complete immunity from civil suit.

The judge reluctantly agreed. Citing the provisions of the 1964 Diplomatic Privileges Act he dismissed the case.

The Fahmys were naturally outraged. Not only were they left with almost £4,000 still owing to them, but they would have to pay their own legal expenses of more than £1,000 which they had also asked the court to award them. Mrs Fahmy said of the court's decision: 'Now he's got a lovely new flat and he has had to pay nothing. The decision means that anyone in his position can say "I'm a diplomat and I'm not paying." '

What does the Saudi diplomat think of the matter? He has generally refused to make any comment. But after the case was dismissed he was asked by a reporter if he didn't think he had taken advantage of his status. His brief and to the point reply was, 'I don't care about that.'

Trying to put the case in a favourable light, a Saudi Arabian spokesman said that the diplomat had wanted to file a counterclaim against the Fahmys and that the idea to question the court's jurisdiction on the basis of diplomatic immunity was completely the idea of his solicitor. The solicitor says her client 'has found this business most upsetting and very expensive. Pleading diplomatic immunity seemed to be the fastest and cleanest way to go about the case.'

What neither the solicitor nor the Saudis say is that under the law, based on the Vienna Convention, the filing of a counterclaim would have eliminated the defence of diplomatic immunity. Had the diplomat filed his counterclaim it would have been up to the judge to decide who was in the right. That would have been justice, apparently not something that either the solicitor or her client wanted.

What was the Foreign Office's position on the matter? As a spokesman put it, 'We have written to the Saudi Embassy asking them to look into the matter. But it is not for us to take sides.'

The problem of collecting debts from diplomats is so critical in the Washington retail community that many stores simply refuse to extend credit to diplomats. Other retailers report bad cheques have been a problem for them, so they make it a policy never to accept personal cheques from diplomats.

Milton Mitchell, a professor of diplomatic law at George Washington University, tells of one ambassador in arrears who didn't like to pay his bills. He kept a revolver in his desk drawer, says Mitchell, and when an impatient creditor came in to collect his money, he'd just hold up the revolver and yell, 'Get out!' Not surprisingly, they did.

Creditors' claims against diplomats are so commonplace that New York City's Commission for the United Nations and for the Consular Corps offers regular assistance to negotiate them. Alan Parker, while an attorney with the Commission, compiled a list of debts which totalled more than $500,000 for the period between March, 1974, and November, 1975. He himself recovered $225,000 in uncollected commercial debts. Parker said the bulk of the debts which remained outstanding belonged to six or seven missions which refused to cooperate with his efforts.

Jerome Glazer, President of Eastern Credit, a Washington collection agency, told of his experience in collecting past due personal debts. 'Most embassies, not all now, are not too cooperative. They just kind of slough you off, like just forget it. If the guy leaves for some country where you can't make any contacts, you've got a nice big closed file.'

Public embarrassment is sometimes the only way to recover on a diplomat's bad debt. One catering service with outstanding embassy bills running into the several thousand dollars mentioned the embassy by name to a newspaper reporter. The reporter included it in an article and a cheque for the full amount was mailed before the ink on the paper's next edition was dry.

One of the State Department's more obscure functions is their confidential and unofficial duty as a debt collection agency. When diplomats and missions don't pay their bills, creditors are forced to turn to the State Department as their only recourse.

In the classical model of State Department credit service, the diplomat will simply ignore the creditor's monthly billing. After several months pass and the bill is severely overdue, the creditor will telephone the diplomat or embassy. The diplomat usually tries the 'the cheque is in the post' gambit. The creditor then waits patiently for the money to turn up. When it doesn't, the diplomat becomes just another bad debtor for a collection agency to hound. Only this time, the collection agency is the Department of State and it's at the taxpayers' expense.

Instead of the usual collection agency notice, filled with thinly veiled threats of a ruined future and a bad credit rating every one will know about, the State Department takes a more gentlemanly approach. No threat of 'serious consequences' as in the usual collection letter appears, because both the diplomat and the State Department are fully aware of the protection provided by diplomatic immunity.

Here is a sample from the files of the US taxpayer-supported collection agency for diplomatic debtors:

A shopkeeper was owed a total of $303 by a Bolivian envoy from two transactions made in November of 1982. The shopkeeper sent monthly statements but they were ignored. Eventually, the salesman himself tried to collect, but to no avail. Then the retailer turned the account over to his usual collection agency.

The credit bureau received not so much as the favour of a reply. Finally, the agency succeeded in getting through to the Bolivian Ambassador. By then fifteen months had passed, and the Ambassador promised the store a cheque would be posted on the 23rd of the month. No cheque arrived, so the store turned to the State Department.

What the shopkeeper didn't know was the less than sterling record of the current crop of Bolivian diplomats. His bill was only one of several the State Department was pursuing that month. The other three accounts were all past due for more than three years.

A group of Bulgarian poets visited the United States in January, 1981, as part of a cultural exchange programme. The American Academy of Poets in New York City hosted a reception in their honour. Discussion of sprung rhythm and dactylic metre flowed freely as the photographer hired by an official of the Bulgarian mission to the United Nations recorded the exchange. Later, the Bulgarian official ordered six prints from the photographer.

The photographer forwarded the prints along with an invoice for sixty-two dollars. By May, the photographer hadn't received the remittance, so he forwarded a photocopy of the invoice. A third and fourth invoice followed fruitlessly during the ensuing months.

The only thing the photographer received from the official in the year since taking the photos was a Christmas card. In January, 1982, the frustrated photographer sent yet another statement. He contacted the State Department because he was starting to doubt he would ever see his money. The State Department collection team took over the case, and the photographer finally collected – sixteen months after the Bulgarian poets had taken their final bows.

Although Iraq had no embassy in the United States, they had an Iraqi Interest Section as part of the Embassy of India. The Iraqis booked rooms for several visitors at a Washington hotel, but when the guests left in November, 1980, they failed to pay the bill. After invoicing the Iraqi Interest regularly to no productive end, the hotel turned to the State Department. When requesting State Department help, the hotel expressed the feelings of most of those taken advantage of by diplomatic parasites. 'Any assistance or advice you can offer,' they said, 'is greatly appreciated as I am at a loss and have exhausted all other means.'

The Iraqis were not such great credit risks either, as it turned out. The State Department was trying to collect on two other debts they hadn't honoured. Eventually, the State Department's 'collection agency' was successful in recovering the money owed.

A Turkish diplomat ran up a bill of $403 in mid–1981. Every month for the next nine months, the supplier sent a polite invoice, restating the past-due amount. Nothing was forthcoming, not even an explanation.

Finally, when the State Department stepped in, the embassy came up with a cheque which they forwarded to the supplier. The company deposited it the same day. Two weeks later it was returned for non-sufficient funds. The company redeposited it, but it bounced again. The company tried to contact the Ambassador but couldn't get through. Finally, in September, 1982, they decided the State Department should handle it.

'Frankly,' the company wrote to the State Department, 'we feel that we have been more than patient and very understanding. We now feel that there is no excuse for this type of behaviour from a man of his position.'

With the help of the State Department's unofficial collection bureau, the company recovered the debt. The process took nearly two years.

Not all of the State Department's collection duties are for these relatively small amounts.

In 1980, the press attaché at the Embassy of Bolivia called at the Washington Hospital Centre with a $10,000 cheque as a deposit towards the treatment of two women severely burned in a Bolivian fire. The envoy arranged for the hospital stay and doctors and told the payment office there was no problem about the bills being paid. The government commandeered a plane and flew the women to the Hospital Centre for treatment.

Upon successful treatment, the recovering patients were released and returned to La Paz. Their treatment left them with a medical bill for $82,408.

Once the life and death crisis had passed, the hospital couldn't get the Embassy to pay the bill. They ended up appealing to the State Department collection agency.

After the Embassy received a letter from the Protocol section, the Bolivians promised that their Ministry of Foreign Affairs would be responsible for the bills incurred. Since the country was having financial problems, they requested a convenient payment plan. Like any good credit bureau, the Protocol staff arranged it.

A similar occurrence involved the Embassy of Turkey. Members of the Turkish Armed Services were brought to American hospitals for treatment of serious illnesses. The Office of the Defence Attaché of the Turkish Embassy made the arrangements and promised responsibility for all medical bills. For one group, nine Turkish patients accumulated unpaid bills totalling $2,217. For another group, the uncollected balance due was $6,243.

In a third case, the outstanding bills were an inch thick and came to $104,406. The patients had various operations, dialysis, transfusions, radiology, and nearly every test known to medical science. After State Department negotiation, the hospital received a first payment of $55,000 and arranged for the $49,450 balance to be paid in easy monthly instalments.

The case of the Frenchwoman and the shipping line illustrates the stubborn denial of responsibility and the reliance on privilege that usually crops up in these affairs.

Foreign diplomats and consular personnel assigned to the United States generally have the privilege of importation of personal and household goods free of customs duties and taxes. To receive this exemption, the foreign emissary has only to fill in a one-page form stating where and when the goods will be arriving. In the case of the Frenchwoman, the State Department spent nine months in pointless negotiation over a few pennies because of her dogmatic insistence on privilege.

A container of household effects weighing 7,716 pounds was shipped via the Steamship Pulanski from Le Havre to Baltimore, due to arrive June 15, 1982. The French Embassy employee submitted her 'Customs Clearance of Merchandise Intended for Foreign Personnel Entitled to Special Privileges and Exemptions' to the State Department for processing on June 15, the same day the ship was due in port. Diplomats are requested to allow two weeks for processing. Even though the completed form was late, the State Department expedited clearance through the necessary departments and sent the approved exemption to the Baltimore customs agent on the 24th.

Since the ship docked on the 15th and cleared customs on the 18th, the unclaimed container was put in storage on the 23rd, a day before the form had cleared. For the first period of demurrage, the charges were $7.70 per day for five days; a grand total of $38.50.

The container was delivered COD to the woman in Washington after her customs agent received the authorized form from the State Department. The woman refused to pay the $38.50, preferring instead that her container of household goods return to the warehouse. She insisted her diplomatic status would exempt her from all storage charges. As the weeks wore on, and her complaints continued, storage charges mounted up.

By August 31, the charges were up to $256.80, but the woman still insisted that she didn't have to pay them. When the shipping company threatened to auction off the contents of the container to recoup their storage costs, she reminded them that because of the Vienna Convention, the container was inviolable. They were prohibited from opening it.

The fight continued into December. The woman hadn't seen her belongings since they were removed from her Paris apartment in the spring. Finally, in January the State Department told her that the charges were legitimate and were a direct result of her not having informed the customs clearance department in sufficient time. She had to pay the charges.

Commercial and residential leases are broken with impunity by diplomats, as anyone knows who has had the misfortune to rent property to one. Diplomatic immunity, in this popular abuse, becomes a simple device for abrogating contractual commitments.

Mario Perez Balladares, Consul-General of the Republic of Panama, signed a five-year lease for his consular headquarters in a commercial building on South-East Second Avenue, Miami. According to the terms of the lease, the rental fee was $36,372, payable in monthly instalments of $3,031. The lease for the office suite began on June 1, 1979, and was due to expire on May 31, 1984.

In July, 1981, with the lease not yet half over, the Consul-General wrote to the landlord. 'We're sorry,' he said, 'but as of August 1, 1981, we are forced to leave our office.' That was three weeks away. 'Therefore,' the letter continued, 'accept our apologies for all the inconveniences this change may cause you . . . Kindly consider our contract with you cancelled as of July 31, 1981. On behalf of our Government . . . we take the opportunity to express the assurances of our high esteem and consideration.'

But you can't take 'high esteem' to the bank when the mortgage payment is due and 'consideration' is meaningless when you have three weeks to find a new tenant for a large office suite.

Normally, a landlord in these straits would use the Florida Statutory Landlord's Lien to prevent the tenant from removing the furniture and equipment from his offices. The aggrieved landlord would also sue the tenant for the balance of the rent reserved under the lease. Unfortunately, the Miami landlord had no such recourse because of Panama's immunity.

Bruce Gussman, the building manager, observes, 'For the Panamanians to just simply up and leave really killed us. Because they had diplomatic immunity, there was nothing we could do. I've got more than ten consulates in this building today. They all have leases that are worthless . . . but I hope they don't know that.'

'This taught me a lesson,' Mr Gussman says. 'The only way I would rent to another large consulate would be if I got paid a year's security deposit.'

When a landlord who has been faced with the problems of diplomatic tenants tries to avoid further vexation, a solution may not be so easy to find. A suburban Virginia property company, The Dittmar Corporation, owned over 1,600 residential rental units. So many diplomats broke leases and left the apartments badly damaged that the company's managers refused to lease the units to diplomats from certain countries. Dittmar's revised policy, in effect from 1970 to 1975, was challenged in court when the Justice Department filed a discrimination suit and forced them to resume renting to all diplomats.

Even when diplomat's don't walk away from their signed leases, they may leave behind thousands of dollars' worth of property damage which the landlord must repair at his own expense.

In New York City, a professor and his wife rented their home to a Guatemalan representative to the United Nations during their sabbatical year abroad. When they returned home, they discovered damage to their home amounting to $14,683. Thinking they could collect for the repairs, the couple contacted the Guatemalan Mission. The Guatemalans offered them a $900 settlement. The professor and his wife felt insulted by the offer, so rejected it. Because of diplomatic immunity, they recovered nothing whatsoever and bore the cost of restoring their home to its prior condition themselves.

At the Bulgarian Embassy and Chancery at 2100 Sixteenth Street in Washington, the tenants removed items worth $4,350 when they vacated the premises. They could hardly have mistaken the items for their own – their plundering included antique wall sconces, door handles, light fixtures and light switches. Besides the theft, repairing and painting the damaged walls, windows and doorways cost $18,700.

Another residential property owner had a signed lease in 1981 with the Iraqi Interests Section of the Embassy of India. Unit number 455, a three-bedroom, two-bath apartment renting for $1,250 per month, came equipped with all the amenities – washing machine, dryer, dishwasher, central air conditioning and a parking space.

The landlord was not notified until the Embassy sent the October rent that the tenant had left the country in September and the apartment was vacant.

Reclaiming the apartment key from the Embassy, the landlord went to survey the apartment's condition. The estimate to repair the damage and return the flat to habitable condition was $11,747. Besides that, it couldn't be rented for the months of November and December because so much work needed to be done. The landlord tried to collect the money from the Iraqi Interests Section but got nowhere. The State Department had to step in and negotiate a settlement. After four months of negotiation, the State Department got the Embassy to pay a $7,750 settlement and the landlord applied the $1,250 damage deposit to the renovation.

José X, his wife and their four children rented a house in a suburb of New York City while José was stationed as a first secretary to the Mexican Mission at the United Nations. The family paid $1,350 per month for the eight-room house where they lived for nearly a year. In June, 1983, the Mexicans decided to move, so they didn't pay their rent.

The family removed three $200 full-length mirrors from the walls. The mirrors were being loaded into the removals van when the home owner arrived. Landlord Harcharan Skiand knew the mirrors were his, so he was able to stop the theft, but after his tenants left, he found almost two and a half thousand dollars' worth of damage to the house. Skiand tried to sue his tenant for the months' rent and the damage, but José invoked immunity and thus avoided having to make any reparation to Mr Skiand, a former diplomat himself.

Mrs Failey Smith, widow of the former head of the Presidential Press Corps, Merriman Smith, leased a home to an attaché of the French Embassy. When that family departed she found the damage they had left behind would cost $11,000 to repair. Since this was before the law changed in 1978, the State Department cautioned Mrs Smith's lawyer against bringing suit because initiating a civil action was a punishable offence.

'They warned me against harassment which might be construed as a violation of statute,' said Attorney Joseph Moran.

Mrs Smith placed a newspaper ad asking those who had had trouble with diplomats to call her. She received seventy-nine calls in a single day!

During the three years between 1977 and 1979, claims for damages totalling $750,000 were made against foreign diplomats, according to State Department figures.

Diplomatic financial irresponsibility can also extend into the contract area. Here, too, the State Department takes on an unofficial role as contract negotiator, not always successfully.

In one case, a company had a $20,000 signed contract with the French Embassy. The company, though, couldn't get the French Embassy to honour it, even though it was fully executed by the Embassy's staff attorney.

The corporation didn't know where to turn for help, so they engaged the services of a consultant who thought he could pull the right strings to reinstate the contract.

The consultant was a retired American diplomat of thirty-three years service. He wrote to the French Ambassador and told him he had spent seven years at the American Embassy in Paris. Along the way, he mentioned that two of his 'very good friends' were President François Mitterand and the Minister of National Defence, Charles Hernu. His spectacular name-dropping proved ineffective in bill collecting. The consultant was forced to involve the collections experts in the Protocol Office.

In the end, though, even the State Department's efforts were in vain. France's immunity made the contract unenforceable.

A Maryland couple, Mr and Mrs Simon Eilenberg, planned to buy a home from a Brazilian couple.

After some six months of searching for the right house in their neighbourhood, the Eilenbergs felt they had finally found it at 4909 Sangamore Road, Bethesda. On April 24, 1977, the Eilenbergs entered into a contract with the couple to purchase the house. The Sangamore Road property was not the couple's residence, but one they had purchased as an investment. A purchase price of $140,000 was agreed upon in a written offer and counter-offer. The contract was secured with a $10,000 escrow payment by Mr and Mrs Eilenberg and was fully executed by both couples. Since their own house was currently in negotiation, they were especially anxious for the deal to go through.

Out of the blue, the couple telephoned the Eilenbergs to renege on the contract. On May 7, after the $10,000 had been deposited in the escrow fund, the couple notified the Eilenbergs by telegram that they were cancelling the contract. If the Eilenbergs had simply walked away from the signed contract, it would have cost them the $10,000 escrow payment.

The wife was employed by the Brazilian Embassy as an economic attaché. Her husband's explanation for the cancellation was that since his wife was a diplomat, she 'cannot be compelled to do anything'.

This was certainly an abuse of diplomatic immunity. Article 31 of the Vienna Convention explicitly states two conditions which were met in this case where immunity would not protect the diplomat.

Article 31 of the Vienna Convention makes it clear that a diplomatic agent cannot enjoy immunity from the receiving state's civil laws in the case of 'private immovable property situated in the territory of the receiving State, unless he holds it on behalf of the sending state for the purposes of the mission.'

Nor is immunity applicable in the case of 'an action relating to any professional or commercial activity exercised by the diplomatic agent in the receiving State outside his official functions.' The Sangamore Road house was not the couple's residence, and since they were selling it at a profit of $50,000, the sale would certainly be described as commercial activity. Still, once the couple had made clear their intention to plead immunity should a suit arise, and since suing a diplomat was still not possible under the law, there was nothing the Eilenbergs could do.

The Eilenbergs did get their escrow funds back eventually, but they were not compensated for their time, their legal fees, nor for their inconvenience. They had to take their own home out of negotiation and start the search for a suitable house anew.

CHAPTER TEN

A Free Ride

In Britain, causing death by reckless driving is a crime normally punished by at least two years in prison. In the last decade, at least three British citizens have died at the hands of diplomatic motorists who completely escaped prosecution.

Forty-three-year-old Sally Kertesz of Langley, Hertfordshire, the mother of two, lost her life to an irresponsible driver protected by diplomatic immunity. In October, 1979, she was killed by a twenty-year-old porter from the Embassy of Finland.

At the junction of Chelsea Bridge Road and Royal Hospital Road, the Finn drove his high-performance BMW through a red light. He smashed into Mrs Kertesz's Toyota and another car. It was more than three hours before the young man arrived at the local police station to be given a blood alcohol test. But even that long after the accident, the reading was 151 milligrams. The legal limit for alcohol in the blood stream is sixty-five. Even three hours after the accident, he was still very drunk.

The young employee of the Finnish Embassy had been on private business. Despite his low status at the Embassy – which might have meant he was entitled to only limited immunity for official duties – he was still granted full immunity and walked out of the police station a free man.

A Finnish Embassy spokesman said of the incident, 'We are sorry that the accident occurred and this woman died. But it was simply an accident and nothing more.' Asked whether there was any question of waiving immunity, the spokesman seemed all but stunned by the idea. 'Dear me, no,' he was reported to have answered. 'This is what immunity is for.' Asked if the man would be sent back to Finland, the spokesman said that he would be rotated back sooner or later, but his transfer would have nothing to do with the accident. 'It is a closed matter,' said the spokesman.

Many reckless driving incidents involving diplomats are attributable to intoxication. For the ten-year period between 1974 and 1984, there were 228 cases of diplomats taken to police stations for driving under the influence of alcohol or drugs. The number who are stopped but not taken in is unknown.

A chauffeur at the Ghana High Commission was arrested twice for drunken driving during 1977, but was never charged. He was released to go drinking and driving again. An envoy of the Zambian High Commission in Kensington was arrested for drunken driving in Earl's Court Road. Officials of the Iraqi, Thai, North Yemeni and French Embassies were also arrested for similar offences in Kensington, where many embassies and high commissions are located. They all escaped prosecution by invoking diplomatic immunity. They all could have taken lives or caused serious injury.

In 1977 alone, 33 diplomats were arrested for drunken driving in Britain. All were released after asserting their immunity. Police reported that it was a miracle that no one had been killed as a result. Many of the drivers had been pursued in high-speed chases and hadn't stopped until their cars smashed into other vehicles. Scotland Yard also pointed out that the number could actually have been higher because it did not include high-ranking dignitaries or ambassadors who were not bothered with a trip to the station.

In a 1980 BBC interview, Sir Anthony Kershaw, Chairman of the Foreign Affairs Committee, pointed out, 'Immunity is immunity, and it depends upon people being civilized and claiming only the immunity that is necessary to them, and not behaving in the barbaric way that has become fashionable in certain parts of the world recently.'

But too many diplomats can't be counted on to be civilized. A representative of the Libyan government had a traffic accident in the Kensington area. As a police officer was taking him in, the Libyan assaulted the officer. Shortly afterwards, the Libyan walked free on diplomatic immunity.

In August, 1980, Nicola, 28-year-old daughter of MP Clement Freud, was driving her small white Renault down St John's Wood Road. In the car with her was her young son, Jack, and her brother, Matthew, aged sixteen. As the car reached the junction of St John's Wood Road and Maida Vale, it was struck sharply from the side by a large car containing four men. The small Renault was thrown a considerable distance and its passengers only narrowly escaped serious injury. The Renault was badly damaged.

There was no question that the car containing the four men was at fault. It should have given way at the junction, but it never even slowed down. Nicola remembers, 'I was sitting in my car still dazed when a man from the other car ran up. He was extremely apologetic and said that the driver of his car had suffered a heart attack, which of course, made me very concerned. But later, when the police arrived, I saw the driver sitting and smoking a cigarette and talking to the police. It was then that I first noticed that the car had CD plates.'

In fact, the car was driven by a cultural attaché at the Saudi Arabian Embassy. Police later told Clement Freud that had the man not claimed diplomatic immunity, he would have faced several serious traffic charges.

Riding a motorbike leaves you wide open to injury – especially when there are uninsured and irresponsible foreign emissaries driving in the same city. Charlotte Owen, a 23-year-old Londoner, was driving her motorbike west on Marylebone Road in January, 1984. Her boyfriend was riding behind her on the bike as they approached the corner of Park Crescent. The light turned green and Charlotte proceeded into the junction. A green Mercedes, approaching the junction from the south, came up against a red light, but the driver drove straight through it. The Mercedes smashed into the two young people on the motorbike and then continued on its way. Charlotte was thrown into the air and across the road. She landed with a broken leg, but the envoy never even stopped to see if she and her boyfriend were alive.

'Just as I passed the light,' Charlotte recollects, 'I noticed the car coming from my left-hand side and it seemed to me going very fast. It hit me right on, and I was knocked off my bike, flung over to the other side of the road. Luckily, I had just bought a new helmet because I landed on my head. And as I was lying on the road, I heard someone saying that the man who knocked me off was running away and that a taxi driver was chasing him.'

The cabbie chasing the hit and run driver lost sight of the car as it sped through Regent's Park. Charlotte was taken to hospital where her leg was set in a cast and she was treated for her other injuries. Besides her broken leg, the accident also had serious financial repercussions.

'Because of the accident,' she says, 'I lost a very good job that I was going to in New York with a photographer. I had been waiting a long time for the job, and because I was in plaster for two months with my broken leg and going to hospital every day, I wasn't able to go. I have still got scars on my legs that will never fade as far as I know, and my boyfriend as well suffered very bad scarring.'

As for her motorbike, Charlotte hasn't set eyes on it since the accident.

The hit and run driver was an attaché at the Kenyan High Commission. The day after the collision, he went to the Marylebone Police Station and admitted what he had done. When he gave police his statement, he also exercised his diplomatic immunity.

'The only time I heard from anyone connected with the Kenyan Embassy,' Charlotte relates, 'was about two days after the accident when I was still in hospital. I received a hand-delivered get well card that was signed "With respects from the Government of Kenya." '

For over a year, Charlotte, her mother, Margaret, and her lawyer tried to get compensation from the Kenyan government or from the Kenyans' insurance company, but they were unsuccessful. In the end, though, Charlotte did receive some compensation for her injuries and her lost wages. 'I finally received a payment after I had appeared on a television broadcast and told my story. But they were very careful to say that the payment was voluntary.'

The man has long since returned to Kenya.

Though even the Royal Family can be held responsible for traffic infractions, foreign emissaries are not. Even though a 1955 study showed that diplomats were involved in minor traffic offences such as speeding twice as often as normal British drivers, they can't be held responsible.

Mark Hampton, a partner in a successful fashion design house in London's West End, was driving along New Bond Street in early 1984. Police were trying to ease the morning rush hour congestion. Mark was waiting for the policeman's signal to proceed through a junction when a black saloon rear-ended him, sending his car smashing into a lamppost. The saloon was going at about fifteen to twenty miles per hour. As he was totally at a standstill, the force of the impact severely damaged both the front and rear ends of his car.

Mark recalls the accident, 'I got out of the car and the police came over. The driver was the wife of a diplomat from Nigeria in a big, black Saab with the diplomatic plates and everything. The police took me to the side and said, "We saw what happened. We'll make out a report, please go ahead with your insurance claim." '

The police gave Mark their names and stations and said they were willing to be witnesses if he needed them for his insurance claim.

At the time of the accident, a policeman told Mark, 'Go after them, but I wish you luck.' He didn't realize the significance of the remark until much later.

'I put in the report to the insurance company,' Mark continues, 'and the insurance company went back to the Embassy. It went backwards and forwards and in the end a year went by and nothing had happened. In the meantime, I had to have my car repaired and I lost my no-claims bonus. It cost me a thousand pounds cash in excess of my insurance policy. In the end it worked out that there was nothing they could do about it.'

The diplomat's wife never offered to pay the damages and by the end of the year the Nigerian couple had returned home.

'The thing was,' Mark says 'the reason why she smashed into the back of my car was because she was looking in a shop window. She admitted to it, apologized and everything. It was nice that she was sorry, but that doesn't pay the bills.'

The British insurance laws are quite simple. All drivers are required to carry unlimited liability policies. According to a spokesman for the consular section of the Foreign Office, this applies to all diplomatic drivers as well. The spokesman also stated that since the 1930s, the major car insurance companies have agreed that if their insured party is a diplomat, they will not plead his immunity or use any plea he himself enters for immunity from possible criminal charges to affect their potential liability.

The system is not without flaws. Any number of different district authorities issue CD plates and not all are as careful as they should be to determine that a diplomat in fact has insurance before issuing the plate. Diplomats in Britain are not required, as they are in the United States, to carry non-cancellation clauses in their insurance and to pay a full year's premium in advance. There is nothing to prevent a diplomat from taking out insurance in order to secure the CD plate, and then immediately cancel it. Further, there is no list of approved insurance companies from which diplomats must buy their insurance, as there is in the US. Therefore, it is possible for them to buy insurance from a smaller company that is not a signatory to the agreement.

'We are working on all these problems,' the spokesman said. 'In the meantime, we have let all missions know that we will take a very dim view of any diplomat becoming involved in an accident not having insurance or trying to use his immunity to avoid liability. Recently, we expelled an African diplomat in just that situation. It came to our attention that he had a minor accident and did not have insurance. He paid for the damage, so we only issued a warning. A few months later, he had a second accident, again very minor, but again he had not taken out insurance. We ordered him expelled.'

For nearly twenty years, EEC countries have required that diplomats produce a 'green card', proof that the car is insured, before it is allowed to enter the country.

Most Western European countries are signatories to the European Convention on Compulsory Insurance Against Civil Liability in Respect to Motor Vehicles. If, for example, a diplomat causes a car accident in Germany and injures a pedestrian, the court proceeds directly against the insurance company. The diplomat cannot be named as a liable party in the suit.

The United States sought to end once and for all the problem of uninsured diplomatic drivers when it passed the Diplomatic Relations Act of 1978. Under Section 6 of the Act, diplomats are required to have liability insurance in order to operate a motor vehicle, boat or airplane in the US, and the insurance company is forbidden from raising a defence of diplomatic immunity even if the policy holder has such immunity.

Despite the seemingly more favourable legislation, many US citizens have come out the losers after being involved in traffic accidents with diplomats. No case has been as tragic as that of Dr Halla Brown.

Saturday, April 20, 1974, was a clear, bright morning in Washington DC. Dr Rosenbaum and Dr Brown had to get up early most Saturdays to get to work, but they were used to the routine. Dr Halla Brown was a professor of medicine and chief of the allergy clinic at George Washington University. Many of her patients could only come on Saturdays, and she was happy to oblige them. At sixty-two, she was vital, energetic and active.

Dr Rosenbaum would drop his wife off at the hospital on Saturdays before going on to work himself. They left the house and were on their way before 7.30. Since there was never any traffic, the ride was always more pleasant on Saturdays.

Alberto Watson-Fabrega also got into his car about 7.30

that April morning. The thirty-year-old cultural attaché was posted to the Panamanian Embassy on McGill Terrace and 29th Street.

The two doctors headed south on 34th Street towards Massachusetts Avenue, near Washington National Cathedral. Arthur Rosenbaum approached the light at the corner of 34th Street and Garfield Avenue, about two and a half miles north of George Washington University Hospital. On the 34th Street side, it was green.

Alberto Watson-Fabrega drove west on Garfield Avenue about half a mile from the Panamanian Embassy. He sped towards the traffic light at the corner of 34th Street. On the Garfield Avenue side, it was red.

The Rosenbaum car entered the intersection. Ignoring the light, Watson-Fabrega's Toyota charged through the red light and into the intersection. The Panamian's car rammed head-on into the side of the doctors' car, colliding with a thundering impact. The folding metal, skidding rubber and flying glass made a frightening sound. The Rosenbaum car was sent skidding wildly across the intersection, finally hitting a tree with a sickening crash.

Two passersby stood on the sidewalk cringing, watching the collision helplessly. The victims barely stirred.

A police siren wailed as it approached. Officer Russell Jackson arrived and called ambulances. The trio of injured were rushed to George Washington University Hospital. Complaint Number 192348, filed by Jackson, stated that Alberto Watson-Fabrega entered the intersection against the red light and was at fault. The two witnesses verified the facts and gave their statements to the officer.

Dr Rosenbaum and the diplomat were released from the hospital within days and suffered no permanent damage. Dr Halla Brown wasn't as fortunate. In the space of a few seconds, Alberto Watson-Fabrega had completely altered her life.

Admitted to the hospital where she had practised with dislocation of the cervical spine between the fourth and fifth vertebrae, Dr Brown was now paralysed with quadraplegia;

she could not move her body at all from the neck down. She has not, nor will she ever, recover her mobility.

During her hospitalization, Halla Brown suffered one traumatic complication after another. Respiratory difficulties resulted in an emergency tracheotomy. She suffered pulmonary disorders, seizures and loss of bowel functions. The nerve endings in the skin from her left shoulder to her elbow were damaged so that the slightest touch of fabric caused her extreme pain. Her blood pressure sometimes dropped to zero. The radical blood pressure fluctuations created a constant crisis situation.

Since Alberto Watson-Fabrega had diplomatic immunity, he was free from charges and from a compensatory lawsuit. He had no car liability insurance. He offered no restitution, showed no remorse.

Halla Brown was in intensive care from April 20 until July 9. She remained in the hospital until November 11, when she was transferred to the Institute of Rehabilitation Medicine, New York City. Her medical bills were staggering and she soon exhausted the limits of liability on her own insurance coverage.

Pleas for some form of financial restitution were made to the Panamanian Embassy. Informal requests were made by the Protocol section of the State Department. Months passed. When the couple finally heard from the Embassy, it was bad news. A letter from the Embassy lawyer, sent eight months after the accident occurred, read: 'The Ambassador authorized me to inform you that he does not intend to make an offer of indemnification.'

After destroying Halla Brown's ability to move, the diplomat turned his back and walked away with the support of his Ambassador.

On November 20, 1975, a year and a half after the accident, Dr Brown was released from the Rehabilitation Institute to her new apartment. Dr Rosenbaum had been forced to sell their home and rent a specially equipped apartment which could serve their new and complex medical requirements.

Halla Brown can read books held by a special book-rest as she lies in bed unable to care for herself. More than ten years have passed since the horrible accident that took everything but her life and her mind. She holds a rubber-tipped stick between her teeth so she can turn the pages herself.

Round-the-clock nurses sometimes shift her to a wheelchair and strap her in so she doesn't fall out. They wrap her body in elastic bandages from her feet to her ribcage to compensate for her poor circulation. They change her body position every two hours to prevent bedsores. They monitor her blood pressure constantly and are always ready to take the necessary measures when it drops suddenly.

As a professional courtesy, many of her doctors did not charge Dr Brown for their services. Nonetheless, her medical bills exceeded $250,000 during just the initial period of her hospitalization. Her loss of income averaged about $50,000 a year, but no amount of money could begin to repay the loss of a productive, happy life.

The couple's attorney, Arthur Feld, summed up the tragic moral of the whole terrible incident: 'There's a big difference between law and justice.'

Watson-Fabrega left Washington for another world capital before Halla Brown left the hospital. After wrecking the lives of Dr Rosenbaum and Dr Brown, he disowned responsibility for his actions. No one could stop him because he had diplomatic immunity.

In 1977, Congress began hearings to reform the outdated 1790 law which guaranteed blanket immunity for every diplomatic employee from the janitor to the ambassador. Halla Brown's plight dramatically illustrated a specific area of abuse that required immediate attention – diplomats' disregard for traffic regulations. The result was the 1978 Diplomatic Relations Act which, among other provisions, requires diplomats stationed in America to carry liability insurance for their moving vehicles.

Dr Brown's case was just one of several serious accidents caused by uninsured diplomats who did not compensate their victims. Twenty-year-old Floyd Dickerson was a passenger in a collision caused by an assistant naval attaché at Washington's Soviet Embassy in mid-July, 1974. The young car mechanic suffered residual pain and a permanent back injury. Though the diplomat was insured by The American Insurance Company, they claimed their client had immunity, so offered no compensation to the young victim. The Embassy offered no compensation either. The diplomat returned to the USSR in December, 1976. The mechanic remains disabled.

Diplomats behind the wheel have been a headache for American motorists practically since the invention of the automobile. During Prohibition, in the late 1920s, a measure was introduced in Congress to provide the President with the power to demand the recall of any diplomat who operated a motor vehicle while under the influence of alcohol. In 1930, Senator Kenneth McKeller introduced a bill to revoke diplomats' immunity when they violated traffic laws. Unfortunately, neither bill was passed. If they had been, perhaps the problem might not have escalated to its present level.

A *Washington Post* editorial of February 17, 1977, conveyed the city's sentiments well: 'Here in the land of foreign dignitaries, the native motorist learns at an early age to be on the alert for the dreaded DPL tag – which is a license to commit all sorts of illegal acts without the risk of arrest or prosecution.'

Washington Police Chief Maurice Turner kept a file on driving cases involving foreign envoys in 1982 and 1983. The file held nine car accidents and drunk driving cases over the two years just within the confines of the federal district itself, an area of only sixty-nine square miles.

On New Year's Eve, 1982, a Colombian, a receptionist at their Washington Embassy, was stopped for reckless driving in Virginia. She was going at seventy-eight miles per hour in a fifty-five mile per hour zone. This is a misdemeanour, for which a citizen could receive a fine of up to $1,000 and one year's imprisonment. Even though the receptionist's immunity was questionable because of her low ranking at the Embassy, she was not charged.

In New York, that same morning, another Colombian – this one attached to his country's UN delegation – was stopped by police for speeding, reckless driving, ignoring a red light and drunk driving. When the State Department confirmed his immunity, he was released immediately. Fortunately, no one was injured.

An employee of the Saudi Arabian Embassy had been ticketed for exceeding the speed limit by ten miles per hour on three occasions within an eight-month period. He was requested to show cause why his driving privilege should not be revoked, but the diplomat didn't appear. Instead, the Maryland Department of Transportation received a letter from the Protocol section of the State Department citing Vienna Convention Article 31, paragraph two, which states: 'A diplomatic agent is not obliged to give evidence as a witness.' The Saudi wouldn't even answer his own correspondence.

The Hit and Run Follow-up Unit of the Washington Metropolitan Police keeps official reports in their files regarding accidents where motorists don't stop after causing accidents. In two separate incidents, one in 1981 and the other in 1982, French diplomats left the scene after hitting and damaging unattended parked cars. Eyewitnesses provided police with the licence numbers of the hit and run cars.

Notifications of the hit and run incidents were forwarded by the Unit to the French Embassy, citing the licence plates of the cars involved, and requesting that the owners, the cars, and their drivers on the days in question appear in court. Both summonses prompted the French Embassy to send letters to the State Department denying any involvement and reminding the State Department that Embassy personnel have diplomatic immunity. Although the letters bore the official seal of the French Embassy, no name or signature was on either letter. Both investigations were dropped.

When Edward Lombard was superintendent of the Washington Insurance Department, he revealed that diplomats usually fail to report their accidents. Not only that, he asserted, 'They deny filing a claim, deny being at fault – deny everything. Anybody damaged by a diplomatic car doesn't have much recourse.'

Prior to 1977, when diplomats caused traffic accidents

victims were rarely offered restitution for their losses. About the only recourse they had was the State Department who were often called upon to mediate. Their policy remains as follows:

First, they urge all parties to try to work it out through their insurance companies. If that can't be done, and a written request is made, State Department liaison officers will make an effort to help. If the diplomat and his embassy aren't willing to cooperate, the cases stay unsettled.

A Congressional investigation revealed that for the three-year period from 1974 to 1977, the State Department was unable to get settlements of monies owed to American citizens for automobile accident claims from the following embassies: Bangladesh, Brazil, Ghana, Iceland, India, Israel, Kuwait, Nigeria, Panama and Senegal. The State Department would not disclose the amounts of the damages.

Too many diplomats have equal disregard for the safety of other drivers and for the law. In August, 1982, a detective assigned to a criminal investigation unit of the Washington DC police department observed the First Secretary of the German Democratic Republic weaving in and out of heavy rush hour traffic at high speed. Though the detective didn't normally issue traffic citations in the course of his duty, he felt the German driver's violations were flagrantly endangering the lives of other motorists. He felt he had no alternative but to issue a citation. Because of immunity, though, the First Secretary neither paid the fine nor answered the summons.

On Christmas Day, 1981, a Bolivian representative to the Organization of American States was observed driving erratically on Route 495 outside Washington. The police officer who stopped him believed the envoy was more than mildly intoxicated, and was a life-threatening hazard to everyone else on the road. The Bolivian was unable to walk a straight line or to maintain his balance, but once his diplomatic status was verified at the station, he was released, without charges, to the custody of his family.

Canadian officials remember well the night in 1981 when

a very drunk envoy attached to the embassy of Upper Volta drove his car through the front window of a crowded Ottawa restaurant. It was only by some miracle that dozens of people were not seriously injured. Police immediately arrested the man and charged him with reckless driving and driving under the influence of alcohol. But as soon as he identified himself as a diplomat the charges against him were dropped and he was released.

The problem of drunken diplomatic drivers is so common, the State Department circulates this document among police precincts to advise them what to do when they encounter a drunken diplomat:

1. Take him to the station or a location where he can recover sufficiently to enable him to drive safely.
2. Take him to a telephone so that he can call a relative or friend to come for him.
3. Call a taxi for him.
4. Take him home.

New York City police operate in a similar, though more informal, manner. One traffic officer who sees quite a few drunk-driving diplomats told me:

> Our procedures are quite clear. As soon as we have identified a diplomat we are supposed to send him on his way. But our duty is also to protect citizens and there is no way we can let a drunk diplomat go if we think he is going to be a menace on the road and a danger to either himself or to others.
>
> So what you do is ask him real nicely if he wouldn't mind parking the car and taking a taxi to his destination. If he insists on driving away, you suddenly have a lot of problems properly identifying him as a diplomat. You get on the radio and ask for a supervisor to be sent to the scene – slowly. That usually takes about twenty minutes. If the guy gets antsy and looks like he might simply drive away, you reach in the car and take the keys.
>
> Then the supervisor arrives. It will take him about three

seconds to understand what is going on and he will ask the guy if he doesn't think it would be better to park the car and take a cab. If the guy still insists on driving then the supervisor will have a problem with confirming that the driver is a diplomat and will very apologetically tell him that he will have to go to the station to be identified and that the UN will have to confirm his identity. If the guy still does not get the message and agree to get in a cab, the supervisor will take him in. This will take an hour or so and by this time the guy should have sobered up. We have wasted a lot of time and effort but at least the guy hasn't killed himself or some citizen.

This kind of service, with the police acting as wet-nurses, is a far cry from the treatment the rest of us would get – arrested, charged with drunken driving, and put in a cell.

At about 5.00 p.m., on Saturday, June 15, 1985, Robert Malakoff, a Senate subcommittee staff member, was driving his car north on the Rock Creek Parkway in the District of Columbia. In the front seat of his station wagon was Malakoff's wife, Grace. Cecile, his 85-year-old mother, was in the back seat. The three were only five minutes from home.

The Malakoffs were in the left northbound lane of the four-lane road which is divided only by a double yellow line. They had just come around a curve north of P Street when suddenly coming head-on towards them was a Ford LTD which had crossed the double yellow lines into their lane.

'The way we all remember it,' says Malakoff, 'as we came around the curve the car was not only directly in our lane but was actually slightly to our outside, meaning it was not only across the centre line but actually two lanes across . . . There was no time to react. The impact was just seconds after I saw the car.'

The crash was unavoidable. The Malakoff's car was severely damaged on its right front and side confirming that the car which struck it was completely in the wrong lane. Malakoff was only barely able to jerk his car slightly out of the way and thus avoid a head-on collision.

'We were all badly shaken up and we could not even get out of our car,' says Malakoff. 'A number of people stopped to help us and within a couple of minutes the police arrived. It was obvious that there was really very little damage to the interior of the other car so most of the initial efforts were towards getting us out of our car, particularly after it was apparent my mother was badly injured.'

US Park Police officers, Sergeant Thomas Moyer and Officer Paul Mitchell, were the first on the scene. Once the process of getting the Malakoffs out of the car had begun, Sergeant Moyer went over to the other car.

The driver of the Ford LTD had not tried to get out of it. In fact, when asked to leave the car by Sergeant Moyer, he refused. Finally he did so and instantly the cause of the accident became apparent. The driver of the Ford was staggeringly, almost incoherently, drunk.

As they noted in the accident report, when the officers tried to question the driver, he could only mumble. He was having a great deal of trouble walking and smelled strongly of alcohol.

The problem was compounded when the drunken driver started to struggle with the two officers. He was handcuffed, taken into custody and transported to Park Police headquarters, about a mile up the road.

Finally at police headquarters, the driver indignantly identified himself as Soviet Air Attaché, Sergei Smirnov, and loudly proclaimed his diplomatic immunity. Upon his identification and confirmation of his immunity, the Soviet Embassy was notified and he was released into the custody of several Embassy officials who quickly arrived on the scene.

In the official accident report, Sergeant Moyer and Officer Mitchell noted, 'The accident was clearly caused by driver Smirnov. Contributing factors would be the consumption of alcohol since he was apparently severely intoxicated.'

The police report added that Smirnov 'could not speak. He babbled, appeared incoherent, and had difficulty walking. He had the strong odour of an alcoholic beverage about his breath.' The report went on, 'We handcuffed subject after he became violent.'

A Soviet spokesman, Boris Malakhov, vigorously denied Smirnov was drunk. His strange actions were the result of the accident. 'He was not intoxicated . . . He was under shock. The car was badly damaged. Why wouldn't the person inside be too?' Malakhov continued, 'It was a sheer accident. It was raining. It could have happened to anybody.'

Malakhov noted that all holders of diplomatic licence plates must carry car liability insurance, and he assumed this would cover the Malakoffs' medical expenses. The Soviet spokesman said Smirnov was clearly exonerated by the fact that 'no one is charging him. Had he been thought to be guilty, he would have been charged.'

Of course, as a Park Police spokesman pointed out, once identified as a diplomat with immunity, Smirnov could not be charged. Had he not had immunity, he probably would have been charged not only with drunk driving but also with resisting arrest.

The most severely injured in the accident was 85-year-old Cecile Malakoff who suffered a serious hip injury, was put in traction and was not expected to leave the hospital for at least two months.

Her only comment on the incident, made from her hospital bed, was, 'They are guests here. Don't they think they ought to honour the laws of the country that provides the hospitality for them?'

The State Department requires all foreign service personnel posted abroad to carry vehicle insurance for their privately owned cars. The head of every US mission is personally responsible for ensuring that all mission employees have the insurance.

In Australia in 1977, a US agricultural attaché, Dr Roger Meisner, was involved in a fatal accident in Canberra. Dr Meisner, whose job included inspecting meat for export to the United States, pulled away from a stop sign and struck a government truck a slight blow. Dr Meisner recalls that he never saw the truck and has no idea where it came from. Though the collision did little damage to either vehicle, it caused the passenger-side door of the truck to fly open. One of the three passengers was jolted out of the truck, landed on his head and died.

A few weeks earlier, a Third World diplomat had been driving while intoxicated and had caused a tragic accident. The drunken diplomat had ploughed into a small group of people waiting at a bus stop. Several died.

Because of the earlier incident, Dr Meisner's accident received considerable media attention. Dr Meisner was advised by American officials to leave Australia until the furor died down, so he returned to the US.

When the Australian government announced it would hold a hearing into the accidental death of the government worker, Meisner returned to Canberra to testify. On the morning of the hearing, he was advised not to attend. The Embassy decided that a staff lawyer should represent him instead.

At the hearing, Dr Meisner was held responsible for the accident, but no criminal charges were brought. At no time was diplomatic immunity claimed on his behalf. Dr Meisner was reassigned to another post and left Australia. His insurance company paid a generous settlement to the family of the deceased.

Soviet-American relations become strained whenever a Soviet representative is stopped in the US. A Soviet consular employee from San Francisco was driving in excess of seventy miles per hour in a fifty-five mile per hour zone in the spring of 1983. A California Highway Patrolman signalled him to pull over. The stubborn Soviet refused at first, but finally came to a stop on the shoulder.

The driver couldn't produce a consular identification credential. When the Russian said he didn't have immunity, the officer wrote a citation. The Soviet refused to sign it, even after it was explained that signing the summons was a receipt for the ticket, not an admission of guilt. While trying to explain clearly, the officer put his hand into the car and touched the consular employee's arm. The Soviet jerked his arm away and signed the ticket. Later, the Soviet claimed the officer had struck him in the face. The Soviet government filed a protest with the State Department, charging assault.

With the proliferation of foreign consulates, diplomatic driving abuses are likely to occur nearly anywhere. The Haitian Consul-General stationed in Chicago was stopped on Interstate 94 in Michigan and given summonses for reckless driving and driving without a licence. Haitian Consul-General Adams objected, telling State Trooper James J. Box that diplomatic immunity protected him from traffic tickets. The Consul was indignant at being stopped for such trivia. He grumbled and told Officer Box that he would 'have to do 90 miles an hour the rest of the way' to get to his destination on time.

Adams also told the state trooper, 'The safety of citizens isn't as important as the meeting I'm going to.' When handed the two tickets, Adams flung them back at the officer. 'I don't want these littering up my car,' Mr Adams said. He drove off.

A few hours later on that July afternoon in 1974, the same car was clocked travelling at ninety-three miles per hour on the same freeway, this time in the opposite direction. Again, the car was pulled over. Adams' brother, Franz, was behind the wheel. Consul Adams told another Michigan State Trooper that he was wasting their time because in the end, he'd beat the ticket. Later, when the incident was reported in the press, Adam not only denied he'd been speeding, he alleged that what the state trooper said was a 'big lie'.

Traffic incidents involving foreign emissaries sometimes approach the ridiculous. In an area outside Washington where a radar monitors passing traffic, a Thai diplomat was stopped for driving at fifty in a thirty-five mile per hour zone. The motorist got out of the car and walked back to the officer. The officer told him he had to sign the citation and contest the ticket later, in court. The Thai then asked to be taken to jail. The officer explained the citation again. The Thai asked to see the radar, but when the officer pointed to where the radar was, the man said it was too far to walk.

The officer asked the driver to get into the patrolcar to take a ride to the station. As they drove off, the man again asked to see the radar. Then he said he thought he had left his car running. The officer told him he would send someone to turn it off. The Thai got irritated and threatened to jump out of the car, which was going at about twenty-five miles per hour. He opened the door of the moving car to demonstrate. The officer stopped the car abruptly.

It was then that the Thai identified himself as a diplomat and claimed immunity. He produced the State Department blue book from his pocket which verified his accreditation to the Royal Thai Embassy. The officer could only shake his head and let him go.

In 1981, the son of former Philippines President Ferdinand Marcos was pulled over on the New Jersey Turnpike for speeding. Ferdinand Jr was a student at the University of Pennsylvania and was driving with a female companion in the front seat. When the state trooper arrived at the driver's window, he couldn't help noticing a semi-automatic rifle on the back seat and a revolver strapped to the leg of the woman passenger.

When Marcos presented his diplomatic passport, the trooper waved him on. Later, a spokesman for the New Jersey State Police said the incident was handled according to 'standard procedure'.

The State Department said that Marcos was not entitled to diplomatic immunity because he was not registered as a diplomatic agent of his country, but that was long after the gambit had got him off the hook.

Historically, diplomats have always been extremely arrogant in how they use their cars. In 1926, a policeman pointed out to an attaché from Ecuador that he was parked illegally. 'If I choose to leave my car in the middle of Sixteenth Street,' declared the attaché, 'it would be none of your damned business.'

The police chief of Takoma Park, Maryland, told his district's congressional representative that his department often learns ticketed cars belong to embassy personnel only after the tickets are overdue and in penalty. For instance, in 1976, six tickets were issued to the car owned by a clerk of the Nigerian Embassy. When the tickets remained unpaid, the police chief sent the usual warning letters, not realizing the car belonged to an embassy employee. Eventually, all the letters were returned, bearing the addition of the official seal of the Nigerian Embassy. A small engraved card was enclosed. It read, 'With the compliments of the Embassy of the Federal Republic of Nigeria.'

In another Takoma Park case, a car bearing diplomatic plates collected twenty-one tickets for parking in a permit-only carpark near Montgomery College. The car was registered to the daughter of an Israeli Embassy official. The police chief personally called the Israeli Embassy to request cooperation to cease the repeated violations. He was told that the young woman had been trying not to park illegally, but whenever she went to class it took her half an hour to find a legal space. So, naturally, the official explained, she had to park illegally.

It is acknowledged world-wide that traffic violations and unpaid parking tickets are the most common abuses of diplomatic immunity.

London, a city laid out long before the advent of the automobile, has simply not been able to handle the traffic congestion that now crowds its streets. Everyone admits there is almost a total lack of parking facilities in central London and illegal parking has reached epidemic proportions. This is especially true among cars with CD plates.

According to official government figures, in 1984 104,690 parking tickets were cancelled because the cars were registered to diplomats. This represented nearly five percent of all parking tickets issued that year, a slight increase over 1983's figure of 102,210. That's twice as many tickets as diplomats received in 1980.

Central London's parking problems are especially acute in Westminster, Kensington, and Chelsea, the areas where most diplomatic embassies and chanceries are located.

Mid–1983 saw the initiation of wheel-clamping, a strategy popular with police in America. The clamp, originally nicknamed the 'Denver boot' since it was first used in Denver a number of years ago, immobilizes the car, forcing the owner to pay a hefty fine for its removal.

In May, 1983, Chief Inspector Keith Brindley of the Traffic Patrols Department, announced a ninety-day experimental wheel-clamping programme for central London. A sergeant, eight constables, twenty-eight 'vehicle removal officers', and eight traffic wardens were assigned to the programme. If a car was found illegally parked, it would be subject to clamping. The car's owner would have to pay a ten-pound fine and £19.50 removal fee.

Chief Inspector Brindley capped the announcement with a statement that brought joy to the hearts of most Londoners: 'Diplomatic vehicles will be treated as any other cars.' If they were illegally parked, they too would be clamped.

Polish Ambassador Stefan Staniszewski's limousine had the dubious distinction of being the first diplomatic vehicle to be clamped as it sat illegally parked at the Brent Cross Shopping Centre on May 16. When the driver returned to the vehicle and found it clamped, he called the Foreign Office to claim immunity and to demand that the clamp be removed. Thirty minutes later, it was.

But the clamping continued. On May 19, six cars belonging to Iraq and five belonging to Kuwait were clamped. On May 24, twenty-nine diplomatic vehicles were clamped. Of those, eleven belonged to France and ten were owned by Tanzania. By June 3rd, 101 vehicles registered to thirty-two different countries had been clamped. By the time the ninety-day experiment was completed, of the 4,358 vehicles clamped, about 400 were found to bear CD plates.

The Traffic Patrols Department declared the experiment a success. They said that henceforth the clamp would become a part of the day to day battle against illegal parkers. At the same time, the Foreign Office announced that it was ordering the clamping of diplomatic cars to be suspended pending a review of the matter. All diplomatic cars were released without paying the £29.50 fine.

The diplomatic community had been in an uproar over the clamping, and the Foreign Office had had to spend untold time smoothing ruffled diplomatic feathers. Diplomats told the Foreign Office in no uncertain terms that if the clamping continued, there would probably not be a British diplomat anywhere in the world who could safely park a car. Wars have been started over less.

Finally, on December 12, 1983, the Parliamentary Under Secretary of State at the Home Office, Lord Elton, announced in the House of Lords that the Foreign Office had reviewed the matter thoroughly and had decided that the clamping of diplomatic cars was a violation of Articles 31 and 37 of the Vienna Convention which forbade the host country from interfering with the 'free movement' of diplomats and would no longer be permitted. Lord Elton also stated that the towing of diplomatic vehicles that were parked in such a way as to constitute a hazard would continue. (In 1984, about 200 diplomatic cars were towed, though none paid fines.)

The clamping experiment had little effect on diplomatic parking habits, as the increase in parking offences indicates. Rising pressure in Parliament forced the Foreign Office to take some action. In late January, 1985, Mr Eustace Gibbs, Undersecretary of State and the head of the Foreign Office Protocol Section, began calling ambassadors from countries who were the worst offenders into his office for stern lectures.

The first visitor was Major-General H. A. Hananiyam the Nigerian High Commissioner, whose mission had accumulated 6,618 parking tickets in 1984. He was followed by Ambassador Hassan Abou Seeda of Egypt whose country was second on the list with 6,294 offences. Ambassadors or High Commissioners from Saudi Arabia (4,800 offences), Cuba, Cyprus, Ghana, India, Italy, Japan and Poland (each with over 2,000 offences), Iraq, Haiti, Bulgaria, St Lucia, France, Greece, Uganda, Algeria, Upper Volta and the Grenadines (over 1,000 each), all made appearances at the Foreign Office.

There was no one left in London representing the Libyans. They had 2,708 offences on record the day they were expelled in April, 1984.

The message all these diplomats received was blunt. Britain's patience with massive illegal parking had limits and those limits were being reached. Beginning in May, 1985, detailed tabulations of parking offences would be kept on a day to day basis. It was not out of the question, the heads of missions were told, that diplomats would be expelled for particularly numerous parking violations.

The reactions to these warnings ranged from a statement from a Ugandan diplomat that an expulsion would result in British expulsions from Uganda to a French complaint that the situation was all Britain's fault. The French pointed out that they had over 100 people in their mission and had been given a total of two official parking spaces, while the British Embassy in Paris had official parking for over forty cars.

Did the warnings do any good? As the government noted in its mid-1985 White Paper, 'Regrettably . . . requests for cooperation have been widely disregarded.'

Diplomatic parking abuses are as big a problem in the United States as they are in the UK. For instance, during a seven-month period in 1976, from April to October, diplomatic employees ignored 22,004 parking tickets worth $235,490 in fines. Soviet Embassy cars amassed the most unpaid tickets – 8,435, amounting to uncollected fines of $101,930. The Israeli Embassy in Washington ignored 2,503 parking tickets with unpaid fines of $19,995.

Washington residents have been troubled for years with these abuses of diplomatic privilege. In 1977, Mrs Kathleen T. Perkins decided to do something about it. Her Citizen's Committee on Diplomatic Immunity came together to pressure legislators for stiffer penalties for diplomats who use immunity to ignore parking fines and disregard traffic violations. She and her group compiled the list of the worst diplomatic parking offenders in Washington. Her results are on pages 234–5.

DC Superior Court Chief Judge, Harold H. Greene, told a Senate hearing in 1978 that eighty percent of the tickets issued to diplomats go unpaid. The serious offenders represent a cross-section of nations economically and politically, he pointed out – developed and developing countries, dictatorships, democracies and communist states.

Whether blocking pedestrian crossings, entrances to buildings, bus stops or fire hydrants, diplomats continue to ignore

UNPAID PARKING FINES OF EMBASSY EMPLOYEES WITH DIPLOMATIC PLATES FOR SEVEN-MONTH PERIOD APRIL-OCTOBER 1976 ($5 TO $25 PER TICKET)

Embassy	Number of tickets	Amount owing
BY AMOUNT		
		($s)
USSR	8,435	101,930
Israel	2,503	19,995
Peru	644	7,230
Nigeria	443	4,500
France	405	3,865
Organization of American States	292	3,430
Togo	153	3,300
Trinidad and Tobago	204	2,880
Argentina	275	2,780
Taiwan	283	2,550
Saudi Arabia	196	2,535
India	261	2,525
Brazil	231	2,395
Cameroon	283	2,290
Iran	218	2,070
Italy	273	1,865
Sudan	236	1,745
Senegal	145	1,715
Libya	147	1,440
Morocco	145	1,290
Ecuador	108	1,275
Spain	104	1,230
Tunisia	161	1,225
Mexico	94	1,215
Jordan	137	1,150
Uruguay	125	1,150
Greece	88	1,000
Liberia	95	970
Haiti	94	960
Zaire	99	925
Guinea	67	915
Hungary	66	890
Poland	83	890
Central African Republic	88	880
Chile	79	880
Somalia	119	875
Zambia	34	850
Qatar	99	825
Czechoslovakia	77	815
Ivory Coast	84	810
Japan	61	780
Germany	76	770
Romania	73	765
Panama	62	745
Colombia	72	715
Kuwait	72	715
Mali	64	715
Gabon	71	705
Yugoslavia	72	705
Ghana	65	675
Malta	29	650
Korea	53	640
Australia	64	630
Venezuela	66	595
Philippines	58	570
Afghanistan	96	565
Indonesia	60	565
Belgium	61	545
Egypt	50	535
Denmark	56	530

Embassy	Number of tickets	Amount owing
BY AMOUNT		
		($s)
Guatemala	49	515
Canada	44	505
Bulgaria	36	495
Kenya	52	460
Portugal	47	460
Bangladesh	39	455
Great Britain	51	450
Mauritius	53	450
Syria	51	440
Netherlands	45	425
Cyprus	38	405
Pakistan	40	405
Burma	44	400
Sierra Leone	41	400
Malaysia	61	395
Austria	39	390
Bolivia	40	390
Chad	51	385
Mauritania	34	380
Lebanon	36	360
Barbados	33	335
Madagascar	32	320
Tanzania	29	320
Singapore	28	315
Paraguay	33	305
Sweden	36	305
United Arab Emirates	30	305
Uganda	26	280
Costa Rica	23	265
Thailand	27	255
Botswana	17	250
Honduras	24	245
El Salvador	21	245
Turkey	22	240
Niger	25	235
Malawi	33	225

Embassy	Number of tickets	Amount owing
BY AMOUNT		
		($s)
Benin	24	215
Upper Volta	20	215
Norway	22	210
South Africa	25	210
Ethiopia	22	205
Oman	16	205
Algeria	14	185
Nicaragua	16	180
Burundi	12	170
Lesotho	23	170
Finland	24	165
Jamaica	16	155
New Zealand	18	155
European Common Delegation	15	150
Iceland	9	135
Swaziland	9	125
Rwanda	12	105
Dominican Republic	7	100
Sri Lanka	9	75
Switzerland	9	75
Guyana	7	60
Nepal	5	60
North Yemen	6	50
Pan American Union	3	35
Bahamas	4	25
Latvia	1	25
Bahrain	1	10
Luxembourg	1	10
Ireland	2	10
Laos	1	5
No Embassy ID	1,367	13,810
Total	**22,004**	**235,490**

thousands of summonses. On a recent typical Tuesday during the evening rush hour, thirty diplomatic cars were impeding traffic in 'No Standing Zones' on 16th Street between L and P Streets. Even though they may have accumulated quite a collection of ignored parking tickets, the cars are not towed away, merely moved around nearby corners onto side streets.

The parking situation in New York City is just as bad, if not worse. In a 1977 letter pleading for congressional reform, Brooklyn Borough President Howard Golden pointed out, 'Our citizens' safety means nothing to these individuals who park in bus and hospital stops and double and triple park in theatre and other congested districts. Complaints from hospital, school and transportation officials and business people are ignored.'

A report to the United Nations by the City of New York which covered the period from March 1, 1974, to January 3, 1975, stated that twenty diplomatic cars during that period had in excess of 360 tickets each. A single vehicle had collected 671. The problem has escalated with the passing years. Recently, during one ten-month period, three Peugeots assigned to the Ugandan mission became outright winners in the parking abuse stakes, with more than 1,700 ignored tickets between them.

Processing and issuing traffic tickets in New York City during 1980 cost $300,000 in direct costs, and caused a one and a half million dollar loss of revenue from unpaid tickets and uncollected towing fees. Each month, about 100 such diplomatic cars are towed away for illegal parking, even though only those blocking major thoroughfares impeding rush hour traffic are moved. No fees are ever collected. That year, 108,000 parking summonses were issued to diplomatic and foreign consulate plates.

The problem is worldwide. Unpaid traffic tickets written to diplomats in Ottawa prove a problem for Canadian law enforcement agencies. In 1983, the most recent year for which figures are available, 4,323 traffic tickets were issued, but only 184 were paid. Nigerian diplomats were the worst offenders, as they are in Britain, paying only two of the 271 tickets issued to cars registered to their embassy. Algeria was second, paying none of their 237 tickets. Somalia was third, ignoring all of their 205 tickets. France was fourth, with six out of 188 paid.

American Embassy officials, contrary to State Department boasts, paid only thirty-one of the 146 tickets they were issued. The best records belonged to El Salvador which paid the only ticket it got, and the Vatican which paid both of its tickets.

When Senator Daniel K. Inouye was chairman of the Appropriations Subcommittee for the District of Columbia, he made a noteworthy observation when he said, 'I find it difficult to accept the thesis that the spirit of friendship between our country and other nations should be deemed to rest on the privileged status of their representatives here in our nation's capital regarding our traffic and parking regulations.'

Surely he is right. But how can the problem be alleviated? Periodically, the State Department sends circulars to remind members of missions that they should operate their vehicles in accordance with local traffic laws and regulations, and that they are expected to pay charges resulting from parking violations. These circulars have minimal effect.

If anything is to change, leadership must come from the heads of missions. The fact is, embassies and their employees can afford to pay their parking tickets. They can also pay the minimal respect to the laws of their host countries and obey the traffic regulations along with everyone else. When they do get tickets for moving traffic violations, they can pay the fine. If they're too drunk to drive, they can exercise responsible judgment and stay off the road. While some embassies do have insufficient parking, diplomats shouldn't have to park illegally as much as they do.

Voluntary compliance is, after all, a relatively simple matter. The Swedish Ambassador to Britain, Leif Leifland, reports that he orders his staff to pay their parking tickets and advocates voluntary responsibility.

As for the invoking of diplomatic immunity: 'I think it's

unnecessary,' says Ambassador Leifland, 'and diplomatic immunity is not there in order to protect foreign diplomats from parking tickets. I have told my staff that I expect them to pay their parking tickets, and they do.'

The problem in London has become so bad that the government had to limit the number of CD plates issued. The issue of CD plates is now restricted to those with full immunity, and limited to one set per diplomat accredited to the mission for the mission's cars. Starting in 1985, the Foreign Office has resolved to crack down on offenders. About 900 cars did not get their CD plates for that year. The total number has been reduced from 6,800 to 5,900 because the status of travel and trade offices has been downgraded. People working in these offices no longer have immunity, nor are they eligible to receive CD plates. Also, the number of CD plates per diplomatic household has been restricted to two. In the past, a single household had been known to have as many as five.

The US instituted a reduction in the late 1960s. In April, 1967, the State Department withheld approval of licence applications for ambassadors or senior diplomats until outstanding tickets were paid. In 1969, seven applications were withheld until payment was made.

The State Department changed its interpretation of the Vienna Convention in 1972 and stopped holding up DPL plates for unpaid tickets. The revised interpretation viewed the Convention as prohibiting the State Department from denying licence plates to diplomatic employees and so the policy was discontinued. The current policy has reduced the number of diplomatic plates from approximately 16,000 to around 14,000. Now, only those plates paid for in full by the country to which the diplomat is accredited will be issued.

In New York City, Israel's representative to the United Nations vowed in 1979 to do something about his country's poor reputation for not paying parking tickets. The reason for his reform was undoubtedly pressure brought by the adverse publicity resulting from the mission's embarrassing performance record being reported widely in the media.

Backed by Israel's Foreign Minister Moshe Dayan, the Head of Mission issued an order to his delegation: pay the parking tickets out of your own pocket and stop invoking diplomatic immunity. As a result, Israel dropped off the list of the ten worst offenders, a position they had occupied for a long time.

Such an incident shows that we are not entirely powerless against diplomats who abuse their privileges. Concerted media attention can bring results, shaming the diplomatic community into action to try and improve its tarnished image. A crusade against diplomatic parking offences seems almost petty in the light of some of the more horrifying incidents described in this book, but it might prove to be the thin end of the wedge as far as diplomats are concerned.

If such a campaign was successful it could mark the beginning of the fight-back against diplomatic criminals and their appalling acts. The time is certainly ripe for action. The citizens of Britain and the United States have suffered these outrages for too long. The murder of Yvonne Fletcher was the final horror, an act that can never be forgiven or forgotten. But it has perhaps taught us one thing, a lesson we hope this book has helped to underline: the abuse of diplomatic immunity is a danger to us all.

AFTERWORD

During the four years since the first interview that prompted this book, a great deal has happened.

The rate of civil and criminal complaints involving United Nations personnel in New York City has nearly doubled according to that city's police authority. Scotland Yard won't give specific details but they readily admit there have been a number of incidents such as thefts and unpaid rents attributable to British-based diplomats and even more often to their servants and families.

In the United Kingdom, Germany, Holland, the United States, Canada, Japan and Australia, there are strong parliamentary efforts to find ways of restricting diplomatic immunity to officials themselves and to exclude chauffeurs, secretaries and children from the so-often abused magic protection.

Various international police organizations are beginning to speak out about the frustrations of their member officers and the demoralizing effect of arresting and then freeing rapists, thieves and killers.

Between now and 1988 the issue will be debated publicly for the first time. Many believe the legacy of Yvonne Fletcher and the other victims you have read about may be a new era of equity – one with respect for the role of the diplomat but which demands that diplomats respect the laws of their host countries.